SUMMIT FOR THE WEEKEND

PETE MAY

ISBN: 9798374080179

Cover design by Andrew Chapman

For Nicola, Lola and Nell

CONTENTS

ACKNOWLEDGMENTS

Thank you to all who have helped on my Lake District journey. Particularly to Nicola Baird for first buying me a Wainwright wallchart, plus Lola May and Nell May for allowing me to drag them to Keswick, Glenridding, Wasdale and Ambleside on annual walking holidays and Vulcan for canine support. Thanks to Andrew Chapman for designing a great cover and to Nigel Morris, Dave Meigh and Hannah Scrase for transport to some of the more difficult fells. Also to John Manning for commissioning some of my words in *Lakeland Walker* and all the members of the *To Climb The 214 Wainwright Fells* Facebook group for help and advice. It's been a marathon not a sprint.

INTRODUCTION

A man approaching sixty has to be honest. I've published a fair few books, but I'm not going to be Charles Dickens, Leo Tolstoy or Nick Hornby. The chance to play for West Ham has gone — well, barring a very bad injury crisis. I'm never going to be an intrepid/idiotic explorer of wilderness like Bear Grylls. But the Wainwright fells — the 214 Lake District fells detailed by Alfred Wainwright in his magnificent *Pictorial Guides* — are still attainable for men like me. Better still, most have a pub somewhere close by. Climb every Wainwright, ford every stream, until you find your dream. As Alfred Wainwright once said, everyone needs a goal in life, and mine was completing a wallchart.

It all began with a visit to Stickle Tarn and the Langdale Pikes on my school's Geography field trip in 1976. For a teenage boy from the flatlands of Essex the Lake District seemed like a magical place. Further trips followed while I was an undergraduate at Lancaster University, and then a few solo outings in the 1980s.

I'd been fascinated by Wainwright since he emerged on Sunday evening TV in the 1980s, an indisputably authentic figure with his pipe, sideburns and anorak in an age of yuppies and designer clothes. He seemed equal parts bluff romantic, gentle visionary, chip connoisseur and cantankerous old git.

A period of more exotic holidays followed, but then, inspired by walking Wainwright's Coast-to-Coast path from St Bees to Robin Hood's Bay and later becoming a father, in the new millennium I spent my summers trying to complete the circular walks in the 1980s coffee table book *Fellwalking with Wainwright*. Like many Lakeland lovers, I had long cherished AW's *Pictorial Guides* as both indispensible walking aids and also works of art. *Fellwalking with Wainwright* linked up many of those individual peaks into dramatic ridge walks.

Then came that summer at the Wasdale Head Inn celebrating my 50th birthday. My wife Nicola bought me a Wainwright wall chart with space for ticking off every one of the 214 summits Wainwright listed, along with the date climbed. I'd completed a lot of them already.

By 2019 I had finished all 18 of Wainwright's circular walks and most of the highest mountains in the Lake District. Helvellyn by the edges, up on the thrilling Striding Edge and then down via Swirral Edge, taking in the perfect peak of Catstycam on the way down; the Fairfield Round from Ambleside that completes eight tops in one circuit; the lovely Coledale Round overlooking some of the best Lakeland valleys and peaks; the Newlands Horseshoe beginning in a delightful tiny church; the majestic High Stile Range overlooking Buttermere; the Mosedale Round from the splendid isolation of Wasdale Head; the Coniston fells and their mining debris; High Street and Harter Fell from Haweswater; the Kentmere Round in three stages (it's difficult without a car); the Langdale Pikes; Bowfell and Esk Pike; Skiddaw via Ullock Pike; Scafell Pike with its legions of walkers; Great Gable from Honister via Moses' Trod; Scafell from Wasdale Head; Blencathra from Threlkeld; Crinkle Crags and the very fell where Wainwright's ashes are scattered, Haystacks, with its peaceful Innominate Tarn in the heart of the fells. It felt like a lot of walking, plus I'd scaled many other individual peaks on my travels. But there were still 85 fells left out of the 214 listed by Alfred Wainwright. Not that I was counting, much.

Next came the Facebook group *To Climb The 214 Wainwright Fells*. Here were like-minded anoraks/aficionados. People posted useful tips about their routes and pictures of their walks. You could see that Raven Crag had wooden duckboards on the final ascent, five Wainwrights could be knocked off starting at Longlands and that Mungrisdale Common was a boggy plateau. Fellow users would happily answer queries about routes and timings. It was a Facebook group that really did have the moral high ground. One thing I learned was that size wasn't everything. At just less than one thousand feet in height, the smallest Wainwright Fell, Castle Crag, was one of the most fascinating.

For many years I had been raging at the dying of the light, usually after a long trek as I staggered down Rossett Ghyll in the 8pm dusk on my way back to the Old Dungeon Ghyll Hotel at Great Langdale. Now I was approaching my 60th birthday and a more literal dying of the light.

My legs still felt strong even if my waistline was expanding, but I could remember my dad's struggles with arthritis in his seventies. My children were heading off to university and my wife was not too averse to a Lakeland yomp. So why not do it? Every man loves a list. If ever I was going to complete all 214 of Wainwright's fells it had to be soon. It wasn't going to be easy living in London and relying on public transport, but it could be done. Or so I hoped.

1. CLIMB EVERY WAINWRIGHT

Date: April-May 2019

Accommodation: Helvellyn Youth Hostel and The White Lion, Patterdale.

Transport: Train from London Euston to Penrith, 508 bus Penrith to Glenridding.

Companions: Solo trip.

New Wainwrights bagged: 4 — Hart Side, Clough Head, Wether Hill, Hartsop above How.

Old Wainwrights bagged: 3 — Stybarrow Dodd, Watsons Dodd, Great Dodd.

Total Wainwrights completed: 133

Total Wainwrights left: 81

The sun is beating down on the cracked concrete and loose grit of Greenside Road. It's unseasonably hot for April. Wheeling my suitcase from the bus stop at Glenridding up the mile-long track to Helvellyn Youth Hostel is proving more difficult than I had anticipated. Particularly as one of the suitcase wheels is broken and the handle is stuck at half-elevation. So I have to lean down to pull my case rather like the Hunchback of Glenridding. I've stayed at the Helvellyn hostel before. But in my memory this road was just a short stroll, now it feels like attempting to scale Striding Edge while pulling a suitcase and carrying a daypack.

But at least I have escaped London. Not that I don't like the place. London is exciting, buzzy, full of culture, but sometimes overwhelming — and it certainly has no mountains unless you count the hill up to Crouch End.

My wife Nicola is at home attending to her freelance lecturing job and editing *Pavement*, a magazine for homeless people. My elder daughter Lola is a student drinking freshly-ground coffee in her shared house in Turnpike Lane. My younger daughter Nell is 17 and busy at home revising for her A levels and will soon be going to university. My career is floundering and the print and publishing industries are contracting. I've been to see a life coach about my lack of a "big idea". The impasse of Brexit rumbles on in Parliament as Prime Minister Theresa May struggles to satisfy the nationalist wing of her party. Our fridge has broken and my income is declining.

Our border terrier Vulcan has been left to chase next door's cat and the urban fox that saunters through our hedge, leaving shredded burger containers and worse. The dentist has cut part of my gum away and I'm getting tired of checking for a few pence per day of AdSense revenue from my West Ham blog. Commissioning editors are rejecting my ideas. Another of my gig jobs (the gig economy sounds much more rock 'n' roll than the low-paid economy) writing potted music biographies for £10 a go is underpaid and unfulfilling, while boxes of my out-of-print books are proving useful as insulation in the attic.

But none of it seems to matter all that much up here in

the Lakes. Sometimes a man needs to get back to something elemental, to escape stabbings and shootings on the London streets, all those notifications and likes on Twitter and Facebook and the latest bad news on Radio 4. Here I am a man with a plan: there are 85 Wainwright fells left for me to climb.

It's good to hear the bleats of Herdwick sheep and the revving of motors. Farmers, quad bikes and dogs are doing *Countryfile*-type things with sheep and pens on the verdant fields across the river valley. On my back is a daypack containing my waterproofs and walking poles. My small blue suitcase is clattering unsteadily over piles of stones on the decaying road, but so what, I'm back in the Lakes after the long dark nights of winter.

One of the benefits of being older is that I no longer travel to the Lake District with just a backpack. A suitcase keeps my clothes flat and it can hold a collection of Wainwright guides without putting undue strain on my back. This system usually works well when I'm dropped off at my accommodation. But as the White Lion in Patterdale was full, I've had to take a detour into youth hostel land. Helvellyn YHA is sited at the former Greenside lead mine, hence the access road leading deep into the fells.

Sweat is now running from my forehead and down my cheeks. Steve Backshall had huge problems getting his gear into the rainforest to explore unexplored South American cave systems on *Undiscovered Worlds*, so perhaps this is my equivalent.

It's been half an hour since I got off the bus at Glenridding. On the journey I noted that the driver had obviously been schooled in compulsory bonhomie as he greeted the locals: "How do! You're not getting on! She's been on the gin… Whisky makes you frisky! She's got the giggles now…" Not the sort of banter you get on the 210 bus for my training walks on Hampstead Heath.

The road improves when the concrete surface emerges, laid for the mine lorries half a century ago. Up, down, stagger along, around the bend. Finally I make it, feeling a little dizzy upon arriving at Helvellyn YHA.

A Jewish family in skullcaps are packing their car, while some Lycra-clad cyclists dismount and a German couple unpack a car boot full of bags and food. The YHA still attracts a rich mix of people, in fact just about everyone apart from youths. The gleaming cars parked outside suggest a decidedly older customer base.

"Can you leave your case outside please, I've just had a new floor put down," says the man on reception. "It's looking good, don't you think?" It is indeed. Encouragingly there are beer pumps behind the counter. Gone are the days when any stay at the YHA involved a tortuous walk to the pub to find alcoholic sustenance after a day out on the fells.

Having checked in and ordered an evening meal I explore the hostel. It's a good feeling to be staying in what was once a dormitory for the workers of the Greenside lead mine. Two rail trolleys full of rocks sit outside the main entrance as a reminder of the building's industrial past. From the entrance the view is of a vast wall of spoil on the side of Sheffield Pike. Hard men once stayed here. Talk to an old miner and they will reveal that many of the workers died horrible deaths from lung disease. Tougher men than me, a soft southerner plugging an iPhone charger into the wall.

For a mere £26 I have booked a four-bunk bedroom to myself. This is perhaps anti-social, but better than enduring the bag rustlers of shared dorms. Being able to book a limited number of solo rooms is a welcome sign of modernity at youth hostels. When a walker reaches a certain age he needs a room of his own.

In the downstairs comfy chair area a wall chart details the miles of tunnels that extend under the whole region, some shafts deeper than Ullswater. "Not everything has changed for the better," read the accompanying rather curmudgeonly history notes. Mining went on here for hundreds of years and some 300 mine workers used to live in Patterdale. The wall is covered with numerous black and white photos of men with large drills and epic moustaches.

My evening meal is at a shared table with Dave from Leeds, who is doing the 192 miles of Wainwright's Coast to Coast Walk in seven days, as that's all the annual leave he has left. We chat about my experiences on the Coast-to-Coast 20 years ago and I'm able to tell him that there are no cafes at Haweswater, but Kirkby Stephen definitely has a chip shop. Dave's a fit man, walking the C2C at a pace that would have flummoxed Nicola and myself back in 1997.

At the back of the hostel I sit and listen to the sound of running water pouring over rounded boulders on the way down the beck to Glenridding. It was here that Nicola, Nell and myself enjoyed a lovely cold drink of wine and beer after descending from Striding Edge and Swirral Edge a few years ago. Happy memories. Then I return to the quiet of my room and a view of sunlight fading on rock and grass.

Next day it's off at 9am to find the path to Sticks Pass. "Should be good views up there today!" I venture to the only other walker I spot, treading past gorse and spoil in the bright sunlight. "They're forecasting rain later, I'm getting up there quickly," he declares. You always encounter a few weather pessimists on the fells. Maybe he's right. But it will take more than bad weather to stop a determined collector of Wainwright summits. Today's objectives are Hart Side and possibly Clough Head, two outlying fells that I'm looking forward to scaling.

Remnants of the old industry are everywhere along the steep path heading up by Swart Beck. A dam made of decaying wood and rusty metal, tumbled down stone buildings, pieces of rusting iron pipe and old wooden roof props. Then a flat area of mounds of spoil and what appear to be old reservoirs. A giant ugly nick has been gouged out of the side of Hart Side in a brutal piece of open cast mining.

Then it's round piles of rubble and upwards on the path that zig-zags towards Sticks Pass. A cyclist is coming towards me, tyres crunching gravel, shooting down the pass with great velocity. He's playing music on headphones as he pedals and I imagine Mr Wainwright's ashes starting to smoulder somewhere up on Innominate Tarn. Sticks Pass is a big thing with mountain bikers. You can find endless videos of Lycra-clad cyclists racing down it on YouTube.

The track is next to the scary looking ravine of Sticks Gill. It looks likely to crack bones should someone fly off the path and fall head first into the depths. The risk is the buzz, I guess, though for me this is one place where you don't need an extra adrenaline high.

Worries start to disappear. There's just the slightly cold air and the sounds of birdsong and boots on rock. Wainwright once wrote about being on Skiddaw and seeing a mysterious red light in the sky that proved to be Liverpool burning in the Blitz. Britain is only metaphorically burning now, but it feels good to escape three years of the Brexit impasse.

I'm not sure what has happened to my country, but it seems to have become an insular, small-minded place since the EU referendum. It's a relief to not wake up to Radio 4's *Today* and politicians chasing unicorns while forgetting to govern. And there's no Twitter up here, where everything is binary and no-one ever agrees to disagree.

Both Remainers and Leavers could be wrong. Perhaps a no-deal Brexit would be wonderful. But right now everyone is shouting at each other, no one wants to beg to differ and right-wing populists are gaining ascendancy around the world. As Frank Turner titled his recent album, *Be More Kind.*

The path levels out to the crossroads of Sticks Pass. A thin track across the grass before the summit of Stybarrow Dodd suggests a short cut to Hart Side, a new Wainwright for me. I'm slightly confused by the summit of White Stones, which has fine views over Sheffield Pike, before realising that the summit of Hart Side is a further walk away to my north.

It's an easy mile-long stroll over flat grassland to the top of Hart Side. There are a few stones on the uneventful green top. It's not an exciting summit, but there is the satisfaction of knowing that I'm now down to 84 Wainwrights left to complete — and there's a fantastic view across to Ullswater, Little Mell Fell and the hanging valley of Glencoyne below. While in the other direction is the brooding black silhouette of a line of Dodds — Stybarrow Dodd, Watson's Dodd and Great Dodd.

On the top of the Lakeland world my thoughts turn to my affinity with the fells. Why do humans walk? Perhaps because it's good to feel insignificant sometimes, a tiny figure clambering up the serrated edge of a vast mountain. Whatever problems you have, they seem lees important when you are out in the elements. Your mind is in the present, concentrating on avoiding the next drop or scrambling over large boulders.

But there are bigger thoughts too. The glaciated landscape of huge lakes gouged out of the earth, shattered rockfaces and scree deposited by ancient ice reminds us that in the geological timescale human life is short, but the landscape seems eternal and unchanging. So perhaps the likelihood of West Ham not winning another trophy in my lifetime is not that important.

Walking gives us lessons for life. Planning is certainly advisable. Weather has to be scanned, bus timetables checked and heights checked. Everything is inter-connected in strange and unusual ways. A butterfly flaps its wings in Borrowdale and it can make you miss ordering a pub dinner in Keswick.

Finding the right path early on is often the most difficult part. The hiker discovers that the journey itself is often as enjoyable as reaching the top, and you don't need to rush to get there. You learn that the biggest peak isn't necessarily the best, just as in life you learn that the loudest voices do not always speak the most sense. Missteps and falls often happen on the way down, when you get a little tired and complacent having obtained your goal.

There is also the frisson of being an everyman explorer. Lakeland has just the right amount of danger. Here there are no man-eating animals or death zones. You don't have to step over bodies as you do on Everest. But dozens of people still die here every year and the environment has to be treated with respect. I always carry a survival bag, compass, whistle and torch, even if some adventurers think I'm a bit over-cautious.

Mountains can help us clear our minds. I've walked in the Lakes while unemployed, having been dumped, having become a father, lost my parents and seen a close friend die. Each time I came down with a greater sense of clarity.

And nothing bad ever comes from walking up a mountain. Mr Wainwright was profound indeed when he wrote that no-one ever planned a robbery or murder on the fells and that all left feeling in some way refreshed.

From Hart Side I now need to walk back to Stybarrow Dodd and then on to Watson's Dodd and Great Dodd, three fells I've completed a few years previously. It's already a lengthy walk back to the youth hostel. But if I trek another two miles to Clough Head it's a new Wainwright. There's a pronounced dip and then a walk along a grassy ridge. I encounter a walker coming up from Clough Head. He's been up via the Fisher's Wife Rake. "Is that the summit over there?" I ask, deciding that I should go for it, as I might not be up here again anytime soon. The man in a red Gore-Tex says there's a good view once you're up there.

The long slow slog seems to take forever as I step up a wide grassy incline and through the odd peat hag. After Helvellyn the range gets decidedly rounded and lacks the spectacular scenery of Striding and Swirral edges. But the reward comes at the top of Clough Head. It's a brilliant view across the valley to Blencathra, with its five buttresses and saddle-like summit. While looking across towards Thirlmere reservoir the mountain ranges stretch into the distance enhanced by the light of a lowering sun.

There's a slightly wonky trig point, as if erected by cowboy surveyors. I eat a Tunnock's Caramel Wafer in celebration — it's my second new Wainwright of the day.

Then comes the long trudge back to Sticks Pass. It's six hundred feet of ascent back to Great Dodd and then another climb to Stybarrow Dodd. By the time I'm descending Sticks Pass I realise that I'm unlikely to make my 7pm dinner pre-booked at the youth hostel, and I really don't want to have to walk the extra mile to the nearest pub, the Travellers Rest in Glenridding. Perhaps I am now experiencing that frisson of danger that the cyclists get, churning up dust as they career down Sticks Pass?

Pushing my body onwards, I finally descend Sticks Pass and stumble down by the stream to return to the hostel at 19.25pm. My phone's health app tells me that I have walked 18 miles and 28,000 steps. "We were starting to get worried about you," says the warden, who has thankfully saved my evening meal on the hotplate. I order a refreshing pint of cold Cockerhoop and take my seat with the only other diners, two cyclists from Burnley who have cycled from Lockerbie to Glenridding today, which seems a tremendous distance. Everyone is fitter than me it seems.

We talk the Lingua Franca of football and how Chris Wood and Ashley Barnes are doing well for the Clarets and Burnley's 3-0 win at West Ham sparked a pitch invasion from protesting Hammers' fans.

One of them is married to a Leeds fan. "She says 'you don't care do you?' when she goes on about Leeds, and I don't!" Tomorrow they are going up the Kirkstone Pass and on to Burnley. I retreat, full of mashed potato, carrots and a pasty, to head for the showers and a blissfully quiet sleep,

The next day my body is stiff, but after a good YHA breakfast — with an extra sausage, they must like me — I walk back into Glenridding.

There's a bus due in Glenridding and although it's only a mile I need to conserve energy. Taking my place in the bus shelter a local man stops to chat. "Where have you been staying? I'm surprised more people don't stay at the YHA, it's good value. We used to only have Helvellyn YHA, and then they built Patterdale." He's a talkative type and it's good to talk to friendly strangers. "In a few weeks the weather will change… It burns your retina off when all the colours come out! Good luck with the bus, they're sometimes packed. At Pooley Bridge there were 30 walkers got on the other day!"

I get off the bus in Patterdale five minutes later and check in at the White Lion, leaving my suitcase behind the bar in order to walk up to Angle Tarn. My legs feel done in though. On the way up to Boredale Hause volunteers from Fix The Fells are doing a fine job re-laying the battered path with large stones being inserted into red soil.

Today is about pacing. Hardly anyone is about and the tiny islands on Angle Tarn look as stunning as ever on the smooth surface of the water. My lunch is interrupted by two noisy geese emerging from the tarn. They chase me away from the edge of the tarn as they protect their young. I must look like *Monty Python's* brave Sir Robin as I run away.

A walk round Satura Crag reveals the rise to Rest Dodd. I'd thought about trying to reach The Nab, another of my unexplored Wainwrights. But it's a mile and a half out from Rest Dodd and then you have to come back the same way, as the rest of it is a restricted access deer reserve. My body has been pushed to its limits yesterday and it's best to save The Nab for another trip as my walking legs have gone.

Back at the White Lion I find *The Professionals* and *The Sweeney* on some obscure TV channel and then eat a good curry in the bar. The landlord is behind the bar talking to a local: "I'm a Conservative and a Brexiteer, but I'm embarrassed by them now! Hang on, I shouldn't be talking politics…"

The following day I'm feeling rested and ready to tackle Wether Hill via the Ullswater Steamers ferry to Howtown. A coach party is boarding the first ferry of the day. In the queue there's an elderly cycling couple in Lycra who say they have been on two wheels for 70 years. Meanwhile there's a Londoner complaining about the vagaries of Lakeland guest houses. "That place at

Ennerdale was like *Fawlty Towers* with the sodium light outside and that thin curtain, and the loo, it was so small I couldn't pull my trousers up!"

Accompanied by a recorded commentary on the sights of Ullswater the boat soon arrives at the idyllic hamlet of Howtown. After a coffee at the hotel café I head up the lane past bluebells and dandelions in the verges and then on to a concrete path signposted to Fusedale.

At Cote Farm people are trundling about on quad bikes herding sheep. The fields are that deep green you only seem to find up north. The farmhouse is white and sheltered by trees, the silage bags in the field shiny black. A set of stonewalled fields nestles between the flanks of the Fusedale valley. It's a perfect walking day.

The path veers around the farm and across a footbridge. Two women with dogs pass me as I stop for a gulp of water. The path climbs up the side of the valley past waterfalls and then a ruined stone building with a bench outside. I take a picture and send it home on WhatsApp, suggesting that this B&B could do with a little renovation.

Soon the High Street range emerges. The path travels parallel to the ridge, then past another ruined house with gaunt holes for windows and rubble in the hearth place. I'm reminded of Wordsworth's poem, *Michael* and the forgotten tales of those who have devoted their lives to one valley, but whose homes become sad ruins when they are gone.

After a 20-minute climb across a smoothish grass flank I make it up to the ridge. It's a flat uninspiring area of featureless grass, but has scintillating views across to The Nab, Rest Dodd and Steel Rigg. A faint path turns left towards a small, rather phallic cairn that marks the summit. It's a mass of tussocky boggy grass, but it's also inspiring to think that the Romans walked up here on their newly-constructed road nearly 2000 years ago.

A group of teenagers emerge carrying voluminous backpacks. Some of them are black and it's good to see a bit of diversity in the Lakes. I discover they are Duke of Edinburgh Award students from Oxford. "Is this Wether Hill?" one of them asks, "We're not sure." I tell them it is Wether Hill, probably ruining their navigational test in the process. They have to get to Kidsty Pike and down to Haweswater to camp. I point them in the right direction.

It's too late to make High Raise as well if I'm to catch the ferry. So it's down to the dip between Wether Hill and Loadpot Hill and an indistinct path that should join up with the path from Fusedale. As I stop for some dried mango and nuts a fell runner thuds past me, gambolling down the steep path.

An unexpected joy on what looks like a smooth mountain is the ravishing ravine of Groove Gill, with trees clinging to its rocky sides and precipitous drops to the fast-flowing stream below. Soon I regain the path to Fusedale and am welcomed by the enticing white homes of Howtown. Then it's the gentle ferry ride back across the serene water of Ullswater to the pier at Glenridding.

On the final day of my five-day sojourn I plan to bag another Wainwright, Hartsop above How, before catching the 19.01 train from Penrith. My route is a mile long trek from Glenridding down the footpath to join up with the path at Bridgend, passing carpets of bluebells in the woods. Then it's a relentless up and down climb along the spine of the fell following a brilliantly-engineered dry stone wall. That wall follows every curve, dip and raise of the ridge and never deviates. How many working hours must have gone into making it?

The views across to Saint Sunday Crag and on the other flank to High Hartsop Dodd increase in magnificence as altitude is gained. After several false summits the top is attained; it's a grassy perch with inspiring vistas of the massive cliffs of Hart Crag and Greenhow End, towering walls of stone gouged and scraped by glaciation. It's just 1871 feet high, but Hartsop above How is a very underrated fell.

The only person I see on the mountain is a man running with three dogs. We exchange a quick hello as he runs down towards Bridgend and then back up towards the summit. Does he never stop? I'm all for ambling myself.

It's a lot easier on the legs heading downwards after four days of walking. Towards the bottom of Hartsop above How there's a May tree (always liked a tree that shares my name) full of white blossom with Saint Sunday Crag looming behind it. It makes a beautiful shot on my phone camera and earns me some kudos and likes with the *To Climb The 214 Wainwright Fells* Facebook group.

Back at Glenridding I collect my suitcase and catch the 16.20 bus to Penrith. A man from Derby is sitting in the next seat and starts to chat. He's a Wainwright bagger too and is camping at Keswick.

"I'm working through the Wainwrights book by book," he says. "I've just completed the book of the Eastern Fells on this trip. Next up I'm going through the Northern Fells."

Now that is methodical, whereas my approach has been scattergun. My new friend recommends the splitticketing.com website for cheap train fares, which is useful. The bus drifts past the road to Little Mell Fell and I ask my bus companion advice on the route from the bus stop. He says it's an easy walk. Yes, I have become the sort of man who discusses Wainwright routes and train timetables.

Soon I am on the train back to London. This year I will be 60 and with four new Wainwrights completed on this trip there are still 81 left to do, not that I'm counting. With judicious planning and several train trips from London could this be the decade when I finally complete them? It's often the more obscure fells that are the most rewarding and surprising. And every time I visit the Lake District it feels uplifting. Each tick on my Wainwright wall chart is an achievement. It's time to do it while I still can.

2. DODD MAN OUT

Date: July 2019

Destination: Keswick Youth Hostel and Dollywagon bed and breakfast, Keswick.

Transport: Train from London Euston to Penrith, X5 bus to Keswick, Scales and Troutbeck, 77 bus to Rosthwaite.

Companions: Solo trip.

New Wainwrights bagged: 8 — Dodd, Eagle Crag, Sergeant Crag, Souther Fell, Bannerdale Crags, High Tove, Armboth Fell, Great Mell Fell.

Wainwrights completed: 141

Wainwrights left: 73

It feels strange to be leaving Keswick for a walk at five pm. But this is midsummer and with five hours of light left, it should be possible to make it across the footpaths to Dodd, an outlying spur of Skiddaw.

From the familiar path to Skiddaw a track turns to the left across the fields. The verges are full of buttercups and foxgloves. Taking a seat on a low branch of a stunted tree I eat a spicy vegetable pasty bought in Keswick. The smell of kidney beans and chilli pervades my nostrils. I'm hungry and every crunch of pastry is delightful.

It's always difficult acclimatising to the Lakeland air after arriving on the train — all that freshness after London's pollution can knock you out. Normally it's my rule not to walk until I've slept overnight, but a long June evening is too tempting to resist. I need to get my walking legs going.

It's on over the odd cowpat and past grazing sheep, through gates and stiles with yellow footpath signs and into the village of Ormathwaite. Then past a farm and over more fields to Applethwaite. Emerging among some delightful cottages, I make a note for my return journey to turn left at Field View and take the path to Under Scar.

The village of Millbeck looks lovely in the amber light of a long summer evening. I pace down a deserted road, past holiday homes and a small white church with a war memorial. Eventually I see a small sign saying "Skiddaw Path". The path is through trodden grass across a broad bank and rises steadily upwards. Soon I'm up towards the Carl Side ridge but worryingly, the rounded and wooded top of Dodd appears to be a separate round knoll to my left. Passing a couple coming off Scafell, they tell me there does seem to be a path towards it. When I find the path, it's a steep drop down towards the track in the valley and then up again to the summit of Dodd.

After a rather uncomfortable descent I emerge on to a forestry commission road, with ominous signs stating that the way down is closed and there is a danger to life as forestry operations are under way. It's all starting to feel a bit *Blair Witch Project*. Despite my unease, I follow the road and take a snaking track through a never-ending pine forest that appears to head upwards. A woman walking her dog emerges from a side track and she assures me that if I keep going there's a track up to the summit. Eventually the trees thin out and a stony path wends its way up through sparse grass.

Finally I emerge at the top, a small cap of grass and white flowers above a forested bulk of mountain. An upturned piece of slate acts as a cairn with several memorial plaques attached to it. The views are spectacular, across to Bassenthwaite Lake and away to Keswick and Derwent Water to my south. It's strange to be summiting at 8pm. But this is day one of my trip and already there's been progress with another Wainwright completed straight from the train.

Getting off Dodd proves more difficult than getting on it. The path takes me through the forest on a road that seems to head downwards towards Millbeck. But more fearsome signs warning of a danger to life point me towards a diversionary path. The faint path stretches across a massive area of clear-felling. I see a solitary red fox but no humans.

It's an apocalyptic yomp, crunching over dead branches and trying not to get my feet trapped in them. At the end of the track a solid fence bars my way. So I head down over more dead wood and over a small stream towards the deadly logging road.

There doesn't appear to be any heavy machinery about to deposit tree trunks on me at 9pm on a Sunday night. The forestry road becomes a path down through woods, but now it's getting dark enough for a Gruffalo to emerge.

A sense of slight panic pervades as my boots stumble down an ever-steeper path and finally emerge on to the road near the Lyzzick Hall Hotel. I've forgotten my torch and the light is going. It's a race to get back to the YHA before the gloaming engulfs this hiker and he's never seen again. Luckily there's only one car on the road the entire journey back as my attire is black and probably invisible to motorists.

It seems much longer on the way back, retracing my

route through Applethwaite and across gloomy fields. But eventually I emerge back on the Skiddaw path and climb up to Briar Rigg and the safety of Keswick at 10pm as night now blankets the fells. It's proved to be something like ten miles and my shirt is sticking to my back with sweat.

The YHA bar is a very welcome sight as I deposit my backpack on a chair and order a bottle of Punk IPA. Is there anything better than a cold beer after a long yomp in the fells? Dodd has been bagged via public footpaths from Keswick, which is an achievement. Who needs a car? Fortified by ale I slump into the bunk in my private room and sleep soundly.

The next morning I head to the Cornish Pasty shop on Lake Road to buy my lunch. According to my not-very charitable wife, "you're the sort of man who could happily sit in a chair eating pies for the rest of your life." Which is why I don't eat pasties in London. But once in the Lakes, and particularly after walking up a fell, a pasty seems a lovely reward for all that exertion. Though I have been known to carry Gregg's baguettes as an alternative. Wainwright baggers march on their stomachs, and my lunch box generally contains dried mango from Lidl, mixed nuts, a Tunnock's Caramel Wafer, an apple, perhaps some caramel shortbread and maybe even a packet of crisps. Similarly the pub dinners and chip shops offer Lakeland treats for the evening. Wainwright was a lover of fish and chips. It's not a great place for anyone on a diet.

Today's target is Eagle Crag and Sergeant's Crag. They look easy on my OS map — so of course they are anything but. The path from Rosthwaite to Seathwaite is surely one of the most beautiful in the Lake District. Stone walls enclose a lane running next to the bubbling waters of Stonethwaite Beck, while ancient moss-encrusted sycamores and oaks shelter the lone walker.

At Stonethwaite the path joins the Coast to Coast path to Greenup Edge and it becomes steeper and more worn. Resting by a lichen-clad rock with a flowering foxglove in front of it, I spot a rather touching plaque on the stone: "This tablet was affixed by Douglas and Michael Doyle in enduring memory of their friend and companion Gordon Hallworth who died in peace under the shelter of this rock in the early hours of Sunday 8th January 1939." Luckily I don't expire in the same spot and carry on walking.

Eagle Crag is an imposing mass of cliff from the path, a striking Alpine-like crag towering over me. My legs are feeling tired after my Dodd exertions the previous night. Consulting my Wainwright book I aim for the easier path up to the saddle behind Eagle Crag rather than the sheer climb by a dry stone wall. The promised ruined sheep fold eventually appears on an island in Greenup Gill. Crossing the gill there's no path, just a tiring traverse across bracken and loose rocks up the side of Eagle Crag until a dry stone wall is reached. Following the wall relentlessly upwards I discover that, bizarrely, the summit is contained by a dry stone wall and metal fencing. Eventually there's a chink in the edifice and I go under some rusting metal and vault up a rock to emerge on the summit, looking down into the Langstrath valley.

Sergeant's Crag is visible half a mile away, a fairly easy grass walk parallel to a wall, into a dip and back up again. There's no-one else around, but clearly some hardcore Wainwright walkers have been here before as an incongruous and sodden crisp packet is on the ground, which I pick up to take down to a rubbish bin.

Once again it's a bizarrely inhospitable top, barred by stone walls and bare rock. At the far end of the path there's a small grass chute where I gain enough purchase to scramble to the top. Looking across to a misty Greenup Edge in brooding clouds it seems that bad weather might be approaching and I feel a familiar sensation of trepidation. Retracing my steps it's another knee-jerking descent down the side of Eagle Crag towards the ruined circular sheep fold before the path to Rosthwaite is rejoined.

As I head towards Borrowdale two twentysomething blokes ask me: "Do you know where Blackmoss Pot is? It's supposed to be great for wild swimming." When they add that it's in Langstrath, I'm able to tell them they should have turned down Langstrath valley and followed the Cumbria Way path some half a mile back. They thank me and I feel a reassuring sense of smugness at knowing the fells better than hipster swimmers. It's taken 40 years, but I almost know my way about now.

At Rosthwaite bus shelter I find two women doing the Coast to Coast walk. "We were just admiring the graffiti," they say. "Well, the local youth do have a long wait here," I reply, looking at the decidedly non-PC graffiti concerning Mark's sexuality and what part of the male anatomy Taylor likes.

We discuss the C2C route to Kidsty Pike and Haweswater as we ponder the timetable and discover that we have all been fooled by the inclusion of a Saturday only bus. So with an extra half hour at hand I head off to the Royal Oak for a pint and then the bus back to Keswick and a rewarding burger in the Wainwright pub.

Both walks have been more strenuous on city limbs than I imagined, so on day three it's an easier trip to Scales on the bus and an exploration of some northern fells. Heading up the lane from the White Horse pub, the verges are full of cow parsley, purple foxgloves and yellow buttercups. The path across the lip of Mousthwaite Comb is fairly gentle in its gradients and Souther Fell is an easy walk across a spongy and forgiving grass surface, dull to some, but a relief to me after the endless angular rocks of Borrowdale.

On the way up to Souther Fell there's a woman about my age, Sue from Newcastle. When I say I'm trying to walk all the Wainwrights she tells me she's on her second round of the 214 fells. "That Mungrisdale Common was an absolute waste of time!" she says. "It's just like a boggy pudding. I don't know why I bothered!" Which makes me want to do it; the outliers, the boggy, weirdest, most esoteric fells are sometimes the most interesting. You never know what you might find and it's rare to find any fell that is completely devoid of interest.

Souther Fell is a flat-topped grassy promenade, but it's surprisingly enjoyable among the cotton grass. To the east I can see across towards Great Mell Fell and the flat plains to Penrith. While looking towards the northern fells there's the surprisingly rocky face of Bannerdale Crags.

Descending from Souther Fell, I cross a footbridge and proceed up the lovely enclosed valley of the River Glendermackin. The grassy declines are pitted with ridges and folds, with occasional spots of erosion exposing the rocks beneath the soil. It's tremendously quiet and peaceful, with a great view of Blencathra's Sharp Edge passing in and out of cloud. Past a solitary sheepfold and the remnants of an old mine then up to the lip of the valley and across the path to Bannerdale Crags. Here the cloud comes down and there's nothing to see from the summit. So rather than trek across the top I retrace my steps. The only other people I see all afternoon are two cyclists on the lip of the valley and a fell runner on the way back to Scales — a relief after climbing some of the more packed tourist fells.

As the Youth Hostel is now booked out, I move on to

a Keswick B&B. Amanda the landlady cooks a delicious creamed mushroom breakfast and tells me about her problems with her mother, who sadly has dementia. My mum had Alzheimer's before she died, and I reflect that at least those days are over for me. Back in the 1980s my mum always said that Mr Wainwright on the BBC seemed a nice old man. He was classic Sunday evening viewing, both my respectable mum and her post-punk son could agree on that.

My next trip is a walk to Watendlath Tarn and High Tove. I'm on the open-top bus to Rosthwaite, behind two men talking about cars and catalytic converters, and then walking up the path to my kind of tarn. Gleaming in the July sun it's one of the Lake District's most idyllic tarns, and most importantly, as it's on an easy-to-follow farm track, it offers a tearoom on the way to High Tove.

The name Watendlath comes from the Norse *vatn-endih-hlade*, meaning 'water-end-barn'. Watendlath Farm was once owned by the monks of Fountains Abbey and nestles next to the tarn. Fold Head farmhouse is a fine example of a traditional longhouse and was the home of the fictional character Judith Paris in Sir Hugh Walpole's *Herries Chronicles* novels written in the 1930s. There's a small boat on the tarn and groups of anglers at its edges. It looks idyllic on a hot day.

The path up to High Tove passes further swathes of foxgloves as it zig-zags up the steep face of the central fells. In summer it's not quite as boggy as Wainwright described and it's a pleasant stroll to the summit, which is just beyond a solitary gate in a now-disappeared fence. Dale Head framed through that ghostly gate makes a great photo. It looks like a painting by Magritte. From here there is a view of Thirlmere on the other side of the ridge. My next target is the legendary Armboth Fell, Wainwright's least favourite mountain.

There are no paths, not even a faint line across the grass. But according to the map the summit is across the rocky area to my right. Soon it gets boggy, very boggy. My boots stand up pretty well, the water never quite covering them, but the best technique is to move quickly. I pace on across tussocky clumps of long grass flecked with cotton grass, on over moss and brown pools of water towards a series of rocks. Even the heather around them is squelchy.

Resting my sticks and backpack on a rock, one of the few solid things on this inhospitable top, I venture up to a slightly higher grey rock, what I assume must be the summit. Then for a moment I can't rediscover the rock where I left my backpack and I envisage dying on this boggy morass and my body sinking deep into the central fells. But eventually my backpack is spotted and I stagger across the bog back to the relative solidity of High Tove and its solitary gate. It feels like miles.

But I know it's been worth it as when I post details of my walk on Facebook, my pal Nigel comments that I must be taking the Wainwrights seriously if I've been up Armboth — with the logical brain of a Wainwright buff he has long championed the idea of writing a book called *From Armboth to Yewbarrow*.

Staggering down from High Tove on a gloriously sunny afternoon I find that the tea room at Watendlath is about to close, but just manage to order a pot of tea and some crisps and replenish my water bottle from the outside tap. Sipping tea under a blue sky, perfect. Then it's back up over the pass to Rosthwaite and the end of anther day of boggy discovery.

My final day in Keswick is another scorching day of 27C. People on the *To Climb The 214 Wainwright Fells* Facebook group all say how wonderful it is, but in terms of climate change it all feels wrong. The Lake District just isn't meant to be relentlessly hot. Is it going to end up looking like Spain?

It's so hot that it feels like there's real danger of heatstroke, so I opt for a smaller new mountain, Great Mell Fell. In the Lakes you never know where the bus stops are, but after consultation with the driver of the X5, I discover that he is stopping by the Troutbeck Inn on the A66. From here it's a short walk down the road and then a trek along a lengthy and hopefully disused rifle range.

The rifle range is long and narrow. I pass a dilapidated barn with upturned floorboards, sheep poo on the ground and holes in the roof. At the end of the range there's another strange ruin. Behind a bank of earth lies a brick and concrete structure that must have been used by the army at some point. The windows are out, the roof is letting in daylight, but it's still relatively intact. My thoughts turn to the young men who practised shooting here before perhaps dying in some foreign quagmire.

Climbing over a stile, the pudding-shaped Great Mell Fell stands before me. A series of indented steps in the grass go straight up, though in the fierce sun I'm soon sweating profusely and have to take frequent breaks, gulping water, sitting uneasily on the steep slopes in the searing sun.

Eventually I emerge on the top. The summit contains a low tumulus, so it's been an important site in ancient times. The views of the ridges of Blencathra are excellent, as is the opposite view of the High Street range. It's the HD version of Lakeland beneath a cloudless sky.

I'm back home soon and I need to earn some money. Things might be looking up on the writing front. I've had a commission from *The Author* magazine to write a piece on the diary of a writing nobody, and perhaps a year in the life of a jobbing writer might make a book.

Unexpectedly, I'm suddenly joined by two walkers

arriving from the other side of the fell. We start to chat and after telling them that I am a writer, I discover that Anthony is a medieval musical instrument repairer and his wife Fiona originally came from Walthamstow in London. They live in Kirkby Stephen and take a walk every week. Anthony has a shop in Saltaire and an outlet in London. I ask him if he's had any famous customers.

"I once repaired a hurdy-gurdy for Pete Townshend. And I've done some work for Sting."

"Though you didn't recognise that bloke from Whitesnake when he came in!" adds his wife Fiona.

"This is quite an unusual discussion to be having on the top of Great Mell Fell," I muse. "You don't expect to meet a medieval musical instrument repairer at the top of a mountain. Or to be talking about Pete Townshend's hurdy-gurdy."

We say our goodbyes and I descend back down to the rifle range. You never know whom you are going to meet in the Lakes, but I now know where to go to if I have any hurdy-gurdy problems.

My trip is over. It's back to Keswick for a bus to Penrith. The train home to London is delayed by a fatality at Wigan and has been diverted. The automated station announcing system is confused, telling us we are at stations that have been bypassed: "It thinks we're somewhere we're not!" adds the human ticket inspector.

Euston seems a strange melee of humanity after standing baking on a solitary fell. But it's another eight Wainwright fells completed in five days — enough to provide some memories and maybe even inspire a plan. They say write about what you know. And I'm starting to think that perhaps my big idea could be writing up my adventures in search of the perfect Wainwright wallchart.

3. THINGS CAN ONLY GET WETTER

Date: September 2019

Accommodation: Charlotte Cottage, Keswick.

Transport: Train from London Euston to Penrith, X5 bus Penrith to Keswick, 78 bus to Rosthwaite, X5 bus Keswick to Dubwath, X5 bus Keswick to Braithwaite. Taxi to Whinlatter.

Companions: Nicola, Nell, Lola, Katy and Vulcan.

New Wainwrights bagged: 5 — Whinlatter, Great Crag, Sale Fell, Causey Pike, Scar Crags

Total Wainwrights completed: 146

Total Wainwrights left: 68

The first week of September sees rain and wind shake Keswick. People shuffle under umbrellas through Market Square, cobbles shine, slate roofs keep off the deluge. We hunker down in Charlotte Cottage, our rented Georgian dwelling in The Seams, which is conveniently close to the town centre. In this homely cottage we find stacks of books, dvds, board games and a huge TV to help with rainy days. The interior decor is tasteful, with shutters on the sash windows and subtle green walls; it's someone's home rather than just a rental space.

It's been a busy August before we left. Nell got her excellent A level results, my sister Pam was over from Australia and I celebrated my 60th birthday with a family meal in Stoke Newington. It's not been too bad a life; I've been a dad to two daughters, got married, bought a house, seen West Ham win the FA Cup twice, written for the *Guardian*, had 15 books published and been treasurer of the Drayton Park School PTA. And more importantly walked 146 Wainwrights and just been published in *Lakeland Walker*.

There's been a heatwave and the temperature has gone up in Westminster too. New Prime Minister Boris Johnson has prorogued Parliament. Before this happened I'd thought it was the Prorogues who performed *Fairytale of New York,* featuring Kirsty MacColl. It's illegal and dodgy, but it seems Boris will do anything to get Brexit done, including purging his cabinet of any talented Remainers.

Thankfully we are on our annual family trip to the Lakes and can avoid the news. I've enticed my wife Nicola, daughters Nell and Lola, Lola's friend Katy and Vulcan the border terrier to the area once more. One day they'll get a trip to Greece. Lola once asked Katy why she thought her family were middle class. "Lola, your family go on walking holidays…" was Katy's simple but definitive reply. So we are now set for some middle-class Wainwright bagging, weather permitting.

Of our two daughters Nell is still quite keen on mountain walking. Lola hasn't been so keen since our debacle on Blencathra's Sharp Edge in 2012. It was my fault as I'd previously been up Narrow Edge and had somehow confused this in my mind with Sharp Edge. The weather was good, though that didn't stop Lola having a vertigo attack halfway along the edge, which was right up there with Striding Edge for scariness. While her hapless dad tried to calm Lola, who had never shown any previous fear of heights, Nell went to see if there was a path to the right as we had hit a rock impasse. She didn't return. Nicola was trying to edge her way up a rock chimney. And then there was the problem of the dog. Vulcan had become scared too and the scrambling was difficult for his tiny legs, so he was now in my backpack, his head poking out and giving the odd whimper. It was all shaping up to be the most unsuccessful expedition since Captain Robert Scott failed to bag the South Pole.

Finally Nell returned, a traumatised Lola managed to move and Nicola had found the chimney to the top of Blencathra. Poor Vulcan was so stressed he began weeing all over the top of Blencathra. Lola wasn't much better and vowed never to go up a mountain again.

We did entice Lola up to Angle Tarn in 2017 on a fine sunny day. But once we got beyond Boredale Hause the black cloud moved in and a deluge of rain hit us accompanied by huge buffeting winds. We arrived back at the White Lion soaked and not even chips and gravy could pacify Lola. Despite my pointing out that I did not control the weather in the fashion of some omnipotent deity, she was clear it was all her dad's fault. Since then she's stuck to walking round lakes and valleys.

Here in Keswick the mountain weather information service is forecasting rain and heavy winds; the evidence of a misty Walla Crag viewed from our bedroom window proves them right.

Day one sees Nicola, Nell and myself taking the easy option of a taxi to Whinlatter, after we discover the 77 bus will take more than an hour to get there via Honister

Pass. Lola and Katy opt for low level activities.

Whinlatter is a kind of adventure camp set in the hills. There's a visitor centre with a shop, canopy walks and lots of marked forest trails for walkers and cyclists. A helpful woman behind the shop counter tells us how to get to the top, "you follow the green trail upwards, at number two go straight across to number 55, walk to the gate and turn right up the hill when the trees stop." I'm a little confused. Strangely there's no printed map for the Wainwright baggers, despite many leaflets on the trails.

As we ascend on mulchy trails through damp pine trees we encounter a carved wooden Gruffalo lurking in the trees. I'm not sure what Mr Wainwright would have made of this – someone even more reclusive and grumpier than himself. Having read Julia Donaldson's delightful story to my own daughters at countless bedtimes, we excitedly take a photo of ourselves with the Gruffalo in the deep dark woods.

As the forest abruptly stops in front of a treeless area, we find two schoolgirls with their parents, who say they are doing a climate change protest at the top of the fell. They have been inspired by Greta Thunberg and the school strikes campaign. At each top they are leaving a painted stone with climate change information on it. Nell is impressed and we offer them our support. Wainwright thought the mountains were unchanging — but with human activity causing the biggest temperature changes for millennia, who knows what this land will soon look like?

It's a relief to be out of trees and see a clear path. We head up to the wide spaces at the top of Whinlatter. It's a better than expected summit, most notably for the fantastic views across to Grisedale Pike and the individual trees slowly colonising the sides of the fells on Whinlatter Pass. The geography of the whole area becomes clear, looking across to Graystones, Lord's Seat and Barf.

We walk from Whinlatter top to the further summit of Brown How. Here there's a curved dry stone shelter where we're buffeted by tremendous winds as we enjoy superb views across to Morecambe Bay. Inside the shelter we find a grey stone painted in bright colours with the words "climate change is real", deposited by the kids we met earlier.

We retrace our steps back through the forest and down to the visitor centre, catching a bus to Keswick with 30 seconds to spare. At 1,722 feet (and much of that is done driving up to the pass) Whinlatter is a relatively small fell, but a surprisingly enjoyable one.

The next day sees more showers, but Nicola, Vulcan and myself leave our tardy teenagers asleep in the cottage and make an early start on the bus to Rosthwaite to try to scale Great Crag. We take the path to Watendlath Tarn. The foxgloves I saw two months before are now faded husks, but the view back towards Borrowdale is as lovely as ever.

At the crest of the ridge we turn on to the path to Great Crag. It soon gets boggy, with our feet squelching through an inch of water with every step. A sign announces that the direct path ahead is closed to protect the wildlife and that we must follow a series of wooden posts. These take a more circuitous route towards the crag as the rain starts. Suddenly my left leg gives way from under me as I fly into the mulch. One leg of my Craghopper trousers is now inundated with water and mud. Time to put my waterproof trousers on, which is difficult, balancing on one leg in a bog while Nicola laughs at me. "It could have happened to anyone," I protest.

We speak to another couple on the way up and ask

them about the path to Stonethwaite. "It's steep and it can get quite technical," says the man. When he's out of earshot we chuckle at this term. Technical, like 'extreme' and 'wild' and 'mindful', is one of those terms that people now use to sex-up old-fashioned hiking. Perhaps I should write a book on *Extreme Technical Wainwrighting*. These days there are countless new buzzwords for outdoor enthusiasts to remember and certainly more wellness editors than you can shake a walking pole at.

Finally we get to the slightly less boggy flank of Great Crag and ascend up a series of stone steps. It's a relief to be away from Boris and his blustering. Up here there's no proroguing. We take in a fine vista of Watendlath Tarn as we look back across the grassy plain to the pass. Great Crag has a series of heather-clad rocky summits. From the cairn we catch a glimpse of Dock Tarn beneath metallic skies.

The rain worsens and Vulcan, wearing the new orange waterproof dog coat that Nicola has bought him, shelters shivering between our legs as we eat bananas and pasties. We opt to retrace our steps rather than walk on to Stonethwaite as Nicola is rushing back to Keswick to paddleboard. Our descent times nicely with the next bus and she's soon at Derwent Water for an hour's paddle, while I head back to light the log burner.

Things can only get wetter in Keswick. Nicola and the three girls are paddleboarding down the river from Derwent Water to Bassenthwaite on an adventure outing. Taking a bus to Braithwaite, I trudge along the path around Barrow to Stair and the start of the path up to Causey Pike. "You can only get wet once, then it doesn't matter," say the only other couple out walking on a grey miserable sodden day. I've never adhered to that, and after an hour and a half of incessant rain and biting wind to get to the start of the walk, I give up and return through the glistening bracken with a saturated Gore-Tex, having indeed got wetter.

Back at the cottage we watch the TV as the country continues to be torn apart by Boris Johnson and his Brexit ultras. First he almost announces an election but doesn't and then there's a live debate in Parliament as the MPs vote on a no-deal crash out of Europe. There's the attorney general booming gravel-voiced invective at the opposition benches and then Boris Johnson refusing to apologise for referring to the 'Surrender Act', surely a dog-whistle to the far right. Wanting to remain in the single market and retain peace in Europe does not make you a traitor.

We find other amusements. Lola and Katy take electric bikes through Newlands almost all the way to Buttermere before Katy snags a tyre on a stone and goes over her handlebars, but thankfully escapes with just bruises and a £100 bill for damage to the hired bike.

With the fells still too wet we spend a great day touring Honister slate mine. Having been up Fleetwith Pike in recent years it's a treat to go inside it. We don miners' safety helmets and take a coach up a dirt track stopping outside a large black hole in the mountain. The rain is pelting down. Our guide takes us in to damp low tunnels with rusting rail tracks. The walls are damp and coated in sludgy grey dust.

Further into the system we admire the huge caverns hacked out of Honister Crag by Cumbrian and Irish miners from the 17th century onwards. Once mining accounted for most of Cumbria's wealth. We exit down a stairway through a sloping seam of the hardest green slate in the world — it lasts 300 years on roofs. And as the tour guide says, remember it's a mine not a quarry. With some glee he informs us that Wainwright mistakenly referred to it as a quarry in his *Western Fells* book: "It's one of the few things he got wrong in his guides."

There's a rare window of light sky when we emerge. In the Honister café Katy has been minding Vulcan and has met some Coast to Coast walkers with a similar dog. On the wall a sign reads: "We have no wi-fi. Talk to each other. Pretend it's 1995."

Our party eschews the bus back in favour of walking down Honister Pass. We take the path down to Seatoller, hopping over swollen streams and slippery boulders. It's the best moment of the holiday, partly because it's unexpected.

At Seatoller Lola, Nell and Katy are fascinated to discover a working red phone box near the bus stop and they phone up Granny Fiona.

"It eats money! Can we have another 50p?"

Granny Fiona isn't that surprised they are ringing from a phone box, but to my kids it's ancient history. We explain that people really did used to live like this and that sometimes you would have to queue to use such a device. They are sad to leave this unsmart phone when the bus to Keswick finally arrives.

With one full day left Nicola, Nell and myself attempt to scale Sale Fell via the X5 bus to Dubwath. The back roads are certainly quiet compared to the speedy A66. Walking through Routenbeck we take the path up the side of Sale Fell, a gentle circular track up to a dry stone wall and then a trudge up grassy slopes to the summit.

But suddenly we're being battered — there's stinging rain and 50mph winds on top. We stop for lunch by some of the few rocks. I try to put on my extra fleece and my Gore-Tex nearly flies away. For half a minute I'm in cold shirt sleeves. "You look like a Spanish civil war partisan!" says Nicola, noting my modish gear of checked red shirt and claret West Ham woolly hat. Vulcan shelters under Nell as we huddle behind our rocky windbreak.

We stagger down the other side of Sale Fell but give up on climbing Ling Fell. Luckily there's a corpse road circling the fell and we take it back to our starting point, stopping to look inside St Margaret's Church. It's a lovely moment; we are finally in a dry space and sit in peace with water dripping off wet coats into the wooden floorboards beneath our pew.

From there we walk on to the Pheasant to dry off. It's a splendid old inn and hotel. Nicola likes the hunting prints on the wall and the bar has a rich patina of polish on old oak walls. It reeks of ages past and Nell falls in love with it. Me less so, when I learn the price of a pot of tea and half a pint of beer, but still, it is the tourist season.

We head back across the A66 to Dubwath and shelter in a solid stone bus stop with a swallows' nest in the eaves. Suddenly there's tremendous rain belting down from the sky. Raindrops ricochet off the tarmac and back into the air. The water spatters closer to our bench but the stone shelter does its job; opposite there's no shelter and a man waiting for the bus to Cockermouth gets soaked before the bus arrives. I wonder if we might be trapped in the bus shelter forever and how we might all sleep in my survival bag, but eventually the Keswick bus arrives as the storm worsens. We look forward to getting the log burner going in the cottage.

My final day sees another go at a solo walk from Stair up to Causey Pike and Scar Crags. I take a taxi to Stair to save some time. Causey Pike is an iconic double-topped chair-like outline from Derwent Water, but I've never climbed it. It's a steep but do-able climb up to Sleet Hause and then a more difficult scramble across heather and rock to the summit. It's a thrill to be on top and the prize is a stunning view of the side of Scar Crags, a massive tilted slab of scree and heather with green, grey and purple flanks that descends all the way to the tiny Rigg Beck far below. I'm happy up here, with my hood up and my nostrils full of the scent of rain, wind and, it has to be said, sheep poo.

After a hasty pasty sheltering just off the top of Causey Pike, I take the path to Scar Crags as the rain and wind sets in again. The summit is a lot flatter than it looks, but the wind is nearly knocking me over. So it's down to Sail Pass, with the zig-zag path to Sail prominent. From here I descend the path down to Barrow Door, finding a great view of Force Crag Mine in the Coledale Valley far below. My mental map of the area is starting to fit together.

It's a gentle ramble down grassy slopes around Underside and back to Braithwaite, where a pint in the Coledale Hotel awaits. Another five summits scaled in a very wet week. So it's 68 Wainwrights left now, with 146 completed. Soon I'll be back in Charlotte Cottage to pack up our poles and waterproofs and prepare to depart. But there's still time for another autumnal trip in October before the clocks go back. As they say on *The Apprentice*, my quest to bag the Wainwrights continues.

4. I CAN'T BELIEVE IT'S BUTTERMERE

Date: October 2019

Accommodation: Buttermere Youth Hostel.

Transport: Train from London Euston to Penrith, 77 bus Keswick to Buttermere and Scawgill Bridge, X5 bus to Dubwath.

Companions: Solo trip.

New Wainwrights bagged: 6 — Whiteless Pike, Wandope, Grasmoor, Starling Dodd, Ling Fell, Graystones.

Total Wainwrights completed: 152

Total Wainwrights left: 62

"It's like bring in prison — only at least you get a tele in prison! I'll wake up and me throat will have been slit…" A lad from Yorkshire is not too impressed by the bunks in the Buttermere Youth Hostel.

He doesn't need to worry too much though, as most of us hiking recidivists are well-past middle-age and unlikely to commit serious crime. My dormitory is on the second floor and sleeps eight male inmates. The hostel should be perfect for exploring the surrounding fells — and it's cheap too. The only problem is I'm sharing a room with seven other men in various stages of sweatiness after longs days of walking and cycling. The odour is a mix of stale perspiration, sweaty clothes and dodgy deodorant.

At least there's a bedside lamp fitted to my bunk, a previously unheard of luxury, plus a wooden partition between my bunk and the bunk opposite. My backpack and clothes can be shoved under the lower bunk. I climb on to a slightly unsteady mattress set on a wire frame and nestle beneath a YHA green duvet cover with my head on a green YHA pillow cover, reminding myself that it's only £15 a night.

Through the night the dorm reverberates to considerable snoring, plus there's the industrial-scale noise of extractor fans and hand-dryers whenever anyone uses the loo next to the room. It's part *Midnight Express*, part Hogwarts. All of hiking life is present when I wake up in the morning. Someone is whistling and singing. A muscular man is doing exercises. Others are bag rustling, one man is crashed out through everything, and someone else is cutting his toenails in the corridor.

After a satisfying full hostel breakfast, I head out for the hills. Today it's a circular route to Grasmoor, the last of the top 20 Wainwrights to complete on my wallchart. The weather is looking good for October and it's a pleasant yomp past Rannerdale Knotts and up smooth grass paths between swathes of yellowing bracken. Despite their 60 years of use my legs are feeling relatively powerful after a summer of walking and by 11am I'm on top of Whiteless Pike. Wainwright number 147 achieved.

The summit has a small cairn and a massive view. The

sides of both Grasmoor and Whiteless Pike are huge slabs of rock covered in scree, moss and heather. They are minus all the usual gullies and crags and slope at 45 degrees down to Rannerdale Beck far below. The grass is an autumnal shade of yellow while a thin wisp of cloud hangs above the flat top of Grasmoor.

The path carries on to Wandope, an area of flat grass with a few stones, but it has a great view of the slopes of Ard Crags and Knott Rigg with the Newlands Pass snaking through Newlands Hause. Plus further slabs of scree and moss on the sides of Scar Crags and Great Crag. This is certainly one of the most impressive parts of Lakeland.

From the pass at Crag Hill it's a well-blazed path up to Grasmoor. The top is surprisingly roomy. There's time for a selfie by a not-very-effective dry stone shelter overlooking Crummock Water. Wind whistles through the gaps in the structure. To the west I can see over to the coast and a mighty wall of scree and gullies on the flank of Whiteside.

My circular route involves descending via Lad How. The YHA warden has warned me that it's steep and some of it is over scree, but my walking poles become good balancing aids and the knee strain is tolerable. Having descended the steep slope of Hartsop Dodd, it's nothing I can't handle. This route also offers spectacular views of the side of Whiteless Pike, a battleground between scree and moss.

At the bottom of Lad How are two brothers, maybe in their forties, waiting for their dad. They ask if they could make it up Lad How and be down for six. As it's already nearly four o'clock I tell them they'd be pushing it, as it's very steep and they'd then have to come down over Wandope and Whiteless Pike.

Which is just as well, as when their dad Tom emerges

it turns out that he's 83. Though he's still game for a walk, and tells me that he first saw the Lake District at the Eskdale outdoor bound centre in 1956, when he was an apprentice and the trip was paid for by his company. We all walk together along the valley between Rannerdale Knotts and Whiteless Pike, an area famed for its spring bluebells. The triangular peak of Whiteless Pike is silhouetted against the blue evening sky like a mini-Matterhorn.

Tom is slowing down and would clearly have struggled to get up Lad How, but how impressive that he is still pacing the fells. His sons discuss Tangle Foot and other beers and their plans for a meal back at the Bridge Hotel. Tomorrow they are off on the bus to Braithwaite to have another go at Grasmoor via the old miners' track and I'm even been able to give them a little advice.

It's been 22,000 paces according to my phone app and I stagger into the Fish Inn for a pint of Keswick Brewery's Thirst Quencher, hoping that my sweaty shirt is not too odorous.

Then it's back to the Buttermere youth hostel. It's a grand old house repurposed, with a nice air of faded grandeur and lots of helpful staff. As darkness edges in I sit on the veranda watching a stunning purple and pink sunset behind the huge silhouettes of Red Pike and Starling Dodd. The car park is packed with four-wheel drives and expensive cars — I'm one of the few hostellers to have arrived by bus.

I've booked in for dinner (£1 off for members). The seating arrangements force hostellers to socialise. Each guest's surname is chalked on a small slice of tree trunk, set by his or her place. I'm sitting with Stefan from Germany, a lecturer at Lancaster University and his wife, plus Stephen an engineer from Huddersfield, who likes cycling and is staying at the hostel while visiting his sister in Cockermouth.

Stefan asks me about Brexit and I say I think it's mad, perhaps unwisely as I don't know if I am surrounded by Brexiteers. Though as a democrat I'm not sure we can revoke it without another referendum. But he has a German sense of logical puzzlement at the whole debacle, while Stephen is also a Remainer. "Is there any industry support for Brexit?" asks Stefan. I can only offer the maverick owners of Wetherspoon and Dyson. We go through the reasons, those left behind, the protest vote, the years of austerity, and the anti-migrant rhetoric of the press. And then the chilli and rice arrives, which is rather good, and we leave off the politics.

Over lemon meringue and ice cream Stefan's wife shows us her many phone pictures of the shores of Buttermere and Crummock Water and an app for learning the Mandarin alphabet. We discuss arriving by train and I tell them there was once a station at Keswick, but the line was closed in 1972, in another strange act of national self-harm. Stefan is interested to know that I was once a student at Lancaster back in about 1643. Later in the lounge he shows me a Lancaster University brochure for his department and we admire the slick student-centric marketing.

After my long walk I can sleep through anything. The next morning the dining room is full of older men breakfasting. Staying at a YHA can be like a *Last of the Summer Wine* convention. It seems there's some sort of CBBC event. Only after I've dined on hashbrowns, beans, scrambled eggs, veggie sausage and toast, a man in the car park reveals that the group is actually from CBC, which stands for Cranleigh Baptist Church. I thought they looked a bit old for TV presenters.

The lady at reception knows all the local routes and gives me advice on Starling Dodd, plus an extra banana in my packed lunch as I've turned down the one-use plastic bottle of water that the YHA strangely still includes in its lunch packs. Any decent walker carries their own water container.

For an hour the rain holds off as I set off on an already soggy path round Crummock Water. But as I head towards Scale Force the drizzle starts and lasts all day. The path follows Scale Beck up past a series of ravines and waterfalls. The rain worsens and enclosed in my waterproof trousers and Gore-Tex jacket and hood, I feel a little like a space-suited Matt Damon in *The Martian*. The Martian feel is accentuated by the fact the stones and soil of the path are running red too. I seem to have found a great deal of water on this red planet. I tighten the Velcro on my cuffs and pull the strings on my hood.

The beck levels out and a long trudge through the rain takes me towards the ridge on the skyline. A couple of lads descending from Red Pike warn me that there's hail and massive winds on top, but I explain that I'm heading to Starling Dodd and will turn back if there's any problem.

After a long climb I reach the Red Pike ridge and bear right across a boggy shoulder of mountain. Paths start and fade in the mulchy grass, but I head in the direction of a ruined iron fence and the path from Red Pike to Starling Dodd. "It's not as bad as it looks really," says an optimistic man with a West Country accent descending from Starling Dodd. Only it is. Most waterproofs can only stand so much rain before water eventually penetrates and now I'm starting to feel damp.

But the trudge up to Starling Dodd is fairly easy and on top I take a selfie, my face hidden by my black hood, standing next to a pile of stones and an *avant-garde* sculpture of upturned metal fence posts. From here I can see a beautiful view of Ennerdale Water with clouds hanging above it in the next valley. But the mist is coming in and the rain intensifying.

Great Borne lies ahead but it's a steep walk down from the summit to Floutern Tarn and then back to Crummock Water. It would add another three miles to my journey and retracing my steps to get back seems the best option. The mist gets a little scary traipsing across the boggy land back towards the Scale Beck path. I made the right decision not to go up Great Borne as it's now disappeared from view.

The waterfalls are gushing and care is needed not to slip on the shining rocks and disappear into the depths of the rapids below. Finally I make it back to Scale Force, where the twin waterfalls have doubled in volume. A dog the size of a house starts to bark at me. It belongs to a waterfall-observing couple, who say he doesn't normally react like that.

The path has become a quagmire and is in places more like a river as I stagger back to Crummock Water. Pursued by the wolf-like canine and its owners, I pace the wettest path in England back to Buttermere, desperate to get dry. A pint in the Bridge Hotel bar helps, though they might not appreciate the soggy patch my trousers have left on their seat.

Waterproofs, backpack, shirt, trousers and boxers all have to be hung up in the hostel's drying room. Then it's dinner with a Mr Harvey from Kendal who is a southern exile but has lived in Cumbria for 44 years. He was going to camp but gave up as the rain set in and has walked all the way from Wasdale Head. He's even encountered Mr Wainwright, I learn. His wife did voluntary work for the Kendal museum and AW once sold a drawing to raise funds for the museum. When my dining companion knocked at AW's door, the great fellwalker gave him the picture and shut the door without further speech.

My final breakfast at Buttermere YHA is taken with a group of late middle-aged men discussing Alexa and how to turn on heating and monitor properties remotely through the Cloud (electronic not Lake District variety). I'm not sure AW would approve. Then it's the bus to Keswick, a check-in to my new B&B and a bus ride to Ling Fell. From the bus window I spot an EU flag hanging outside a house in Braithwaite. Even here Brexit is polarising people.

As with Sale Fell, it's a gentle meandering trail to the summit up the grassy corpse road from near Wythop Mill. After passing the tumbled stones of disused grouse butts I reach the trig point from where the outline of the Galloway coast in Scotland is clearly visible. A dog scampers up to try and steal my apple. The dog is followed by its owner, who says he lived in Rickmansworth, Herts, for 16 years and his wife is from down south. He points out to his house on the flat land towards Cockermouth and says he has a view of Ling Fell and several other mountains.

As one visitor descends another appears. A couple from Maine come up. "We flew in to Glasgow yesterday. It's a shame we missed the heather… how do they get power in those villages? You know Maine has similar hills, but we have 10000 acres of woodland."

I mention that I know Maine from reading *The Cider House Rules* by John Irving and the Maine man is impressed. He asks me how long it takes to drive from London and I tell him that I've come by train and bus. "We're behind on a lot of things, we don't have high speed trains. We're the country of the car, it's a funny time with Brexit and Trump. Boris and Trump seem to get along, though I'm not sure that's a good thing."

My new friend and his wife chuckle as they ask, "Why is it called a Corpse Road?" I explain the path down really is called the corpse road and that's where bodies used to be taken to the church. "I guess us Brits aren't too good at marketing. Americans might have gone for some branding that was a bit less ghoulish."

My walk continues round the lower slopes of Sale Fell and back to the main road for the X5 bus back to Keswick. The day ends with a fine pint of LB 1000 and a falafel burger at the Wainwright pub in Keswick.

On my final day I'm booked on the 7pm train home from Penrith, meaning there's still time for a bus ride to Scawgill Bridge and a climb up to Graystones. Debouching from the bus I admire the fine old arched bridge in what seems to be the middle of nowhere.

The path to Graystones goes up over an old quarry and then follows a dry stone wall relentlessly upwards. Wainwright is rather dismissive of it as a route in his guidebook. But the advantage is that it's right by a bus stop and is only 900 feet of ascent. Had Wainwright been a Wainwright bagger he might have opted for speed over aesthetics when there was a bus to catch.

There's a sheep skull embedded in the dry stone wall half way up which makes it all seem a bit like a David Lynch movie. But eventually the path flattens out to an amble across the grassy summit. I meet a pair of walkers from the Lorton side who tell me there are two summits: "This one's a Birkett and that's a Wainwright." I touch both of them and then eat my pasty.

It's a difficult walk and slide down the steep incline, but I'm quickly back at ground level. While waiting for the bus which is 90 minutes away I take the path through Darling How to Spout Force, which is slightly more visible than in Wainwright's day — a mysterious ravine and torrent through the leafy mass of forest in front of the viewing point.

A couple of workmen are fitting a new bridge across

the beck, and have left a quad bike by the riverside seat near the bridge. It's a peaceful spot and I sit admiring the river, the old bridge and the tree-specked flanks of Grisedale Pike.

Only suddenly 100 schoolchildren emerge, clutching measuring instruments. Two coaches are parked by the bridge. "I bet you thought you were in for a quiet afternoon!" laughs a teacher. "Is that your quad bike, mister? Can we ride it?" ask several teenage boys, clearly hoping I'll let them career off into the valley.

When my bus finally arrives it struggles to get past the school party's coaches. Then a group of cyclists emerges coming up the Whinlatter Pass and a car comes down the other way. Gridlock in what I thought was the most isolated of areas. It feels more like the Seven Sisters Road in Finsbury Park.

But the bus eventually takes me into Keswick and then it's on the X5 to Penrith and the train back to London. It's been a satisfying October sojourn. Six more Wainwrights completed, 152 done overall and 62 left to go. The clocks are going back soon and winter walking is best left to the locals who can choose their days. It's time for a break and then I'll be back in spring 2020. What could possibly go wrong?

5. SUPER GRASMERE

Date: March 2020

Accommodation: Lake View Country Hotel, Grasmere

Transport: Train from London Euston to Windermere, taxi to Grasmere.

Companions: Nicola and Vulcan.

New Wainwrights bagged: 3 — Steel Fell, Raven Crag, Seat Sandal.

Old Wainwrights bagged: 3 — Calf Crag, Gibson Knott, Helm Crag.

Total Wainwrights completed: 155

Total Wainwrights left: 59

A pandemic seems to have hit the UK. We're not sure if we should be going to the Lake District at all. The coronavirus stories are becoming ever more alarming. But our trip was paid for back in February, the trains are running and surely it can't get much worse in four days? We've left younger daughter Nell on a university skiing trip to France, not knowing if it will be cancelled for safety reasons once she gets there.

But should it all go corona-shaped there are coaches in place to return her to our home in London. Older daughter Lola is safe in Turnpike Lane having returned from a mini-break in Barcelona. At least we are in Britain and being stranded in the Lake District wouldn't be at all bad.

West Ham's game has been postponed along with all other football, so Nicola, myself and our dog Vulcan take an earlier train than anticipated to Oxenholme on a Sunday afternoon. It's mid-March and the train from Oxenholme to Windermere is virtually empty compared to the summer season. Those that are travelling are certainly friendly. "Is that a border terrier? I knew it's a northern dog!" says Mark, a bearded man in his twenties nursing a can of lager and stroking Vulcan. He's possibly had a sniff of the barmaid's apron. We learn that he lives in Burneside, but grew up in Kendal. He used to walk his family Alsatian on 200 acres of land.

"I've been to Lancaster for a KFC. We used to have a KFC in Kendal but they closed it down. Mind you, I've not been there just for a KFC, I had a drink and a day out," says our new friend.

We mention that we plan to get a taxi to Grasmere as we'll have missed the last bus. "I used to be a taxi driver. It's a bit like being a priest, you can't say what you see. People with people they shouldn't be with."

Nicola asks him about troublesome passengers. "No offence, but it's the middle aged women who are the worst, they're like your mum!"

He finishes his lager and tells us that he doesn't have a ticket and no-one has asked him for one, even though he has the cash ready, which is a bit of a result. Then he retreats on to the darkened platform at Burneside, full of the joys of ale and KFC.

"He called me a middle-aged woman!" mutters an indignant Nicola. As we draw into Staveley I tell her that it has a decent pub and a chip shop. "Not any more! They're looking for a buyer," says the woman sitting opposite us. We learn that she's been to London to see the musical *Pretty Woman* and the National Portrait Gallery to see David Hockney.

It's proving to be a talkative journey. At every stop the guard walks down the train to open the doors. Nicola says he must be getting fit walking up and down. "Normally I'd have walked all the way down. I'm taking it easy today, I'm self-isolating with my coffee in the cab." We ask him if he thinks the train service will be stopped soon with all the viral panic. "I don't think they'll close us down, we've just been told to carry on. The rest of Europe's closing down and Boris wants us to sing happy birthday twice and wash our hands…" We grin.

At Windermere station we meet our pre-booked taxi. Like everyone else he's talking about corona: "People think 'I'm a tough northerner it won't get me' but I get flu every year in this job, you pick up bugs. I took someone yesterday who was about to fly to Marbella. If we don't have lockdown in a couple of days a lot of people will die. I'm worried about my parents… I don't think young people will isolate, they're used to thinking of themselves, they're selfish."

We arrive at Grasmere and find the Lake View Country House. It's a beautiful room, with a stone-lined wall. We unpack Vulcan's dog bed and then settle down on the comfy sofa to make a night of it watching *Last Tango in Halifax*.

In the morning we find there's a stunning view across a sheep field to Grasmere's lake, with a yellow-brown ridge of fell behind it. Geese take off from the water and coronavirus seems a long way away. Even better, there is real coffee in our room, with a cafetiere. We head off for breakfast at the hotel's sister-pub, the Good Sport, which is five minutes away. We're careful to sit at an isolated table and wash our hands for 20 seconds. The waitress asks us to wait before ordering because she is taking her daughter to school next door. When she returns we enjoy eating porridge and cheesy mushrooms on toast..

The day's objective is to climb Steel Fell from Grasmere and then walk down via Helm Crag. After a stop at the Co-op to buy lunch, we head down Easedale Road and turn right down the lonely road past Thorney How Youth Hostel.

As we walk daughter Nell sends a text from France saying her trip has been cancelled because of the virus and Nicola rings her back from the roadside, probably to the chagrin of the people in the holiday cottage nestling behind us. It seems Nell is getting a day's skiing in before her student party have to get the coach back to London the next day. It will be a relief to us when she is safely back in Britain, though she's disappointed to be leaving so soon.

The official advice seems to be changing with every day, as the virus erupts. Nell's disappointed to miss out on a week in the French Alps, but she is safe. "What doesn't kill you only makes you stronger," I tell her, echoing the words of Nietzsche, another keen walker who might perhaps have described Wainwright as his *ubermensc*h (aka superman).

At Ghyll Foot we find two cottages and the track to Steel Fell. It's a wide grassy path without too many rocks to impede progress. Nicola stops to watch a farmer on a quad bike and his dog round up a herd of sheep. Vulcan looks interested in the view too, but is held tightly by his lead. It's real-life *Countryfile,* as pockets of sheep make bids for freedom before being headed off by the dog or farmer. The grey sheep look like moving pieces of scree in the distance as they head through a gate, led by one braver sheep, and on to the farm.

"Are we in the way if they come up this track?" worries Nicola. "Should we help?"

"I doubt if the farmer has been thinking all morning I wish I could come across a couple of clueless Londoners," I quip. "And if he's anything like Gillian in *Last Tango in Halifax* he'll tell us to f**k off!"

We head off up the path. I'm puffing as it's the first walk of the year. Nicola is faster thanks to her paddleboarding-induced solid core. We stop on the rather saucily-named saddle of Cotra Breast for a lunch break of cheese and tomato sandwiches, looking across to the A591 and the great slopes of Seat Sandal and Great Rigg. The traffic seems reduced today as Britain's shut-down continues. The ascending ridge of the fell lies behind us and in the distance Windermere is now visible.

With renewed energy we soon make it to the summit. I can see the ridge route to Helm Crag and in the distance Greenup Edge is pitted with white dabs of snow. The air is cold but the sky is bluish behind darker clouds and the weather holds. We feel like proper walkers being up here in March. And who knows when and if we will return if the virus continues to spread?

The summit is a small mound of rock topped by a triangular metal fencing pole. A ghost fence of poles stretches across the fell, relics from the days when it was thought that metal might tame the fells more effectively than dry stone. We take celebratory photos with the white flecks of snow all over Ullscarf making a dramatic backdrop under grey clouds. It feels a long way from viral worries up here. And having looked at the contours of Steel Fell all winter on a map there's something very satisfying about finally standing on it.

My second wind returns with making it up another Wainwright summit. It's an easy stroll along the line of the dead fence towards the circular route down via Helm Crag. In the cold of March it's not quite as boggy as Wainwright described. We veer left by the nameless but permanent-looking tarns that AW quite correctly thought should have been featured on his OS map. Vulcan is starting to pull on his lead so we switch him to his harness. Perhaps he wants a pint back in Grasmere. Soon we are on top of Calf Crag. We last walked this section as part of our epic Coast to Coast walk in 1997, pre-children.

"We walked up from Borrowdale over the Helm Crag ridge and down into Grasmere," I tell Nicola.

"We had to dodge thunderbolts and lightning all the way over. It was terrifying!" she says, less enthusiastically.

"Thunderbolts and lightning, very very frightening? But at least we survived. And I seem to recall you thought that as a farmer's son I should know how to stave off a lightning strike... but I didn't, funnily enough."

In my memory it was a short ridge walk from Calf Crag to Gibson Knott and Helm Crag back in 1997. But it's a lot longer and more up and down than I recall. Still, the mosaic of dry stone walls far below in the deserted valley of Easedale looks magnificent and to our left we can see the craggier side of Steel Fell.

We reach the final peak before Helm Crag. We haven't seen anyone since we encountered a solitary man on Steel Fell. Nicola decides to take a loo break, telling me to keep watch as she crouches behind a boulder.

Suddenly, from nowhere, a couple emerge from over the brow behind us. "Hello, erm hello! HELLO!" I shout, trying to sound the alarm, hoping Nicola will hear. "Er, Nicola!"

"I'm so sorry!" gushes Nicola leaping up guiltily from behind her boulder.

"Just taking a comfort break," I mutter.

"We all have to take a nature wee," laughs the rather understanding woman in Gore-Tex.

"We hadn't seen anybody on the ridge until you arrived!"

We get chatting and it emerges that they were meant to be skiing in Switzerland, but it was cancelled yesterday due to coronavirus, so they opted for the Lakes instead. "Who needs the Alps when you have this?" I say.

It starts to get very windy as we approach Helm Crag. The bad afternoon weather that was forecast is approaching and we feel small as we're blown into the fellside by fierce gusts. There are two outcrops of upturned rock on Helm Crag. I mistake the first upturned slab of volcanic rock we see for the Lion and the Lamb, until we emerge at the actual landmark. Appropriately a sheep is munching grass beneath the ready-to-pounce lion.

We descend down the ridge towards Grasmere. In front of us is a man in a red hat who must be 80-odd and shuffling gently downwards with small steps. You're never too old to climb a fell. We rest on the steep path down as Nicola's knees start to hurt, before the path descends to the much gentler gradient of Easedale Road.

We're almost back at Grasmere and its inviting pubs. Then Nicola's phone goes off by the gently murmuring Easedale Beck. It's our eldest daughter Lola phoning in a viral panic. And now the rain is starting to fall.

"Lola says that Boris Johnson has announced we should avoid pubs," declares Nicola.

"But I've been dreaming of having a pint of beer all the way from Calf Crag!" I exclaim. It seems there's a conspiracy from my wife and daughter to stop me enjoying my reward for a nine-mile circular walk.

"It's not about socking it to the Man, it's serious,"

says Nicola. "We'll go to the Co-op and eat in the room."

"But we would never have received that message if you hadn't answered your phone! Nothing good comes of mobile calls in the Lake District. I'm going to have a pint — it might be the last one I ever have before lockdown. And the pub's open, whatever Boris says!"

While Nicola shops at the Co-op I take Vulcan — and my life — in my hand by ordering a hasty pint of Golden Swan ale from the Inn at Grasmere. It tastes excellent. Then Nicola arrives, has a swift glass of wine but ushers me out of the pub when she hears a woman at the next table coughing. Outside the rain is pelting down.

Dinner is cold Co-op wraps, a cold quiche and crisps in our room. But it feels cosier and cheaper than the bar meals we now have to avoid. The room feels like we are at sea as rain lashes the windows and gales howl down the valley.

"Are you a bit worried about this virus then?" we overhear one of the staff say at breakfast. It seems a suitably low-key Cumbrian response to the worldwide plague stories emerging on BBC News. The room is empty but another breakfasting couple sit right next to us — the messages to keep your distance aren't getting through yet. Still, Nell should be arriving home this very day and soon our family will be re-united in London, as we are booked to leave in two day's time.

According to the Mountain Weather Information Service the weather is going to be bad for most of the day, so we opt for a relatively low climb to Raven Crag. This involves taking a bus and exposing ourselves to more people, but at least the 555 is fairly empty. After annoying the driver by ringing the bell too soon, we are deposited at the end of the road to Thirlmere Dam.

Nicola soon forgets about social distancing (maybe it's not as important outside) and starts talking to some

Duke of Edinburgh Award sixth-formers leaving a caravan park carrying large backpacks with rolled-up mats strapped to them. They are from Newcastle and were going to go to Wales until that trip was cancelled because of coronavirus. Now they are on a Lakes alternative heading up to High Tove, which will be a boggy walk.

Access across the dam is closed to vehicles, with large slabs of concrete placed across the road. But walkers are allowed through and we admire the splendid 1890 stonework that holds back a huge amount of water. On the other side of the dam there's a mysterious castle-like tower behind a padlocked fence. The Victorians always did water stuff well.

A giant tractor is blocking the road. We can hear the sound of electric saws. "It'll be a tight squeeze," says a man in a high-vis jacket. He explains that there's a tree in the reservoir that needs to be removed. Nicola asks if that matters. he says it does, because the trunk will get swept down the overflow. We squeeze past the giant tyres of the tractor and head on to the path up to Raven Crag.

The crag itself is massively impressive for a fairly diminutive Wainwright of 1512 feet. It's a sheer buttress of rock that towers overhead, a temptation to climbers and a fatal 500-foot drop for any unwary person who happens to walk off the edge at the top of the crag.

A sign announces that there is no climbing because of nesting peregrines. We go upwards through some clear-felled woods, past damp tree-stumps and then over a forestry road and further up into a pine forest. My thighs ache after yesterday's exertions.

But soon we are at a neat wooden deer fence and gate and head left up a set of wooden steps into the forest. When the path levels out a series of duckboards take us across the boggy ground and on to the top. One of the more unusual approaches to a Lakeland summit.

A wooden fence atop a viewing platform suggests you shouldn't wander out towards the precipitous drop. But several charred pieces of wood in front of us indicate guerrilla bonfires and people prepared to take a risk of a fearful plunge if they have a can of beer too many. It's certainly memorable as one of the few wooded Lakeland summits.

It's a really impressive view down the length of Thirlmere. To the north is the angular wall of the dam and an aerial view of the 'Lake District-in-miniature' fell of High Rigg. We sit on the duckboards with Vulcan and eat sandwiches from Tupperware containers as grey clouds threaten rain.

Nicola begs me to say something interesting to distract her from knee-pain as we descend. But I didn't get where I am today by being interesting. After I fail to inspire, she says she needs distracting and gives me a Radio 4-style lecture on Cervantes and *Don Quixote* as we descend, me the faithful Sancho Panza following behind her, but without a donkey. We make the bus as the rain sets in for another stormy night.

On our final day in Grasmere blue skies return and Nicola, suffering from knee pain, opts to take a low-level walk with Vulcan round Grasmere and Rydal Fell, while I attempt to climb another big fell, Seat Sandal. Frustratingly, I've been past Seat Sandal after hitting Grisedale Tarn on the way to Helvellyn in 1982 and also on the Coast to Coast path, but in pre-Wainwright bagging days had never bothered to climb it.

The news is more ominous, with a *Guardian* found at the newsagent revealing more deaths and that stringent measures such as closing schools could be on the way. I try not to think about it.

Walking past the Travellers Rest pub I take the path

past the deep ravine of Tongue Ghyll. It's pitted with hydroelectric huts and dams and today its torrents are powerful indeed. It's rained all night and the path is almost a river. I'm squelching in an inch of water once it reaches a grassy incline. It's also empty on the highway to Helvellyn. It's so deserted I start to think I'm in the 1970s apocalyptic TV series *The Survivors*. Being told not to visit pubs and restaurants or take unnecessary journeys has had its effect.

The trek takes a long time but eventually the path reaches the impressive depression around Hause Moss, which Wainwright says is the remains of a dried-up tarn, and is certainly filling up with water today. Rocks are strewn all over the flank of Seat Sandal beneath Gavel Crag and it's an eerily peaceful spot.

As I ascend the lip of Grisedale Tarn another walker appears. "What about yer!" He launches into a long monologue in a broad Northern Irish accent and I hardly understand a word. He's having problems with my Essex twang too. Should this be the end of times it would be ironic to be stuck here with just the two of us struggling to understand each other's regional dialects. He asks me if I know Alcock Tarn. At first I wonder if this might be some form of innuendo, until I realise Alcock Tarn does exist on the flank of Heron Pike. I think he's come from there. I do my best and smile and mention the sparse number of walkers. "You're either well or you're not!" is my friend's opinion, as he heads off back to Alcock Tarn.

Grisedale Tarn is the striking body of water at this fellwalking crossroads. Three people are sitting on the path having lunch, but I practice social distancing and eat my sandwiches some distance away. I'm tantalisingly close to my third Wainwright of the trip, but also possibly my last for some time.

A stony and steep path ascends by a broken wall up

the side of Seat Sandal. It looks more difficult than it is and soon I'm looking back towards a thrilling view of Grisedale Tarn, Dollywagon Pike, Fairfield and St Sunday Crag, with Ullswater gleaming at the end of the valley.

The wall up Seat Sandal is broken but would once have been a feat of near-impossible building by skilled artisans. In places it's still intact and big foot-deep slabs of snow have piled up. The temperature is now nearly freezing and it's time for gloves to warm my hands.

The top has two cairns, a tumbled shelter and excellent views across to the snow-lined tops of Scafell Pike, Great End, Great Gable, Pillar, High Stile, Dale Head and Grasmoor. There's a very distinctive view of the shoulder of the mountain heading back down towards Grasmere. My mobile buzzes into life as Nicola sends WhatsApp pics of her delightful excursion on a Wordsworthian tour around Grasmere, Dora's Field and Rydal House.

Meanwhile it's a very steep awkward descent that I tackle with extended poles, occasionally having to run down the steeper sections. At the bottom a shut gate seems to end my progress and I veer left through an open gate and follow a dry stone wall past a padlocked barn and around a boggy field, suddenly slipping and getting a mud-encrusted wet leg. There doesn't seem to be a way back on to the Tongue Ghyll path, so I have to climb over a barbed wire fence and jump down a stone wall at the ford. A couple of women walkers look as me as if I'm a bit on an idiot, which I might be, as there's a stile through the giant wall one field further down.

Three new fells is something of a triumph I'm thinking as I pace wearily back into Grasmere, my poles retracted for the bar. I'm about to have a pint of Grasmere Stout at the Good Sport, which has safe tables outside, when Nicola phones me. Her friend at the boat club says

London is about to be shut down completely. She wants to get the train home immediately while there are still trains and no armed checkpoints on the M25. I'm not inclined to believe that the government would do London lockdown without notice, but it seems I am destined to never get a pint.

Back at the room it's a hasty bath as Nicola uses her laptop to buy new tickets and then the 7pm bus to Windermere instead of a final relaxing night in our peaceful room by the lake. At Oxenholme station we use the waiting room for an hour. "You'll have to move once I've done these seats over here, but don't worry, these ones will be dry soon," says a friendly man who is spraying all the seats and door handles with disinfectant. He is wearing an Avanti high-vis jacket with a tasselled leather jacket underneath. A sort of Lemmy of the gig economy. We learn that he used to work at Sainsbury's and this is his first week with the train company. Nicola says he could be saving lives. "At least I'm helping," he says modestly. He thinks the service will soon be reduced but not stopped.

We catch the 8.24pm train to London and there's a woman with an insistent dry cough in our carriage. Eventually we move. Corona has us all suspecting each other. We stagger out at Euston and take a strangely quiet Victoria line tube to Finsbury Park.

We're back in the madness of London as panic sets in and tube passengers wear masks like we're in a medical drama. My Wainwright completion programme can't survive this. But hopefully the memories of the fells will sustain us for a long and difficult period when travel is banned. Who knows when we will return? The world is about to change. Pubs and restaurants and even the streets and parks are now forbidden. We're at the start of a real-life Plague Year.

6. LOCKED OUT OF THE LAKES

Date: March-July 2020

Companions: Nicola, Nell and Vulcan.

New Wainwrights bagged: None

You don't know what you've got till it's gone. Thanks to coronavirus tearing through the population my walking district is now the local streets of N4. Amid a global pandemic we're locked down and only allowed out to walk the dog, shop or take one hour's exercise a day. The plague might kill one in a hundred people and we don't yet have a vaccine. At 60-years-old the odds are still just about in my favour, but I could be one of the unlucky ones.

Days seem to merge. We have our youngest daughter Nell at home, sad to be missing out at York University and now doing online learning from her computer. Our house is a bubble, while Lola is locked down at her student house in Turnpike Lane.

I get bread and buy the paper while wearing a facemask. We become very familiar with features of certain TV shows, like Connell's medallion in *Normal*

People and Joe Exotic's mullet in *Tiger King*. Inspired by the *Guardian's* top ten Tom Hanks films we watch *Sleepless in Seattle* and *You've Got Mail* on Netflix, the days of 1990s rom-coms and basic email seeming like a much simpler age.

This was meant to be year when I finished scaling all the 214 Wainwrights. But now I don't know if normality will ever return. Our 'bubble' family of three getting on our bikes and cycling to Blackfriars Bridge now seems like a massive adventure. London is my locale and nowhere else. It's not even that important when hundreds of deaths from Covid-19 are being announced every day, but I miss the Lakes.

It's surprising how much I'm missing the freedom of being able to jump on a train (National Rail's journey planner's labyrinth of fares permitting) and get out at Penrith or Oxenholme, the gateway to the Lakes. Things I took for granted. No-one thought this would end. There will be no more B&Bs because everything is shut and the Lake District National Park is saying don't visit. And for someone like me who relied on buses to get around, will the risks of coronavirus and social distancing mean I have to hire a car if I ever visit Lakeland again? Watching *Contagion* on Netflix doesn't fill me with optimism.

I'm thinking of missed chances, the mountains I climbed when I didn't know I was trying to bag all the Wainwrights. When I climbed Scafell but didn't walk on to Slight Side or walked straight past Cold Pike on the way to Crinkle Crags. The family trip up Red Screes where we could have taken a short detour to Middle Dodd. I could have bagged High Raise if I hadn't had to get back to How Town for the ferry. Having got to Thornthwaite Crag I should have carried on and scaled Gray Crag before returning to Troutbeck. And what about the fells I scaled as a student when I went out with the hiking club at Lancaster University? I remember Scafell Pike vaguely, but on several other walks no record was taken of the fells we climbed, usually while hungover after a gig the night before.

All I have now is my mournful scrolling of the *To Climb The 214 Wainwright Fells* Facebook group. There's a post from someone who lives in Morecambe and can only look across the bay towards the outlines of the Coniston fells. A picture of an eerily deserted Keswick Main Street and another of Buttermere with no tourists. The locals are lucky because they can still exercise on their mountain doorsteps. But the rest of us are excluded.

Instead I'm looking at YouTube videos of walks from Armboth Fell to Whiteless Pike. I'd forgotten how many of them chose sometimes iffy songs to go with their walks. It might be plinkity-plonky new age music, Dire Straits, AC/DC, or Coldplay, but we could do without the overdubbed portentous music.

It's a good time to plan new routes to fells that are presently just a bunch of contours on the map. I've watched a lot of videos by tattooed couple Leona and Chris Pye, who have climbed everything and talk about 'clag' a lot; plus The Taxi Driver who is avuncular, northern and has a catch phrase of, "we keep going!" Graham Saunders' Fat Boys on Tour are three cheery blokes from Southend, who often end with a beer. They laugh at seeing one of their number fall in a stream and are gobsmacked when they meet Joss Naylor on Middle Fell.

Other people use drones to give an aerial view of their walk. Some use computer-generated 3D route maps. Some very professional videos come from Joe Jackson and his Lake District Guided Walks, complete with soothing music, aerial footage and detailed route maps.

It's even interesting to look at videos of Mungrisdale Common, universally cited as Wainwright's least favourite fell. It's shaped like a pudding and a rare boulder such as the Cloven Stone is cited as a landmark. The summit cairn is in a pool of water. Yet I'm finding it rather interesting that in his *Mungrisdale Common Explained* video, Andy Beck, the author of *The Wainwrights in Colour,* claims that the summit cairn is in the wrong place. So he has filmed himself taking a stone and placing it 50 metres to the north at the point Wainwright marked as the spot height of 2068 feet in his guide (though modern survey techniques suggest it's now nine feet higher).

There are people who have put up videos of every fell and many include useful maps and routes. There's something rather charming about seeing what they have for lunch and feeling you could sip a beer with them at the end. Not to mention the videos of night-camping and cyclists careering down Sticks Pass at incredible speed.

Thanks to YouTube I can see what the elongated emerald valley of Longsleddale looks like and plan a circular walk of Tarn Crag, Grey Crag, Selside Pike and Branstree. If I can ever get to Troutbeck again I might be able to follow the Taxi Driver on his circular walk up Troutbeck Tongue and back down Ings Lane. But right now getting to the supermarket is a risk and I'm trying to keep shopping to a minimum. Buying loo paper could kill me, if it was in stock.

I have my maps and my Lakeland poetry to protect me. Tracing out the contours of a steep fellside means I can almost picture the scene. It looks possible to walk down that lane from the A591 to Binsey. There's more time to look at interlocking routes and dream of just what a daub of blue that's labelled a tarn might look like when I'm actually there.

What lockdown is teaching us is to celebrate everything that we value. Reading *War and Peace* in the unseasonal spring sun of our small back garden I'm transported to Russia and the time of Napoleon; music sounds crisper and cathartic; a chat in the street to a neighbour in a mask seems like a lifeline; my wife Nicola is by my side in our bed; my younger daughter Nell is close by in her room and bored but healthy, while my other daughter Lola is safe in her shared house.

My stored walking poles hang from a peg in the extension and my newly-waxed Zamberlan boots are on the windowsill. And it would be so good to get away from the miasma of panic and lose some worries on the mountains. The Lake District is still out there and one day I will return.

7. ANCHORED DOWN IN AMBLESIDE

Date: July 2020

Accommodation: The Gables, Ambleside

Transport: Train from London Euston to Windermere, 555 bus Windermere o Ambleside, 516 bus to Dungeon Ghyll, taxis from Ambleside.

Companions: Solo trip.

New Wainwrights bagged: 7 — Sour Howes, Sallows, Little Hart Crag, Middle Dodd, Holme Fell, Troutbeck Tongue, Cold Pike.

Old Wainwrights Bagged: 1 — Red Screes

Total Wainwrights completed: 162

Total Wainwrights left: 52

Euston station feels strangely dystopian. We're slowly coming out of lockdown. The adverts on the tube escalator have gone, replaced by government posters telling passengers to wear masks and stay safe. Matt Hancock and Chris Whitty are watching us. Most of the shops are closed on the concourse, bar W H Smith, which is still offering expensive snacks. People gather outside by the shops around Euston Square Gardens so that they can remove their masks, gasp some fresh air and grab a cup of coffee.

For March, April and June we've been confined to home, walking the dog once a day, making masked trips to the local shops and wondering if a vaccine will ever be found for a virus that has killed thousands. At least I managed to finish *War and Peace*. Now summer is here, the R rate is down, restrictions on hotels have been eased, and at last the Lake District beckons again.

On the train to Preston passengers are allowed window seats only and masks must be worn all journey. This feels clammy but not too much of a problem once I lose myself in my OS maps and Wainwright guides. Then from Preston it's the slow train to Windermere and a bus to Ambleside.

At the Gables B&B, where I've stayed many times before, owners Sharyn and Mark have introduced several sensible Covid-aware precautions. These include booking in at the later time of 4pm to allow deep cleaning, sanitiser placed by the entrance, digital registering, no cleaning of rooms by staff while you're staying, a one-way system in corridors and the breakfast room being available to eat takeaways in, though you must then disinfect the table.

In the morning breakfast arrives in a bag placed outside my room by Mark. At first this feels rather luxurious, as I eat cereal in a wooden bowl and a bap full of egg and veggie sausage, rounded off with a flask of coffee, all without leaving my room.

After buying a Greggs baguette for lunch, day one of my return to the Lakes begins. I'm taking the path from Ambleside to Troutbeck. During my long incarceration in London I've found myself inventing new ways of walking to Troutbeck so that I can cut out public transport. Wainwright recommended the Skelghyll Woods path in his guidebook so let's give it a try.

The path skirts round Wansfell and turning off Old Lake Road I soon find myself in a delightful forest with sun streaming through a roof of leaves and emerald moss encrusting the stone walls. When the trail opens out there are great views to Windermere and the boats at Low Wood. The walk ends up at High Skelghyll Farm, then descends a hill, crosses a bridge and turns uphill across open farmland. Passing sheep and bullocks I reach Robin Lane, offering a pleasing descent into Troutbeck.

At the Post Office I don my mask, order a coffee and take a seat at an outside table. The owner serves in a mask, joshing with a young girl who wants ice cream. He then starts talking about hunting with an earthy-looking country lady. She's saying that the Victorian huntsman John Peel, immortalised in song, was from Troutbeck (though the Troutbeck mentioned in the song is more likely to be the one near Blencathra) and that back in 1977 his grave in Caldbeck was vandalised by hunt saboteurs. The owner diplomatically says he's not from the country so he doesn't know a lot about country sports as the country lady gets on to the ethics of hunting. She says southerners don't really understand it and that for many farmers it's a form of conservation. "A fox takes two weeks to die naturally and it's often by a watercourse!" Not the sort of conversation I'm used to hearing in north London, our foxes tend to get mange or be run over.

There's no problem social distancing on the fells, though one dilemma is the numerous footpath gates opened by lifting up a catch. They must have been used by a lot of people and are vital for farmers not wanting to lose stock, but do involve a lot of touching. I take out my bottle of sanitiser and apply it to my hands before eating my lunch, which is a potato and butter pie. I'm sitting by the sad memorial to the 'Great War' at Troutbeck Church, reading the names of the fallen. So many young men from one tiny hamlet.

Then it's over the main road and up the Garburn Pass. This is mainly churned up, uncomfortable stones, though purple and yellow dot the verges, as foxgloves and greater celandine signal new life after Covid. At the wooded site of a former quarry I spot some steps going over the dry stone wall towards Sour Howes and make a decision to tackle it from what appears to be a direct route. I'm soon up on the skyline among a series of grassy mounds and noting the view across to Dubbs Reservoir in the distance. Spotting a female walker I ask her where the summit might be and she points out where she thinks it is. We briefly discuss my Wainwright-bagging project and she says that since she's moved here she's taken the fells for granted a bit and doesn't walk them as often as she should.

Sour Howes offers fine views across to Wansfell but it's not a classic fell. It's a long meandering wander across a wall and over various lumps until the next Wainwright summit, Sallows, comes into view. It rises above a marshy expanse of flat ground and is marked by the spoil from disused quarries on its flank. Crossing a wall a path takes me to the summit. Wainwright writes about the small rocky outcrop looking like an ancient tumulus, though it's actually a natural formation. Taking a direct path back down to the Garburn Pass it's a rather uncomfortable descent, punctuated by the sound of my boots displacing numerous loose stones on the path, and back up the steep lane towards Troutbeck Post Office.

Now I'm familiar with the path back to Ambleside it's a glorious if tiring evening walk, with the full length of Windermere glistening beyond emerald fields in the dusk.

Down to the cattle grid and up to the farm, through the shadowed woods and on to Ambleside. My phone tells me that I've walked 16 miles and 22,000 paces. It's mask on and into a Chinese takeaway to order a chow mein to take back to the hotel's dining room. Then slump on my bed in front of the TV. People often ask if I enjoy travelling alone and I do. There's contact with plenty of walkers on the fells and nothing more satisfying than the heavy tiredness of a long day's walking. And I wouldn't want a companion to smell my shirt after the rigours of the day.

Sour Howes and Sallows were duty fells for the Wainwright bagger, but day two sees a more exciting trek down the Scandale Pass and towards three new fells that I'd long desired to set foot upon.

Taking Sweden Bridge Lane out of Ambleside is always a glorious amble. Through the woods it opens up into a wide valley with the bulk of Red Screes to my right and the not-very-imaginatively named Low Pike and High Pike on my left. The sides of the mountains are covered with lines of stone walls stretching to impossible heights. The air smells fresh, sunshine beats down on pasture, the sky is blue and all seems well in the post-Covid world.

Climbing up to a small ridge by a wall for my lunch break, I'm concealed from a group of five walkers going past. I hear a snippet of conversation: "You can get accused of sexism and racism. The nature of conflict is never polarise yourself…" Would Mr Wainwright agree, I wonder. It's always interesting to note how many people discuss their work on the fells. There's something about the peace here that brings clarity to work disputes.

The pass is wet in places and was always too boggy for a road, but it's a pleasing alternative to ascending to Hart Crag and its companions from Glenridding.

Hundreds of trees have been planted in protective plastic cylinders at the head of the valley, perhaps to replace some of those lost to deforestation and Storm Desmond in 2015.

As the path becomes a wide-walled track rising to the head of the valley, I encounter a family encouraging their daughter to hop over stepping stones at one wet point with cries of "Go Melissa go!" and the promise of an ice cream. I ask them if I get an ice cream for going over the stones as well.

Little Hart Crag isn't little at all. It's a pleasing mass of rock, a proper mini-mountain acting as a sentinel over the pass. I head up past its pock-marked flank and on towards blue sky. The top is a fine double summit, graced by a glorious view of Brothers Water, which from here looks much more like a lake to rival Ullswater.

The triple ridges of Hartsop-above How, St Sunday Crag and the scree-lined Birkhouse Moor stretch away to the north. Then it's a swift descent back to the saddle of Scandale Pass and then up the other flank to Red Screes. It's a long tedious climb by a seemingly never-ending collapsed wall. But eventually I reach Red Screes and then excitingly descend on to the promontory of Middle Dodd.

It's a bit like taking a seat on the bridge of a ship. On Middle Dodd you feel like you're in command of all the surrounding panorama, a kind of Captain Kirk of the fells. I talk to a couple eating sandwiches about walking the Fells without a car. "Ones like Caw Fell are difficult even with a car," says the man. Then it's back up to Red Screes, which I first ascended three years ago with my family. The small tarns on top feel peaceful as I walk back towards Ambleside with the knowledge that I know the way down, always a good feeling.

A fell-runner in a yellow vest passes me on the way up

to Red Screes. The day is cooling as three chatting women in black shorts and tops walk up the track. Twenty minutes later they pass me as they jog down. The path takes me through a dry stone wall avenue and eventually I find my way on to the Kirkstone Pass road. The tarmac seems to go on forever as I stumble into Ambleside.

Eventually the sight of the White Horse pub is too much to resist and after giving the receptionist my phone number for Covid security, it's straight in to enjoy a burger and chips with a pint of Wainwright. Completing Little Hart Crag and Middle Dodd has filled in some of the nagging gaps on my wallchart and has all been accomplished without using public transport and risking any contagion. Another 14 miles done and a good day all round.

After a good night's sleep my thighs still feel tingly and it's time for a gentler climb. Breakfast in a bag finished, I order a taxi to Holme Fell. The drivers don't seem bothered about masks up here, as the country relaxes after lockdown, but at least the window is open. I'm dropped off at Yew Tree Tarn on the road to Coniston. This is a fake but attractive tarn, formed when the landowner dammed Yewdale Beck in the 1930s and turned an area of boggy ground into a trout fishery.

Moving round the tarn a path winds through pine trees and then bracken up towards Uskdale Gap. Here the panorama opens out, with the heather-clad twin tops of Holme Fell visible and also the path down towards the wooded quarries of Hodge Close.

The summit of Holme Fell is only 1040 feet high, but it's an interesting place, all lumps of rock nestling in the heather and splendid views of imperious neighbours like Wetherlam, Coniston and the Langdale Pikes. Across 200 yards of heather plateau is the second summit of Raven

Crag. I hoist myself up a steep path, which involves a bit of scrambling.

"You surprised me there!" says a male voice, "Most people come up the easy route." To my surprise there's a tent, and a dad and a mum carrying a baby in a sling. They're spending their second day up here they tell me. We have a chat about provisions and baby supplies and it seems they've come up with a great alternative to avoiding the fells when you have a small child. Climbing a relatively small peak and staying in a tent is better than confinement in a flat with sleepless nights. And the child is drinking in the sounds and smells of nature in true Wordsworthian fashion.

Taking the easier route off the top, it's back down through the heather as I aim to take the path back to Stang End and then Skelwith Bridge. I can see a small white house and a lane in the distance. The path heads by a moss-lined dry stone wall and then seems to veer into a series of water-filled quarry pits. After going round in a circle I find a kindly woman by a gate, who directs me to the car park at Hodge Close.

Suddenly I'm confronted by a gaping white hole of massive proportions. Behind a low fence a huge chasm can be glimpsed through some trees. A vast chunk of mountain has been removed and the sheer drop descends perhaps 500-feet. A deceptively calm green lake has filled the event horizon of this great gulch. The quarry at Hodge Close is more impressive than anything I'd imagined. There are caves, arches and rusting machinery. Quite a few divers have lost their lives here testing their skills in the submerged shafts. By the car park people are getting under the fence and taking selfies by Lakeland's own grand canyon.

My straw poll of several tourists fails to identify the way to Stool End, but eventually I spot a footpath sign.

The walk takes longer than I'd imagined, but finally I hit the Cumbria Way and turn on to the small road leading to High Park, where a couple are enjoying chilled wine in the evening sun on the patio and looking at their full glasses it would be nice to join them. On through woods, weathered iron kissing gates and a descending path into Skelwith Bridge. The bus has long gone, but after a dash of hand sanitizer it's a chance for a cold pint of Cumberland Ale in the Talbot Bar of the Skelwith Bridge Hotel, and then a call to a taxi and a short drive back to Ambleside.

Thursday sees a Lakeland heatwave. It's more than 30C as I get out of the taxi at the hamlet of Town End in Troutbeck. Walking past several attractive stone cottages, which are probably now holiday cottages, I reach Ing Lane. The stone barns in the fields are looking glorious in the sunlight and a heat haze hangs over the Kentmere fells. While the fields are radiant green. My short-sleeved shirt is soon dripping with sweat and the sun beats down relentlessly on my exposed skin.

After a mile or so Ing Lane ends at Troutbeck Park Farm, which was purchased by Beatrix Potter in 1923 and then donated to the National Trust. Moving past the sheep at Ing Farm a track rises to run parallel to Hagg Gill and along the lower contours of Troutbeck Tongue. Two lady walkers tell me it's quite steep coming off the end. Yellow flowers dot the side of the fell. Near the end of the cigar-shaped lump of fell I climb up to the ridge where there are prehistoric cairns. Troutbeck Tongue is covered in archaeology though it's difficult to tell one mound of stones from another. The cairn I find might once have contained an ancient burial, but now looks a little like a badly-maintained summit shelter.

Then it's an easy walk up the fell to the summit headland where there's an exhilarating view back to

Windermere and a pleasing feeling of enclosure by the surrounding mountains. The Tongue is at the centre of things and you can see why ancient humans made it an important spot. Then it's a steepish descent back to Ing Lane. I'm half tempted to join the sheep in the metallic gleam of the stream. After the steep climb into Town Head I stagger into the Queens Head and after giving my phone number order a pint of Dizzy Blonde from the table service. It tastes wonderfully cold and refreshing.

It's too hot to walk the long path back to Ambleside so I phone a taxi, renewing my acquaintance with Ferenc, a Hungarian taxi driver who has driven me before. The driver is now married to a Polish woman and they live in Kendal with their baby. He proudly shows me a picture of his child.

"This is best view in the world," says Ferenc, as we pass Windermere. He was travelling round South-East Asia and South America when he visited the UK and settled in the Lakes: "It's the best place for lockdown. The police stopped me while I was kayaking, but I was able to say it was my exercise."

Moving into Ambleside we discuss Hungarian politics. "Victor Orban knows how to use fear of migrants, people will vote populist when fearful…" We say goodbye and my mind turns to a takeaway Chinese and bed.

Waking up on my final morning to yet another knock on the door and breakfast in a bag, my legs feel tired and my body dehydrated after yesterday's sun. But days here post-pandemic are too scarce to waste. It's a bus ride to Great Langdale as I need to knock off Cold Pike.

From the farm at Stool End I take the path to Crinkle Crags, moving through Oxendale then climbing by the ravine of Browney Gill. A stream descends from the heights in a ribbon of falls, tumbling past mossy grass and shattered rock. My new lightweight Osprey backpack, brought from Blacks in Ambleside, is proving comfortable and I send a picture of it to Nicola. There's nothing she likes more than a picture of walking kit. Reaching Red Tarn I turn right on the route to Crinkle Crags, heading up to peaty grassland.

There's a fantastic view across to the stumpy tops of the Langdale Pikes, but my muscles are weary and I'm not enjoying it as much as I should be. Like Wordsworth in *Ode: Intimations of Immortality* I've lost my mountain mojo. Five days of walking without a rest is proving a bit much for my sixty-year-old body. My visionary gleam has been left back in Ambleside.

But Cold Pike is not far from the main path. Frustratingly I could have climbed it when doing Wainwright's Crinkle Crags circular walk back in 2005, but back then I had no plans to climb every mountain and ford every ghyll. It's a short detour to the summit and it's worth some tired limbs. Wainwright describes the top as a mini Crinkle Crags, a series of bumpy splintered rocks. I'm completely alone and the view is spectacular; down to Red Tarn, across to the Coniston fells and looking towards Crinkle Crags and the grey grooves of Bowfell links.

Despite its frosty name, Cold Fell is not particularly cold, though it is pleasantly windy after yesterday's heatwave. I'm not sure too much thought was put into the naming of this particular summit, but that's part of the joy of the Lakes, the sometimes gloriously literal names created by earthy farmers.

Then it's back down to Oxendale on a new path of unforgiving stone laid by Fix the Fells, which is effective but feels hard on my feet. Numerous families are coming down from Crinkle Crags. Back at Langdale it's a short wait for the bus, at what must be the best bus stop in

Britain with its views of Middle Bridge, where a shot from *Brief Encounter* was filmed, plus Bowfell and Rossett Pike. The bus doesn't have any windows open raising my coronavirus concern, but at least it's not packed. It's very easy to forget infectious disease when you're among the sublime.

Back in Ambleside I watch Arsenal win the FA Cup in my room and then enjoy a final takeaway meal of chow mein. Tomorrow it's back to London. I never thought I'd get back to the Lakes this year. Seven new fells completed. This feels like a renewal. There will be a second wave of coronavirus at some stage if the scientists are right. But summer is here now and we can relax for a time. The Lakes will endure and outlast all this. I'm back walking with a post-pandemic purpose.

8. ANOTHER GREAT COCKUP

Date: September 2020

Accommodation: Skiddaw Cottage, Keswick.

Transport: Train from London Euston to Penrith, X5 bus Penrith to Keswick, 78a bus to Rosthwaite and Seatoller, taxi to Longlands.

Companions: Nicola, Nell, Lola, Michael and Vulcan.

New Wainwrights bagged: 7 — Longlands, Brae, Great Sca Fell, Meal, Great Cockup, Ullscarf, Base Brown.

Total Wainwrights completed: 169

Total Wainwrights left: 45

Having survived lockdown our family is finally heading for a week's holiday in Keswick. Adult daughters Lola and Nell have been tempted by a free holiday and Lola's boyfriend Michael is also joining us. Nell has sparked alarm by having to have a Covid test after her friend's flatmate in Leeds caught the virus, but thankfully she's negative.

We have to wear disposable face masks for the three-hour train journey to Penrith. And then it's masks on again once we board the bus to Keswick after a refreshing coffee in the grounds of the castle. Our holiday bungalow is close to Booths supermarket in the centre of town, so we immediately stock up on provisions and eat at home to avoid Covid-19.

The cottage has all we need apart from a third bedroom (Nell has to sleep on an inflatable mat), including a conservatory and a back garden with an apple-bearing tree in a fenced off enclosure.

I open the gate in the fenced apple tree area. "Erm, Nicola, things are looking a little grave," I suggest.

"So that's why it's fenced off," she answers.

We are observing two headstones bearing the words "Mum" and "Dad". A grave wasn't mentioned on the website, but it's rather touching that mum and dad wanted to be buried within sight of Skiddaw. They must have really loved this house.

On day one it's time to ease Michael, who has previously only scaled the Arsenal Emirates Stadium, into the world of fell walking with a short trek up Latrigg. It's also a good walk for Lola, as it's free of vertigo-inducing ridges like Sharp Edge. Stocking up on pasties helps (two beef and chilli, one cheese and onion, one chicken and mushroom and one spicy veg) as we take the path to Skiddaw through the woods on the other side of the A66, and then turn up the grassy path to Latrigg. It's steep and a bit of a slog for city legs, but soon we're sitting on a summit bench overlooking Keswick. I've been up Latrigg before, but like so many mountains, it feels a lot better the second time.

Nicola is impressed by the epic view across Derwent Water to Catbells and Causey Pike and wonders why I've never taken her up Latrigg before. We take pictures of our daughters sitting in the 3-D clarity of the Lakeland light;

Lola in her yellow Hunter jacket and Nell in her white and claret shirt gazing out over the tiny houses, the wooded islands of Derwent Water and the rigid outlines of the mighty ranges.

Latrigg has a surprisingly revolutionary history. In September 1897 there was a mass trespass by 2000 people demanding the right to roam after landowner John Spedding, acting on behalf of a female relative, closed the traditional footpath to the mountain claiming he had, "the absolute right to exclude everybody". Among the protestors were Canon Hardwick Rawnsley the founder of the National Trust and Samuel Plimsoll, later famous for saving counting lives at sea through preventing overloading with the 'Plimsoll line'. Luckily people power won.

As the others walk back to Keswick Nicola myself and Vulcan take the Cumbria Way in the hope of making it to Mungrisdale Common. My wife loves the path as it's relatively level but with great views across the valley and of Glenderaterra Beck below us. We meet a nice looking couple of university lecturer types on the Cumbria Way, who have been camping. Nicola is convinced it is Raynor Winn author of *The Salt Path* and husband Moth.

The Cumbria Way is longer than we thought and seeing the size and distance of Mungrisdale Common we decide to turn round and beat the dark. We'll treat today as a fact finding mission. A man rushes past who has come all the way from Calderdale, declaring. "I've been walking into this wind all day, I'm on automatic pilot." The wind isn't too bad for us though as we make our way back to Keswick. Shafts of sunlight come through the clouds, illuminating Derwent Water as we round Latrigg once more. We make it home for a pasta feast purchased from Booths and cooked by Lola and Michael.

The next day it's time for my grand plan, a five-fell

expedition on the isolated northern fells starting at Longlands. Our taxi driver is a friendly lady who tells us all about painting her shed. She doesn't know the fells though, like most taxi drivers, and hasn't heard of Longlands, so I show her the spot on my OS map and we decide to head in the direction of the Over Water Hotel.

At Over Water we turn left instead of right and head back towards Uldale as I struggle with my map. But that proves a blessing. At Uldale we try a new route and drive across Aughertree Fell, a great expanse of flat moorland that looks like it should be in the Yorkshire Dales. Then down a wooded lane. A cluster of parked cars reveals the hamlet of Longlands and the start of the footpath.

The taxi only costs £30, which is pretty reasonable for a 45-minute journey. Nicola, Nell and myself unpack poles, adjust clothing and set off along the Cumbria Way, before turning to go up the slopes of Longlands. Wainwright wrote that, anyone who could not manage this short climb, "is advised to give up the idea of becoming a fellwalker." It's a straightforward grassy track, but fresh from the taxi and on another hot day we find ourselves puffing towards the top, which must mean we're not fellwalkers.

Just before the Longlands summit we meet a sweating man from Barrow on his way down. "Look out for the flying ants. There's more ants than I've ever seen up there!" he warns us. Two fell runners and a show off dog zoom past us. Up to the small summit cairn, which has a mysterious silver shimmer to it. As we approach it moves and we realise it's the ants. They buzz around our heads menacingly, landing on any exposed piece of flesh. We take a hasty photo, admiring the view of Over Water, Bassenthwaite Lake (the only lake in the Lake District) and Skiddaw in the distance as the ants attack again.

We skirt around Lowthwaite fell and head across a

river valley up towards Great Sca Fell. Nicola and Nell wait on the path and compose poetry while I take a 20-minute detour to bag Brae Fell. Half way along the path as it gets wetter the flying ants return. They actually seem to be attacking me. I put on my hat, but they are getting down my neck. I'm hauling up crushed ant bodies from my chest and beating my arms in the fashion of a man doing mad semaphore signals.

By the summit cairn there's a further silver wall of ants. Good view though. This really feels like the edge of the Lake District. The land extends northwards across craggy farmland and moors towards Hadrian's Wall where the Brittunculi ("wretched little Brits") are probably still lurking wondering what the Romans ever did for us.

Nicola and Nell don't seem to have noticed my near demise at the hand of homicidal insects. They have kept hold of my backpack and suggest I eat a pasty, which I do after removing more dead black blobs from my torso.

"I was attacked by flying ants!" I complain.

"Ants are lovely, they don't attack people," replies Nicola. "We saw you doing a mad dance."

"But they were getting down my shirt and into my trousers!"

"You can't be scared of nature!"

Somehow I don't think my wife is going to appreciate the harassment I've suffered. We take a short walk up to Great Sca Fell and the third summit of the day. We can see the circuit now though it's not as obvious as on the map. There are up and down treks to Meal and Great Cockup to come, while Knott looks a peak too far for today.

It's a steep descent down the grass towards Meal, where we meet a man and woman walking the opposite way. They look like middle-class southerners and we have a chat, discussing the merits of which way to do the round. "Like most men you've probably swallowed a Wainwright book," suggests Nicola, not entirely tactfully. But maybe our new friend has done just that. He says he's discovered a website for doing all the Wainwrights in 36 walks. I'm very interested.

We trot down the steep side of Great Sca Fell and then up the grassy bank of Meal, where there's a rock shelter on top. You do wonder where some of these fells got their names. Did it earn its moniker simply because some cartographer had his lunch there?

The Longlands circuit is flat and grassy, but in many ways those sinuous curves make the declivities of the river valleys look even more impressive. Descending from Meal there's the confluence of Frozenfell Gill and Burntod Gill in the lovely sheltered haven of Trusmador. We walk up the edge on to the side of Great Cockup and the three of us lie down on the grass, pleasantly tired as we take in the sun and listen to the sound of running water. Nicola says it is one of her favourite Lakeland walks. Vulcan sits down too, senses on the alert, looking into the distance.

We pace on up Great Cockup and admire the view of Bakestall, a mountain with a giant chunk taken out of its side at a spot called Dead Crags. It's flanked by Dead Beck — someone seems to have been rather gloomy when they named this area.

Soon we reach the top of Great Cockup and think of Boris Johnson. The flying ants are back too and Nell doesn't like them as they follow her away from the summit cairn. We take an ant-harried selfie and walk on. We almost make a Great Cockup coming down, taking a wrong turning at a dry stone wall, but eventually we find our way out at Orthwaite and on to the tiny lane.

We pass a couple of farms but there are no other signs

of humanity. Reaching Peter House Farm we phone Davies taxis but the number is engaged. We decide to take the footpath to Bassenthwaite where we can wait in the pub. It looks easy on the map, just across this field by the farm. "We can't go in there it's full of bullocks!" declares Nell, who has never recovered from her bovine trauma when we were charged by a cow in Wiltshire. Or the snorting bull when she was seven on the Hadrian's Wall path. Or the frisky cows by the seawall on Canvey Island.

"We'll have to, it's the only way of getting to Bassenthwaite village," I counter. "It will be fine."

We climb over the stile into the field and it isn't fine. The bullocks are running around in circles. They look remarkably frisky, like they've just been let out. We hug the right hand fence. "Dad, they're coming towards us!" I hold up my walking poles and make myself look big while shouting. It works for a few seconds. As the bullocks charge for the far corner of the field we increase our pace and make it to a corner of the field, although ominously there is no yellow footpath sticker. We climb over a fence by a large tree and into another bullock-free field. We cross that but there's no sign of a footpath. Night is coming down. Should we veer left to the farm buildings? We decide that if we can't find the footpath we will have to turn back and reach the road. "I'm not walking through those bullocks again. We'll die!" says Nell. "We don't have much choice, I'll protect you and we can leap over the fence if necessary," I counter, with false bravado.

It seems we've made yet another Great Cockup. We return to the bullock field and enter when the group of marauding teenage bovines are at the far side. We hug the fence by the farmyard ready to conceal ourselves behind rusting pieces of agricultural equipment. After an agonising trek we reach the stile. "Get over quick, they're coming, they're coming!" says a panicking Nell as the bullocks run up again. Relieved, we slump by the roadside and realise that it's going to be dark in half an hour.

"Where did the footpath go?" I mumble in the fashion of a Vietnam war veteran with PTSD. The taxi number is still engaged. Then, incredibly, a miracle taxi appears in the lane. How did that happen? We flag down the driver.

The taxi stops and the driver says he's out on a pick-up somewhere down a lane that he can't find and that if we want a call-out we'll have to wait two and a half hours as they're fully booked. He radios the office and tells them to send us a cab to the Sun Inn at Bassenthwaite at 9pm, before disappearing across a farm track. All we have to do is get to the pub before night falls. Looking at my OS map there's a small lane that takes us to Bassenthwaite, even if it is longer than the footpath route.

Tired after 12 miles we saunter down the lane as Nell rings sister Lola to tell her, "Mum and dad tried to kill me, they made me go through bullocks twice!" At Walk Mill bridge we find a secluded lane that takes us through a wood and past the gentle murmuring of Chapel Beck. It would be a lovely walk if we weren't racing against darkness. We carry on down the winding road, past a set of shut-up farmhouses that look like something from *Straw Dogs*. It's nearly dark. "Dad, there will be wolves!" worries Nell.

The lane seems to bend around corners forever. Nell's phone app says we're only ten minutes from Bassenthwaite, though we're walking so fast it now seems to be marking our progress with a car symbol. We take one final turn and then miraculously the village appears. Civilisation at last. Here are cottages and a village green and finally the Sun Inn.

We stagger exhausted and relieved towards the door. "I hope you're not wanting food! We're fully booked out!" says a man who looks like an ageing biker standing by the door. Not quite the welcome we were hoping for after 14 miles.

But it's a lovely old pub, dating from the 16th century. Inside it has low oak beams, somewhat at odds with the Perspex screens now installed as Covid-shields at the bar. Gratefully I order a very welcome pint of Bassenthwaite Beauty, glasses of Sauvignon for Nicola and Nell and crisps and peanuts. The car park has been turned into an area for safe drinking and so we take bench and zip up our coats, as Vulcan sits on a spare fleece. It's such a relief to be at a pub tearing open a packet of dry roasted peanuts. We buy a second round and finish off the lunchtime food in our Tupperware containers.

"That was the most exciting thing that's happened since lockdown," says Nell of her escape from deadly bullocks, suddenly high on an adrenaline rush. I tell her she's got four new fells to put on her Wainwright wallchart, while with the addition of Brae I have five. Many an evening I've sat in London with my map pondering this inviting circuit and now it's completed. The most dangerous part has been the low level escape to Bassenthwaite.

We watch some tourists head back to their rented cottage and then a man walks past exercising a pack of hounds. All of village life is here. At 9pm a Davies taxi draws up. It's the driver we saw earlier we note as we put on our masks. "In all my time I've never had any passengers flag me down on that road," he says. The driver is a nice man. He admires our dog and then talks about the floods and the volume of water that inundated the pencil factory in Keswick. He used to live in Keswick, but his wife died of motor neurone disease and he couldn't stand to be in the house, so he moved to Pooley Bridge.

The taxi drops us off by our rented cottage and we're relieved to finally be flinging off boots and socks by the door as we are greeted by Lola and Michael who have cooked dinner. It's been an adventure, five of the more inaccessible northern Wainwrights have been tackled and we've visited the Sun, a Lakeland pub I've always wanted to sample. We fall into bed in a happy daze.

After a well-earned rest day my next objective is Ullscarf, the last of the Central Fells that I've not climbed. We all want to go to Watendlath Tarn to sample the café and on another fine day we're soon up over the pass from Rosthwaite. Everyone is walking down towards the tarn chatting happily when a Hyacinth Bucket-lookalike mutters, "Don't get out of the way then!" We don't seem to be doing anything wrong and it's a wide path. It's unusual to find unpleasantness in the Lake District, but perhaps she's just spooked by Covid. Or a misanthropic *Daily Mail* reader.

Soon we're sitting down in the tea garden drinking coffee and munching cake. Leaving the others to walk down the road to Ashness Bridge it's time for a solo amble up to Ullscarf. There's an initial steep climb up the path towards High Tove, but then a fairly flat detour along the side of the valley. Sitting in a hollow by a dry stone wall I break open my vegetarian chilli pasty for lunch and admire the view back to Watendlath Tarn, its smooth waters nestling between the two ranges.

Soon the path becomes less distinct and more boggy. That familiar squelch means that I'm surely passing the notoriously liminal Armboth Fell. It's a lonely walk up here, pacing on over spongy emerald moss as eventually Blea Tarn comes into view. It has a desolate beauty, overlooked by the rocks of Standing Crag.

Past the tarn a set of fence posts stretches up to Standing Crag and on to the summit of Ullscarf. There's also a dim path to Armboth in the opposite direction, which I won't be taking, as Alfred Wainwright warns: "Wear thigh-length boots… ordinary words are inadequate."

Passing through a brand new wooden gate I follow the forlorn fence over more solid ground, then up through a grassy gap in the defences of Standing Crag. After a slightly confusing detour around the crag the fence comes into view again. The fence seems to go on forever, now just a straight line of rusting metal posts. What folly to think that modern hi-tech fencing could conquer the mountains.

The top is a plateau of coarse grass that is four square miles in area. Wainwright described it as "a cheerless place, even in sunshine", although today the views are good to Borrowdale, the Scafells and Helvellyn. The fence turns at a right angle and I follow a dim path towards a cairn. This is the summit. It is indeed bleak, but I still take the obligatory selfie satisfied to have completed the final summit in Wainwright's *Central Fells* guidebook. A lone walker arrives while I'm there and asks if he has time to make it to Watendlath and I'm able to advise him that it's doable but boggy.

Following the fence I spot the tops of Sergeant Crag and Eagle Crag and head towards where I should be able to join up with the Coast to Coast path to Rosthwaite. A woman fell-runner passes me as I cut around Lining Crag. It's a steep descent through a striking landscape of rounded drumlins. Eventually I get down to the circular sheep fold near Eagle Crag, but it's going to be a push to make the last bus at 7pm. Tired legs protest over stony ground. Past the ruined barn and then down to the tree-lined enclosed charm of the path to Rosthwaite.

Agonisingly, after my walk of 14 miles, I miss the bus by ten minutes.

So it's into the Royal Oak for a much-needed pint and a mobile call to Davies Taxis. "Aye, we can send a cab, but it's the Borrowdale Roadworks at eight, if the road is closed you'll have to take the long way round via Grange," warns the man at the cabbies. He makes the Borrowdale Roadworks sound vaguely apocalyptic.

At 7.45pm the woman who drove us to Longlands two days before arrives in her cab. She's not sure she can beat the Borrowdale Roadworks, but she'll try, she says. Piles of roadwork signs and bollards are sitting by the road as we reach Derwent Water, but miraculously the Borrowdale Roadworks are bereft of roadworkers. If the Borrowdale Roadworks are the biggest threat to Lakeland life then, perhaps I could live here. Back at the house Michael and Lola have bought takeaway curries and so ends another fine day in the Lakes.

Nicola has managed to get in a couple of days paddleboarding during our trip so it's been a successful holiday all round. Our final walk is to Base Brown. All five of us take the bus to Seatoller and stop for a mid-morning coffee on the terrace at the Glaramara Hotel. Then it's a pleasant stroll down the side road and a low level footpath to Seathwaite. It's another bright day and the lane to Seathwaite Farm is absolutely packed with cars.

Opposite the farm we ascend the path by Sourmilk Gill. The waterfalls cascade in the sunlight and by Seathwaite Slabs we see a brave climber inching his way up the black rocks next to a lethal-looking drop into the gill. As we rest Nicola chats to a fit-looking man who passes us heading down to the valley. He says he's come straight from working his night shift in IT, and has been working his own way across the heather from the Great

Gable circuit. “A couple of cans of Red Bull should get me through tonight’s shift,” he laughs.

The path takes us to the plateau of Gillercomb as we look back at the tapestry of fields in the Seathwaite valley far below. Lola opts to sit by an eroded gulley next to Sourmilk Gill as she doesn’t fancy further altitude after getting a bit spooked by some of the drops on the way up. Michael, Nell, Nicola, Vulcan and myself plod on, taking the easier route around Base Brown rather than the more fearsome path up its craggy front and past the precariously balanced Hanging Stone.

It’s a mistake to cut the corner by the col and head straight up the flank of Base Brown as I find myself puffing relentlessly up the steep grassy slope. But eventually we all reach the top and Michael, who has only previously climbed Latrigg, is finding his mountain legs.

The summit is a good place to be, looking towards the lumpy outlines of Green Gable and Great Gable. While looking back it feels like you could leap straight off the end of the airy fell into Seathwaite. We descend the direct route down the rock face and back towards Lola. It’s quite hairy at times, with a couple of scrambles around cliffs and down rock chutes. But Nell has found a path marked on her SnapChat phone app, which helps. It’s quite incredible that even fell paths can be found by satellite, though Mr Wainwright’s ashes might be glowing red by Innominate Tarn at the prospect. Finally we’re back with Lola by the gill.

On the path to Seatoller we see the Borrowdale Yews, a set of stubby and twisted ancient yews once mentioned by Wordsworth. They might be 1500 years old. We have enough time before the last bus for a drink in the Glaramara Hotel. Taking a seat at one of the socially distanced tables outside we feast on peanuts, crisps, wine and cold beer in the yellow light of the fading sun.

Incredibly we have had a week without rain in the Lake District. Michael still hasn't bought a proper waterproof coat despite our claims that it rains all the time in Cumbria. Perhaps he is some sort of rain God. Soon we will be returning to London. Coronavirus seems to be increasing in the northwest again and there might be another lockdown on the way. But at the start of the year in Grasmere it seemed doubtful there would be any visits to the Lakes at all in 2020. I've completed another seven new fells and gained some background knowledge for further trips next year. That's if the virus doesn't get any of us. Wainwright paced these mountains at times of global crisis and now we are doing the same. It will take more than a global pandemic to keep us away.

9. MUNGRISDALE COMMON PEOPLE

Date: May 2021

Accommodation: Elterwater Hostel, Mill Inn, Mungrisdale

Transport: Train from London Euston to Windermere, X5 bus to Keswick, taxi Keswick to Mungrisdale.

Companions: Solo trip.

New Wainwrights bagged: 4 — Great Carrs, Grey Friar, Bonscale Fell, Mungrisdale Common.

Old Wainwrights Bagged: 1 — Bannerdale Crags

Total Wainwrights completed: 173

Total Wainwrights left: 41

After a cancelled Christmas, three months of another lockdown is sort-of over, the hotels are open and having had two jabs of AstraZeneca vaccine, I'm now back in the Lakes at the Elterwater Hostel (formerly a YHA youth hostel). The weekend has ended perfectly with myself among the 10,000 fans at West Ham on Sunday to see the Irons beat Southampton 3-0 and finish a staggering sixth in the Premier League, therefore qualifying for the Europa League. It's my first live football since March 2020, with all the other games having been played behind closed doors.

After an expensive taxi ride from Windermere station it seems slightly unreal to be at Elterwater in the early evening. From the stand at the London Stadium and the pubs of Stratford to perfect calm. I'm in a simple two-bunk room with a sink, but it has a splendid view of the fells through the window. Walking outside I listen to the sound of cooing wood pigeons and then the murmuring water beneath Elterwater Bridge.

The supper club in the hostel is a strange affair, conducted behind a Perspex shield. There's only one other participant, Alice, also from north London. She had booked to do Wainwright's Coast to Coast walk when lockdown started, so this is her compensation. She's going to Grasmere tomorrow and looking for some wild swimming spots. I also talk to Andy the hostel warden, who serves a good baked sweet potato, and likes a spot of fell running. He says that he can get up to Great Carrs in two hours and that he likes to go up the Greenburn mine route. Clearly he's a lot fitter than this out-of-condition Londoner.

In the morning I head up the bridleway to Little Langdale. Over a stony track, past moss-encrusted stone walls, through oak and sycamore trees. All is shrouded in green apart from a carpet of bluebells in a glade by the track.

Then it's down across farmland to Wilson's Place, where there's the Wilson's Arms pub and a few cottages. Another path takes me over rocky fields to Slaters Bridge. It's in two parts, flatter slabs heading to a boulder in the middle of the River Brathay, then a Tolkien-esque arch of slates, just wide enough for one person and their packhorse, but with an iron safety rail for the unsure of balance. It was built by the 16th century slaters who needed to get over the river with their packhorses to work at the quarry. Here is a good spot to explore Cathedral Cavern in the disused quarry, though today time is pressing and I carry on towards Great Carrs.

The Cumbria Way path then takes me past the Yorkshire Hiking Society's cottage and past the not-very accessible Little Langdale Tarn. The day's objective is in view once on the path up the Greenburn valley. Wetherlam dominates to my left while the end of the valley is blocked by the steep ends of Swirl How and Great Carrs.

The ruins of the Greenburn mine are a short walk up the valley, so I take a detour. They are the usual industrial mess of spoil heaps, tumbling stone walls and shafts covered by metal grilles. Looking towards the end of the valley I conclude that the man at the youth hostel must be some kind of superman to go straight up the steep slope of Broad End to Great Carrs. This is my first walk since last September, eight months ago, so pacing is required. I head back to the footbridge and start up Wet Side Edge.

Despite its name the path is reasonably dry, though it's a long haul upwards and round the valley, but soon there are rewarding glimpses across the Wyrnose Valley to Pike O'Blisco and Cold Pike, separated by Red Tarn. Having climbed both in recent years, the jigsaw pieces are starting to fit. A mini-bus slowly trundles along the pass far below.

Wisps of white cloud hang over the top of Great Carrs. It's proving a hard slog. I'm never quite sure why a full English breakfast is considered the best preparation for a day's walk. It feels like I'm carrying an extra stone in baked beans and hash browns. But the views get better and soon Greenburn valley is way below with Greenburn Tarn in the distance and beyond that Little Langdale Tarn nestling beneath Lingmell.

The mist comes in around the summit of Great Carrs. Amid the clag I find a memorial to the WW2 plane crash, when a Halifax bomber crashed into Great Carrs in 1944, killing all the eight crew. What strikes you is the age of the people who died, ranging from 19 to 33. Most of the rusting wreckage that is left can be found on the path up from Broad End, while the undercarriage is on top of the fell. It's a sad spot on this lonely fell.

The cloud up here is getting more dense and it's really impossible to see where the path to Grey Friar is. The ridge to Swirl How is visible as an outline but it doesn't seem safe to leave the path and the valley edge. I'd caught a brief glimpse of Grey Friar on the way up when the cloud briefly cleared but now it could be anywhere. Sitting it out in the hope of the cloud lifting my fingers start to tingle with cold until I put on my gloves.

Eventually I give up and start to make my way back down Wet Side Edge. But there it is, a vague plateau of grass but with something big amid the cloud. This is the Grey Friar at prayer. Feeling a burst of adrenaline I yomp across a pathless area of grass and head for the lump of rock. On top it's quite ethereal, fingers of rock pointing upwards in the mist. But I can see down to Wrynose Pass and so it's another Wainwright scaled. My biggest concern is getting off in the right direction. The way back is just about visible.

Soon I'm back on Wet Side Edge and the long descent to Little Langdale. It's six o'clock and the day has disappeared. Eventually it's back over Slaters Bridge and then trying to beat dusk, trekking along the cycle track to Elterwater, with every rounded stone hurting my battered feet. By nine I'm back at the hostel and it's too late to get dinner, but the substantial flapjack from my packed lunch is enough to keep me going. My phone says I've walked

17 miles. I stagger to the Britannia Inn and have a satisfying pint.

The following day is for transport, a bus to Ambleside, coffee at Esquires, a bus to Keswick and then a taxi to stay at the Mill Inn at Mungrisdale. It's a pleasingly remote pub in a tiny hamlet that has a village hall and a church, plus a few houses. Wayne the landlord comes from Telford and used to work on the London Underground before moving to somewhere very much overground. A double bed, private shower and TV are rare luxuries after hostelling.

After a good night's sleep my energy levels feel good and I set off for some northern fellwalking. Wainwright mentions the enticing view down the footpath to Mungrisdale, that will appeal on sight to walkers, "because of its arresting skyline and obvious variety of routes." The pyramid of the Tongue (which is a part of Bowscale Fell) is central to the vista, with the flanks of Bowscale to the right, Souther Fell to the left and Bannerdale Crags terminating the valley. It's down this path that I walk, the sky a cloudless blue above the fells. My route goes around the Tongue and then up the side of Bowscale. Wainwright describes it as the easiest route to any summit over 2000 feet in Lakeland. The gradient is indeed gentle and the biggest difficulty is being buzzed by two low-flying RAF fighter jets.

Bowscale Fell is a flat grassy top with a small stone shelter, but becomes much more interesting when a short stroll reveals the substantial Bowscale Tarn half way up its northern side. It was very popular in Victorian times and was said to have two immortal fish, which was probably very believable after a few pints of Bassenthwaite Beauty. It's flanked by steep crags and Wainwright says that it is, "wild and romantic and very impressive."

The other star of the summit is the view of Carrock Fell. Unlike most of the northern fells it's strewn with scree and the steep sides look much more of an obstacle than they appear on the map.

From Bowscale my next move is to trek round the side of Bannerdale Crags to the col above the River Glenderamackin. Here begins a path on to Mungrisdale Common, a fell shrouded in clouds of Wainwright mythology claiming it to be the worst of them all.

Initially the path is fairly solid and clear. A fellow walker passes me going off the fell. "You must be a Wainwright bagger," I suggest, "as no-one else ever comes up here." He is indeed a bagger and we discuss whether it's worth it. I suggest that every fell has its merits and he answers, "well it does have a great view of Derwent Water, I'll give it that."

The path ascends the side of Wainwright's "upturned pudding" and becomes fainter and much much squelchier. I'm grateful to have waxed my Zamberlan boots but still need to dodge pools that would submerge my boots completely. Football-sized clumps of moss are everywhere. Should future archaeologists ever excavate Mungrisdale Common they will perhaps find hundreds of submerged Gore-Tex-clad bodies, and conclude that it was some kind of sacred spot of ritual activity where human sacrifice was commonplace.

The vague path extends on and on. Squelch, squeeze, slurp. It's all the same. The fell is so featureless that a rare boulder, the Cloven Stone is marked on the map. There's nowhere safe to sit and rest either. I spot a bagger with a black beard leaving towards Blencathra. He tells me, "The cairn's up there to the right though they could have put it anywhere. I think Wainwright put it in as a joke, he was a cantankerous old sod!"

On past the clumps of brown and green moss. Then I

find a couple who look like they might be from *Geordie Shore* in soaked Adidas trainers. They ask me about my boots and I earnestly recommend buying a pair. “We’ve done Cross Fell in these trainers and we’re on our 11th Wainwright,” they say cheerily, while navigating with a wrist watch app. Perhaps they have a point. Your feet can only get wet once.

Finally the summit comes into view, an apologetic mound of a few stray stones amid a pool of water. But as the man said, there is a spectacular view down to Derwent Water and across to the Borrowdale fells, and also across to Lonscale Crags and the Cumbria Way Path.

Atop of Mungrisdale and its magnificent rounded profile, I take a picture of my lunchtime pasty on top of the cairn, surrounded by water.

Posting this to the *To Climb The 214 Wainwright Fells* Facebook group gets a rapid response. My comment reads: “A pasty on Mungrisdale Common today. Though had to eat it standing up. Not saying it’s boggy but it makes Armboth Fell feel like the Sahara.”

Replies include: “Well you’ve all really sold me on this — I can’t wait to get up there!”; “I was there yesterday. Won’t be doing that one again lol”; “On a sunny day after a dry spell it's a lovely walk. Great views, solitude and skylarks”; “I was there on Monday....decent views but I won't be back”; “Aaah but so quiet, remote and peaceful, and wonderful views on a good day! After the mayhem of Blencathra it's a wonderful place for a pasty”; “A most boggy place! But at least good weather today”; “I was thinking about it this weekend, then I remembered we've had the wettest May on record and it stopped raining yesterday. Decided it wouldn't be dry by Saturday”; “It’s easy did it last year nothing worse than splashing through but firm underneath”; “I'm off sick this day!”; “Armboth was a swamp when I was last there!

That looks grim too! Well done." Best of all is from Linda Bloggs, who posts a very similar picture of her sandwich on top of the similarly-sodden summit cairn.

"Precious holiday hours should not be wasted here," warns Wainwright. But it's not without charm and in a way it's so bad it's good. Mungrisdale Common is a saturated badge of honour for the bagging fraternity.

After hastily eating my pasty while standing up I get across the mulch as quickly as possible. Back at the col I take a detour to the top of Bannerdale Crags having previously only explored it in mist. Then it's down the secluded and beautiful V-shaped valley of the River Glenderamackin. Past the old mine and sheepfold, water running below, looking up all the way to Sharp Edge. Masses of trees in plastic tubes line the riverside as I reach White Horse Bend. The path rounds Bannerdale Crags and it makes a great circular walk, ending up back in Mungrisdale.

"What can I get you pal?" says the lad behind the bar at the Mill Inn. I'm back in time for a falafel burger and pint before a soothing hot shower. On WhatsApp I explain to my groundhopping friend Matt that Mungrisdale Fell is like visiting an obscure but very credible non-league ground.

My final day is a chance to explore the route to Carrock Fell. The road from Mungrisdale is almost deserted. Cuckoos call, crows cry, the farms have grand arches in their barns and there's a smell of sheep and blossom. I have a sandwich on the disused bridge at Mosedale, just as a group of elderly motor bikers in black leathers shoot past.

Carrock Fell looks intimidating, but there's a vague path from the Swinside Road. It takes me across the fell through endless clumps of heather. What I should have done is try the route from Stone Ends Farm. After a 17 mile walk and then a 15 mile walk my body isn't used to a new season of Wainwright bagging. Emerging at a featureless plateau with a long way to go up and looking at the very steep route down to Stone Ends Farm I realise that I don't have the energy to get down this side or do the circular walk on to High Pike and Knott. Cutting my losses I decide to walk back to Mungrisdale and the pub, Carrock Fell can wait for another trip.

Mungrisdale takes some leaving as there's no public transport, I have to order a £25 taxi back to Keswick, then take a bus to Penrith and the train. But it's a peaceful part of the Lakes, seldom ever troubled by masses of tourists. It feels good to be back in the swing of bagging having dodged Covid and reached the back of Skiddaw. I've been doing what Mungrisdale Common people do. Four new fells completed and a lot more to plan.

10. GIVE ME A MELLBREAK

Date: June 2021

Accommodation: Buttermere YHA

Transport: Train from London Euston to Penrith, X5 bus to Keswick, 77 bus to Buttermere.

Companion: Nicola.

New Wainwrights bagged: 4 — Knott Rigg, Ard Crags, Mellbreak, Hen Comb

Total Wainwrights completed: 177

Total Wainwrights left: 37

It's June 2021 and the third wave of Covid, featuring the more infectious Delta Variant, is now under way. Not big yet, but doubling every week as the government races to get all adults vaccinated. As always dark times create humour. One of my Facebook pals suggests that the Delta Variants would be a cool name for a 1980s synth band.

Nicola and myself have had to rush to get away; Nicola was frantically dealing with paddleboarding bookings and a subbing job last night while on the train up I'm having to text PR ideas for a guerrilla ad campaign. But by Penrith peace returns. Then it's a bus to Keswick, followed by the 77 bus to Buttermere.

We booked Buttermere Youth Hostel back in March as rooms were going quickly. Demand from the new staycationers has seen it sell out for the summer, even though Covid precautions are still in place. We're on our own in a room with six bunks, which is a big improvement on the old days of packed dorms, full of bag rustlers and snorers. We have to pre-book a shower for 7-8am the next morning, packed lunches are no longer on sale, the lounge is closed and breakfast is now a sausage in a bap. Nicola notes the absence of youths, just middle-aged men in new cars. We're the only people to arrive by bus.

But it's still good to be sitting on the claret-painted veranda listening to birdsong and looking across to the vivid outline of the High Stile range. We take a walk down to Buttermere lake from the path close to the hostel, walking through a couple of fields of sheep and past oak and silver birch trees. It's still sunny but occasional gusts of wind suggest bad weather is on the way as waves lap against the shingle beach.

One area of the path is closed to avoid disturbing sandpipers. The advantage of having Nicola with me is she knows about trees and birds — all that Robert Macfarlane stuff which I've never been good at. We sit on a patch of grass and eat our pasties carried from Keswick. Nicola spots white pignut and studies the yellow buttercup-like flowers in the grass and looks through her book of wild flowers. It has five petals instead of four so might be a hoary cinquefoil. She wonders if the oak, ash and alder in front of us have been deliberately planted by the shore. A sadder view is the sickly trees that are suffering from ash dieback disease further along the shore.

We move on to the Buttermere Court Hotel and enjoy a drink before walking to the head of the lake. Sitting on a giant rock we look at the perfect outline of Fleetwith Pike and Honister Crag tapering down to the water at the far end of the lake. Clouds are slowly moving behind Haystacks and a parliament of crows (or could it be jackdaws or rooks?) noisily assembles above the lake looking for evening insects.

The following morning fog covers the lakes and heavy white cloud hangs over all the mountains. The Mountain Weather Information Service estimates only a ten per cent chance of cloud free summits, so we opt to walk round the lake. Signs warn us, "three lambs killed by dogs, don't make it four" and "Keep all dogs on leads (even little fluffy ones). Sheep worrying is an offence. Dogs caught worrying sheep will be shot." We resolve not to mention Covid, climate change or England's right-back dilemma in front of the sheep.

It's a lovely walk along the northern shore, through trees and moss-encrusted crags. A rock tunnel was cut through the crag by a Victorian mill owner. It's dark and damp inside and suddenly Nicola screams as she trips over a rock on the ground. "I thought it was a ghost," she explains.

We walk over Peggy's Bridge in the shadow of Fleetwith Pike and on to the other side of the lake, where the path is wider and more geared towards tourists. You could wheel a buggy down it. Despite the signs, no-one has their dog on a lead and there are plenty of sheep and lambs around. Everyone assumes it must be somebody else's dog doing the sheep worrying. We're missing our border terrier Vulcan, at home with our daughters as hostels don't allow them, but we certainly wouldn't let him loose were he here.

Lunch is in a strip of pines by the Lake. The upper

reaches of High Stile are still shrouded in mist and look like something from *Game of Thrones*. Then we reach the shore near the village of Buttermere. It's a fine four-mile walk and a good alternative when the clouds hang heavy over the valley.

The next day it's perfectly clear again and the hanging valley beneath Bleaberry Tarn is back in 3D vision. After the hostel's average coffee we discover the Sykes Farm café, which serves a superior brew and has some enticing homemade pies. We sit on the white garden tables outside, looking at the farm dog as Nicola at last finds some wi-fi that works. It's not always a good thing to contact home, as she discovers on Facebook that a friend whom she knew from her days of working as a volunteer in the Solomon Islands has died at home in Yorkshire. It's not unexpected, but still very sad news, as we have stayed with her and know her now-adult children. We're in the right spot to ponder mortality, a place where humans feel very small.

Today's Wainwright bagging objective is Knott Rigg and Ard Crags. Should we walk up the road to Newlands Hause or take the footpath over the flank of Robinson? Nicola says she hates road walking and so we opt to take the path.

"Have we made a terrible mistake?" asks Nicola half an hour later as we struggle up a relentless carpet of steep grass.

"We might as well carry on, it should turn left soon and descend to the pass," I suggest, hopefully.

The view to the twin lakes of Buttermere and Crummock Water is rewarding and eventually, climbing above the twisting grey road way below, we reach the brow and find ourselves on Buttermere Moss. It's a wise thing in the Lakes to be suspicious of anything called a Moss. I remember descending from Robinson by this boggy morass. But luckily we're skirting most of the moss and descending to Newlands Hause. The road would have been much less effort, but we get some good glimpses of the Moss Force waterfalls cascading down Robinson. We can also see the clear outline of Knott Rigg and Ard Crags ahead, a distinctive pair of peaks with sloping ends and a flat top, isolated from the fells around them.

After much pole use and a steep descent we find ourselves in the car park that is Newlands Hause. The occupants of a van full of cyclists are passing round drinks and putting on Lycra.

"That's a cute car!" says Nicola, spotting a 1950s MG sports car parked in the layby. "It's not a cute car!" jokes the offended male owner, as his wife laughs along.

The path to Knott Rigg is clear from the Hause. A couple of hundred yards up the track is a picnic area with stones stacked to make barbecues. Nicola has become our Lakeland litter monitor and is fixing the fells by picking up any detritus. She's upset to find a half-full bottle of lager, compounded by the fact that several dead beetles are floating in the stale beer, having drowned in it. There's also a can of Fosters and quite a few other bits of rubbish, which she places into a blue plastic bag. You would think that people in cars could take their rubbish away.

The climb to Knott Rigg can be done by seven to seventy-year-olds, claims Wainwright. It's not quite that easy, but the path is up sloping grass and after a few false summits we're on the top. It's the views into the valleys that make the walk special, particularly the V-shaped plunge down to Sail Gill and the massive scree-strewn flanks of Whiteless Pike and Grasmoor.

Near the summit of Knott Rigg — it's a small pile of stones — we lie down for lunch on the tussocky grass.

We listen to larks, the buzzing of large brown horse flies and the odd explosion from what can only be a working quarry somewhere below. And then the huge roar of a couple of RAF jets shooting through the valleys and later a helicopter.

The skies are full of activity. Two paragliders are floating in the air by the summit of Robinson. Nicola chats to six blokes in technical gear who are walking back from Ard Crags. One has been paragliding and they discuss what gear you need, including an emergency parachute. I won't be taking it up, preferring to take a walk on the mild side.

The further we go along the ridge the better the views to Crag Hill and Grasmoor. A path zig-zags across to the top of Sail from Scar Crags. Tiny walkers move across it. There's also an impermanent looking path through the scree on the lower flanks of these giants.

Part of Causey Pike is completely grey and denuded of vegetation, perhaps caused by a fire? A bit of later research reveals that in 2020 some 40 firefighters tackled a blaze here, possibly started deliberately and exacerbated by the dry conditions. This was during lockdown and it's a pertinent reminder that one bit of stupidity can ravage something as big as a mountain.

Ard Crags has two summits, so we visit both, gazing down into Newlands and a prosperous looking farm with large new barns gleaming in the sun. Newlands is one the Lakes' most unspoilt valleys and its homely farms contrast with the inhospitable gulches nearby.

We retrace our steps and descend to Newlands Hause. Nicola's knee starts to hurt on the steep drops and she experiences a pain in her leg she's not felt before. We take it steady until reaching flatter ground.

From the Hause we walk on the road down into Buttermere and the gradient is much better than our approach over the side of Robinson. Nicola continues to Womble free, picking up some energy gel dropped by a cyclist and a crushed tin of water, but even she baulks at picking up used tissues in the Covid era.

At last we're in the Buttermere Court Hotel eating vegetarian chilli and sweet potato fries. But it's turned into a holiday of three deaths. A phone message reveals that our friend's husband has died. Meanwhile one of Nicola's distant cousins has also departed this life. Best to stay offline and not get any news from the world outside. At least here there is a dry stone wall in front of us and Fleetwith Pike beyond the lake; things of beauty in an impermanent world.

By the church and the lonely street junction sign Robinson is suffused in yellow evening sun. After a thigh-busting trek back up the short hill to the hostel it's the big event of the evening. We have both booked a shower for between six and seven pm and enjoy washing away the sweat of our sojourn. After dinner we break some YHA regulations by taking the mattresses off our bunks and making an impromptu double bed. Not bad, even if there is a chasm the middle. Sleep comes easily after the day's exertions.

Nicola causes consternation at breakfast by asking for off-menu tomatoes in a bap rather than a processed veggie sausage, but she gets her wish and some expertly-sliced tomatoes. We have a coffee at Sykes' Farm café, buy more lovely-looking home-made pies, and head down to the water.

By the lake we see a warden in a National Trust fleece. Nicola tells him that it must be the best job in the world. "Not always," he says, before recounting tales of illicit camping during lockdown. "We had to clear 68 tents left last summer, people leave barbeques, sleeping bags, fridges, everything." The locals have clubbed together to now pick up the rubbish themselves, he adds, before continuing to mark ash trees with numbers, perhaps ready for culling.

The walk along the edge of Crummock Water is beautiful and less wet than in autumn. Nicola is excited to see some paddle boarders out on the serene water including one man with fishing lines attached to his board. The voices of two women swimming carry across the lake. We can see their orange tow floats as they slowly move across to the far shore. Three youths with backpacks are also swimming off the spit at Low Ling Crag.

Cuckoos are calling as we cross Scale Beck and the path to Floutern Pass. Soon we are walking by the lake, the path tight against the imposing bank of Mellbreak. It's a mighty block of rock, an impenetrable-looking giant with steep drops from crag and cliff. At the end of the lake we head along a path and then down an idyllic track followed by a foray into Arthur Ransome-style lanes.

I've always wanted to visit Loweswater. After finding what Mr Wainwright would term a few habitations and passing some kayakers by their car, we reach the white-fronted Kirkstile Inn. We step inside for a lunch of salad and a sandwich, washed down with orange juice.

Nicola manages to avert a near disaster when an off-lead Alsatian springs at a small child. The woman who owns it takes the dog outside while the grandmother and mum with the child don't seem to have noticed how close their child came to getting bitten. "That's your heroic deed of the day done," I tell her.

As Nicola's knee is still hurting going down slopes she decides to walk back via the flatter lake shore. I'm going over the top of Mellbreak. Outside the inn I find the famous negative sign that Wainwright drew, reading "No through road to the lake" in both directions.

The climbable end of Mellbreak lies down a stone-walled track going past Kirkhead Farm. I note the ancient horseshoe-shaped earthwork that AW says the walker should observe. It's seen more clearly from further up Mellbreak and was obviously some kind of Neolithic tea-room for fell-walkers, probably doing a nice sideline in souvenir Langdale axeheads.

The mountain is a pyramid from this end. After a stroll across grass the path moves up a brown scree face. It's more difficult than anticipated. It takes me half an hour to negotiate and it's a struggle, boots sliding everywhere. The rocks are loose, the earth is crumbling and heather comes away in my hand as I try to get some purchase.

For a time it seems like I'll never get up. But then heading to the edge of the crag, the path becomes a thin trail through heather looking across some steep drops. Knowing how fragile the soil is here I'm now suffering vertigo. A promontory offers a chance to rest and admire the vista, where I can see the bay at the end of the lake far below and what might be Nicola by the shore.

Eventually the path levels out among a plain of heather. Within a few hundred yards the summit cairn appears. I sit down and take a drink of water from my canister before taking a selfie. My new Mountain Ridge technical top is less sweaty than my normal cotton shirts and it looks sportier, so that's something for my Facebook credibility.

Mellbreak is a lot less grandiose on top compared to the view from ground level. It's a fairly nondescript expanse covered in heather with a large dip in the middle rising to a second summit. But the views are excellent. It has a clear view of the isolated lake at Loweswater and on the southern side the meandering river and marshland of Mosedale, with the rising slopes of Hen Comb opposite. While on the Buttermere side there are splendid glimpses of both lakes and Fleetwith Pike.

There's no one up here apart from a solitary hang glider above my head. It's a trek across peaty ground to the second and official summit, then a long steep descent down to Floutern Pass and back to Crummock Water. My phone suddenly gets a signal and Nicola is ringing. She's close by having gone for a wild swim in the lake. Having said that middle-aged women do this fashionable activity to cure their pain I wonder if she's experienced something similar. "You'll certainly be able to hold your head up in north London," I suggest, "put it on Facebook at once."

We meet in the valley of the cuckoos, near the bridge over Scale Beck, and walk in the early evening past the delightful shallow brown river to the Buttermere Court Hotel. My cheese and onion pie is now dinner, furtively eaten in between pints of Golden Plover and Corby Blonde.

On Saturday morning something is stirring. A gazebo with a Berghaus logo has been erected at the bottom of the Newlands road offering food and drink sachets. A quick enquiry to the servers reveals it's the Ten in Ten race. As in ten peaks in ten hours. I tell them that we did two in ten when we climbed Knott Rigg and Ard Crags. Opposite the Bridge Hotel is another table providing refreshment. Runners start to arrive, numbers on backs, some walking, some jogging.

I show Nicola the path to Rannerdale, where she plans to do a solo walk along the valley. It's changeover day for holiday lets. A lady who is shaking rugs outside a cottage tells us what a privilege it is to give people so much pleasure and how the same couples keep coming back year after year to her property.

Today I'm planning to bag Hen Comb. It's along Crummock Water again and then up the Floutern Pass path. I take a minor detour to Scale Force. It cascades a long way and is the highest drop in the Lake District, but really, though impressive, it's not as spectacular as many falls I've encountered on less well-known walks.

My only companions are the cuckoos. Soon it's past the path descending from Mellbreak and over the brow is the flat marshy plain of Mosedale. A faint path follows an ageing fence. it's a jumble of metal and wood fence posts sinking into the ooze. The wire is rusting away; taming this landscape with modern fencing has long been pointless as the ground always seems to win.

There's a wonderful feeling of space in this deserted spot. Across the valley a family are making their way along the harder ground by the foot of Starling Dodd. Is this the correct route? And I'm not even sure if there's a path up to Hen Comb from this side, though the man in the youth hostel kitchen said there was.

After a long trek across an undulating, unstable surface I reach firmer ground. And there's a walker coming the other way. He tells me to just follow the fence to get to the summit of Hen Comb.

By an incongruously pristine metal gate I turn right and follow a steep path upwards by the fence, stepping in footholes ground out by legions of Wainwright baggers. It's a lot easier to get to the top than Mellbreak. The summit is a very fine place. I can see the drop to the lower reaches of Hen Comb — it really is shaped like the head of a chicken — and beyond it a glimpse of the lake at Loweswater. Down in Mosedale I spot the famous Mosedale Holly tree, the only individual tree to be marked on an Ordnance Survey map of the Lake District. Floutern Tarn is still hidden but to the south is a good view of Great Borne and I assess likely routes for another trip.

A couple have emerged from the Loweswater path. "You know, Wainwright was quite disparaging, but the views are great," says the woman, before discussing routes with her partner Bob. Wainwright commented that it was pleasant enough, "for anyone who doesn't want to get excited." AW must have been having a bad day. Perhaps he was getting fed up with Wainwright bagging. He came up via the Loweswater route, but from this side it's much better than his description.

I retrace my steps back to Buttermere where Nicola is on the path by the river. We watch small fish dart through the brown water. She's had a good day in the valley at Rannerdale and painted a picture of her boots in her notebook. Even better she is carrying pies and cakes from Sykes Farm tearoom. If I was Don Quixote, she would be my peerless Dulcinea del Toboso. We sit on a slab of stone and enjoy our dinner. From the path back to the pub we have the perfect view of the outline of Knott Rigg and Ard Crags in the distance.

London is calling the next day. After more breakfast baps we remove our bedding and return our keys. It's a basic room looking over the YHA campers' 'Lav Shack', but it has served us well. We head downhill to the bus stop by the Croft House Farm Café and find ourselves chatting to two Sunday volunteers in high-vis jackets, there to supervise the parking as there are now double the number of visitors. Ironically both had to drive to get here. We learn that Michelle gave up walking after the menopause gave her vertigo. Chris says that he moves campers on with tact. He's used to being abused as he's a teacher and a union rep, but even so he tells us with some incredulity about the dog walkers who complain about being asked to use a lead to safeguard the birds on Walney Island, off Barrow-in-Furness.

We're the only passengers heading to Keswick and the 78 bus feels like a private taxi service. In Keswick there's time for one more adventure. We have a coffee in Java and then hire two electric bikes. It's great fun shooting through shadowy country lanes with the turbo gear taking most of the strain of going up hills. We see the Swinside Inn and head down to Braithwaite for yet another pie from the village shop, then a detour to Stair and a glorious tree-lined lane back to Keswick.

Soon we're on the bus to Penrith and then the train to London with a glass of wine and a pint of Hawkshead Blonde. Our dog and children wait at home. For all the shower restrictions and the bunks, it's been a good stay at a reasonable price. and another four names from the map scaled. Now we are heading home and writing condolence messages to friends and relatives as reality returns. It's tempting to stay in Buttermere for much longer.

11. HIGHWAY TO HELVELLYN

Date: August 2021

Accommodation: Helvellyn Youth Hostel

Transport: Train from London Euston to Penrith, 518 bus to Glenridding, Hartsop, Watermillock and Brothers Water.

Companions: Solo trip.

New Wainwrights bagged: 4 — Gray Crag, High Raise, Little Mell Fell, High Hartsop Dodd.

Old Wainwrights Bagged: 5 — Thornthwaite Crag, High Street, Kidsty Pike, Rampsgill Head, The Knott.

Total Wainwrights completed: 181

Total Wainwrights left: 33

After the serene train travelling of Covid days when you got your own double seat, it's now back to having passengers sitting side-by-side. Which feels a little worrying as the virus isn't over yet, whatever the government says. Masks are optional until Scotland on the train to Glasgow, but I make sure mine is on all journey.. As we approach Penrith I'm listening to the compulsive talker in front telling a student about his days in the merchant navy and a man who sounds like Begbie from *Trainspotting* telling his young son to "Stop it!", who in turn cries, "It's not fair!", seemingly ad infinitum.

But after a long three hours I'm back in Penrith and on the bus to Glenridding. Helvellyn YHA isn't that convenient for the fells I plan to walk, but it's all that's available at an affordable price. Two years ago I'd struggled up Greenside Road with a case and it's just as difficult with a backpack and daypack. It feels like a long walk — up past the Travellers Rest pub, past the bench, left through the cattle grid, by the cottages, then the trees, round the bend along the long level bit, then upwards past the car with a 'Trax' logo on it and through the entrance to the YHA. At last I'm in situ, with four bunks to myself in a solo room, ready for my supper club meal and an early start the next day.

After a veggie sausage in a bap for breakfast at the hostel (why has no one come up with anything else in a bap?) and a refreshing coffee in Glenridding at the Helvellyn Kitchen, it's on to the 10.10am bus to Hartsop. When I arrive at Hartsop there's a full car park at the end of the lane. Sadly I'm the only person on the bus despite the fact the area is suffering from the record numbers of staycationers. With packed roads and an overheating planet it's a shame more people don't use the summer bus service.

After adjusting my poles at a convenient bench there's a good track up to Hayeswater reservoir. The day is overcast but the rain has held off and hey, I'm back in the fells. The rounded shoulder of Gray Crag soon appears. As the pump house comes into view a faint grassy path leads upwards. It's steep and hard on my London legs, but after a long climb my spirits rise with a view of

Hayeswater reservoir far below. On the other side of the valley the Straits of Riggindale are a little reminiscent of the Wasdale screes, a wall of intimidating grey and green topped by an inviting flat ridge.

Eventually I'm on the grassy finger of turf that stretches out from Thornthwaite Crag. After the inevitable false summits a modest stone cairn emerges. A hundred yards to my right a man on a mountain bike zips past. It's hard to believe he won't fly off the nose of Gray Crag and down into Hayeswater, but clearly he has a plan for getting down the steep incline.

First Wainwright of the trip ticked off. I stop for a satisfying Thai curry pasty. A bird of prey circles above me, though you'd have to ask Chris Packham what it is. Next objective is Thornthwaite Crag, an easy stroll of a mile and a quarter across the plateau.

Soon I'm at the distinctive ten-foot tall rounded stack of stones that marks the summit of Thornthwaite Fell, a work of hilltop art. A German couple are sitting down for lunch as I take a selfie in front of the cairn. Being here brings back memories of the last time I was at this spot, back in 2015, having ascended via Yoke soon after the death of my old schoolfriend Paul, who died at just 55. Always visit the Lakes when you want perspective.

It's a grand Lakeland crossroads, with the full Kentmere Round on display and a lovely sweeping ridge path heading over the top of the Straits of Riggindale. Soon I'm strolling above the head of Hayeswater and it's peaceful and glorious.

I pass Laura, a 20-something with blonde plaits and flowery leggings and ask her if she's walked far. She's come an impressive 30 miles and explains that this is an alternative holiday — "I was meant to be in Switzerland, until the government changed the travel rules."

A short detour takes me across a tumbledown wall to

the trig point on High Street, which I climbed when Nicola was pregnant with Lola, some 24 years ago. This is Racehorse Hill, where they held annual horse races. It's also where the Roman legions marched to avoid the Brittunculi ("wretched little Brits") — or maybe they were just trying to get away from the crowds in Bowness-on-Windermere.

The path curves around Hayeswater and dips as it joins the Coast to Coast path near the Knott. It's been a long day, but viewing the sharp-angled tip of Kidsty Pike, I decide to bid for another untamed Wainwright, High Raise. We must have walked close to it on the Coast to Coast path back in 1997, but it's not been ticked off on my wallchart and this is my chance.

The path takes me almost to the top of Kidsty Pike and then veers over open grassland towards the raised mound of High Raise. It's after six but I'm up for it and in half an hour I've reached the top — and unlike Loadpot Hill and Wether Hill it is, as Wainwright says, a summit the walker will have an affectionate regard for, because unlike most of the High Street range it has a welcome quantity of stones.

It has a large cairn and a rough wind shelter among the proliferation of white and brown rocks. Half a mile away at Low Raise a mound of white rocks mark an ancient tumulus, rebuilt by walkers to form a cairn. From the top I can see down the range towards Pooley Bridge and then the flat fields stretching to Scotland way beyond.

Having enjoyed the peace of the summit I start to descend only to hear, bizarrely, the roar of an engine. On the summit is a man in leathers on a scrambling bike. The bike is silhouetted against the sky for a couple of minutes before roaring off back down the range towards Pooley Bridge. Unless it's some sort of mechanical mirage in the fashion of a Brocken sceptre. Thank goodness Mr

Wainwright isn't alive to see such a sight — it would surely have resulted in assault and battery of a biker by a man armed with a pipe and flat cap.

From High Raise I take the path to Rampsgill Head. On our Coast to Coast trek in 1997 it was just an area of grass in a hail storm. But reaching the summit it's a surprise to see rugged crags dropping down towards Rampsgill plus excellent views of the Nab and the valley where protected deer live way below. I'd always been slightly unsure if I could count it on my wallchart after getting close on the Coast to Coast trail, but now there's no doubt.

A thin path stretches across the fell to re-join the Coast to Coast path at the Knott. As Wainwright writes, you must be pretty tired if you can't scale the 65 feet to the cairn on the Knott, so it's yet another Wainwright added to the day. We walked past it on the Coast to Coast in 1997 and I'd claimed it for my wallchart, but without doing that final short climb. So now my conscience is satisfied, the actual summit is bagged.

It's been an epic walk covering two new peaks in Gray Crag and High Raise and five more familiar friends Thornthwaite Crag, High Street, Kidsty Pike, Rampsgill Head and the Knott.

But it's a long trek along the Coast to Coast path back to Patterdale. I try to note where the paths are to Rest Dodd and the Nab for future use. Where a stream crosses the path I find an old deer antler, which I pick up to take home for Nicola, a lover of what the *Guardian* has recently termed goblincore.

I walk on over the unclear rocky bit, though a gate, round Satura Crag and eventually reach Angle Tarn. It's looking good in the evening light beneath a bed of silvery clouds. Several tents have been pitched at different points around the tarn and I can hear children playing and a mum shouting that dinner is ready. A man is fishing and a flock of geese take off over the water.

Rounding Angle Tarn I meet a couple with full backpacks doing the Coast to Coast. They've come from Grisedale Tarn and are camping up on the fells tonight. As I head down towards Boredale Hause I pass Jamie, a Scottish Wainwright bagger preparing to sleep somewhere up by the tarn.

"I prefer it when it's like this," he says, gesturing towards the clouds. "Last week I had heatstroke, I thought my mate would have to carry me down… You're doing the Wainwrights? I finished on Haystacks. Where are you planning to end?"

"Wherever I end up," I answer. "Probably somewhere round by Wasdale, it's all been pretty unplanned. I should have chosen Great End I guess. But who knows?"

Then it's a painful 15 minutes down from Boredale Hause to the end of the lane at Patterdale. Plod, plod, plod. It's 8.45pm when I stagger into the White Lion.

"She's outside having a fag," says a cockney customer, referring to the bar staff. The bar staffer returns five minutes later and tells me it's a Sunday and they stopped serving food at 7.30pm. It's all reminiscent of Ernest Hemingway's *The Old Man and the Sea*, long hours of endeavour that end up in a futile denouement, a metaphor for human life. I settle for a pint of Wainwright and a packet of cheese and onion crisps. The cockney customer helpfully rings up the Travellers Rest at Glenridding and they say they stop serving at nine, so it's doubtful I'll get there in time. I feel like the dad in Cormac McCarthy's dystopian novel *The Road,* desperately searching for any signs of food in a post-apocalyptic world.

Fortified a little by my pint of Wainwright I walk on for a mile into Glenridding, and up the hill to the

Travellers Rest. They have indeed stopped serving, and I'm reduced to another pint of Loweswater Gold and a packet of salted peanuts. Then it's the godforsaken trek to the YHA, past the seat, left to the cattle grid, by the cottages, then the trees, round the bend along the long level bit, then upwards past the Trax car and through the entrance to the YHA at 10.10pm. My phone tells me that I have covered 41,913 paces and 20 miles. I collapse on to my bunk, have a quick read of my *Far Eastern Fells* Wainwright guide and enjoy the sleep of the just too late for dinner.

The following morning my legs are very stiff and it's painful to get downstairs for the obligatory sausage in a bap served in the YHA reception area. Still hungry from my lack of dinner I order some extra hash browns. Time to do something much more moderate and climb Little Mell Fell. At least the walk into Glenridding is downhill and a coffee at the Fairlight café helps revive me. Then it's on the bus towards the Pooley Bridge end of Ullswater.

It's a 20 minute climb up Little Mell Fell if you have a car, but by public transport it is more difficult. Getting off the bus at Watermillock I take the back road towards Little Mell Fell. It's fairly safe for a pedestrian despite the lack of pavements and provides an interesting glimpse into the lives of second home owners in plush houses, plus a couple of holiday caravan sites. There's also a fine church as the fell comes into view, where I sit and eat my lunch on a bench among the gravestones overlooked by Priest Crag.

With tired legs, the climb up past woods to The Hause seems to take forever, but eventually I find a stile and the path straight up the flank of Little Mell Fell. A family have just started the ascent and I stop to eat a Tunnock's Caramel Wafer in order give them time as the white-haired grandfather, back bent and finding it a struggle, is slowly making his way up the steps in the turf. Even in extreme old age people feel the urge to get up a fell — that might be me in a few years.

It's an easy if steep climb to the summit cairn. There's not too much to admire about the grassy rock-free summit, but the views are splendid, particularly across Ullswater towards the High Street range and across Great Mell Fell towards Blencathra. A bearded man and his wife arrive from the direction of Great Mell Fell and ask which is the way to the Hause: "They said it was easy but we've been climbing over walls and all sorts," says the lady rambler. I'm able to direct them to the Hause where they plan to walk back to their car.

On the route back I take a small country lane towards Bennethead and Wreay. It takes me past some idyllic homes with large glass windows overlooking the fells. In the middle of nothing much someone has installed a metal seat by the road so walkers can look at the view of Ullswater, which is a considerate touch. At the bottom of the lane The Brackenrigg Pub miraculously comes into view. I stroll up to the bar and enjoy a pint of the pub's home-brewed Brack 'n' Brew ale while waiting for the bus back to Glenridding.

Day three of my bid to knock off all the missing Wainwrights around Ullswater sees me tackling High Hartsop Dodd. As I'm walking from the hostel down towards Glenridding at 9am two sets of walkers setting out for Helvellyn ask me if I've been up already. "Yep, Striding Edge was quite something, perfect day for it," I lie, for once able to pass myself as a turbo-charged macho walker who gets up at 5am. It feels rather satisfying.

Taking the bus to Brothers Water with a group of local women discussing London musicals, I discover a massive camp site behind the Brotherswater Inn, complete with a shop. It's full of families and kids in replica Leeds and Stoke City shirts. I hope any swimmers are careful, a week ago a man drowned in Brothers Water and another swimmer from Newcastle died in Crummock Water. On hot days like this it's tempting to leap into the water, forgetting that the shock of the cold deep water can kill.

Crossing a field and then turning left at Hartsop Hall, an old building with mullioned windows, I'm soon at the site of the triangular stone barn mirroring the shape of High Hartsop Dodd behind it — the picture of Hartsop Dodd that makes all the guide books. The large stones in the field look unusual and some research reveals that there is indeed an enclosure here, with standing stones incorporated into its walls. Clearly the view of High Hartsop Dodd piercing the blue sky inspired awe both then and now.

Wainwright suggests avoiding the steep direct climb and coming at the Dodd via Scandale Pass and Little Hart Crag. So I walk past old stone barns and through trees to the fine enclosed valley of Calston Glen. It's a great climb by Calston Beck, trees clinging to rocks above cascading waterfalls as the glen narrows towards a col on the horizon. Through bracken, over damp bare rock, past a dead ash tree and up to the place where sky meets fell. Eventually I can see over a stonewall to the other side of the pass and the path to Ambleside. Turning right I head up to Little Hart Crag and its twin rocky summits. Going straight over the top I head down to the adjoining High Hartsop Dodd. It's a grassy stroll over a wide plateau with a small cairn at the end of the top and excellent views of Brothers Water and Caudale Moor. Rather movingly someone has left a white heart-shaped piece of china on the cairn with a memorial message.

Then it's straight down the nose of the fell, with my poles working overtime. It's unrelenting but quick and after dodging some bovines in the bottom field I'm back at the barn and the stone circle. It's been a searingly hot day and a bottle of cold Coke from the camping shop is very welcome. The 4.12pm bus takes me back to Glenridding and after a rest in the sun by the bus stop, it's off to the Travellers Rest for a burger and chips, served at the tables that now cover the former car park.

Three days of walking have left me feeling exhausted. I know I'll never make The Nab (my last fell left uncompleted in the area) on my final day, so opt to go up to Red Tarn from the hostel instead, and avoid the walk into and out of Glenridding.

It's a pleasure to sit by the tarn and rest my aching body, while not having to worry about finding the energy to climb Striding Edge. Red Tarn has to be the most spectacular of all tarns with the huge rock wall of Helvellyn at one end and Striding Edge and Swirral Edge on either side.

People come and go in the sunlight as I lie down by the water's edge. Dads skim stones off the water, dogs splash through the shallows, a swimmer wades in and swears at the cold, kids look at tiny fish in the clear water. Above a procession of tiny figures are moving across Striding Edge.

A group of swimmers with orange tow floats head out to the middle of the tarn. "You're now swimming in Lakeland's highest tarn," announces their guide. "If you put your head under the clouds look insane!" Someone on the bank offers to video them. Eavesdropping on their conversation I learn that the outdoor adventure company took Paul Merton and his wife out canoeing and it's on Channel 5 soon. When they get out I can see that the punters are clad in wetsuits, but their leader is just wearing a two-piece swimsuit, which in the Lake District is pretty heroic. Wild water women indeed.

After pottering for an hour or two by Red Tarn I return to the hostel for 4pm, do some reading, and join the supper club at seven, ready to get the bus and train back to London in the morning. Four new fells completed — Gray Crag, High Raise, Little Mell Fell and High Hartsop Dodd so a satisfying trip in good weather. Wainwright's *Eastern Fells* book has been completed though The Nab remains a stubborn fell to crack and is my last remaining objective from the Patterdale area.

A few days after returning home a souvenir of my trip emerges — a vicious eye infection. Back in 1985 I had a cold sore on my face and the virus got into my right eye through a contact lens, necessitating treatment at Moorfields Eye Hospital. *Herpes Simplex* is a nasty infection (though thankfully it's not the genital version) — it lies dormant for years on end but can then re-emerge at times of stress or when your body is rundown. It came back in 2009 after 24 years and after a day of tests at Moorfields Eye Hospital it emerges it's back again after a 12-year gap this time.

It might have been the exposure to sunlight but I suspect it's pushing myself too hard, at the age of 61, on my 21-mile walk to Gray Crag and High Raise. The infection is scary as I lose clear vision in my eye and the pressure is way up. But after being prescribed tablets and three sets of eye drops it subsides over the next ten days, even if the virus does make my whole body feel exhausted. It's not exactly Scott struggling to reach the South Pole with frostbite, but my exertions have exacted a price. I now have 33 Wainwrights left to complete, but I need to give myself proper recovery time next trip and not push myself beyond my city limits. It's onwards and upwards, but maybe a bit more carefully.

12. GET OFF MY FELLBARROW

Date: September 2021

Accommodation: Meadow Cottage, Keswick.

Transport: Train from London Euston to Penrith, X5 bus to Keswick, 77 bus to Low Lorton and Seatoller.

Companions: Nicola, Nell, Lola, Michael and Vulcan.

New Wainwrights bagged: 4 — Fellbarrow, Low Fell, Binsey, Rosthwaite Fell.

Total Wainwrights completed: 185

Total Wainwrights left: 29

At last our family holiday in Keswick has arrived. We've travelled up with daughter Nell and meet elder daughter Lola (who has now moved to Edinburgh) at Penrith station. Now we're in Keswick on a Saturday evening lugging a lot of cases, plus Nicola's inflatable 9ft 8ins paddleboard, along Crossthwaite Road and then turning into Brundholme Road. It's quite a trek, but it becomes easier once we learn of the short cut to town across the park.

Meadow Cottage is everything we hoped for, three bedrooms, a good living room, a front garden seat overlooking Fitz Park and a back garden that's overlooked by Skiddaw. There's the Pheasant pub within walking distance and the Filling Station Café with its fancy brunches. Fortified by supplies from Booths we enjoy peanuts in the garden and then carbonara cooked by Nell, followed by a sampling of the Pheasant's ales.

Sunday morning arrives and we're ready for our first excursion. It's Fellbarrow and Low Fell today. Stocked up with pasties from the Cornish Pasty Shop in Lake Road we take the 77 bus to Low Lorton, getting off at the Wheatsheaf. After a short stroll we are soon away from the tight and busy main road admiring the bridge over the River Cocker.

We turn into a lane heading upwards. It becomes a tree-lined off-road track as Lola, Nell, Nicola and myself head up towards the highest point of the lane. I adjust my poles. Nicola stops to pick blackberries and Vulcan enjoys some roadside fruit too. There's grass down the middle of the track and a rusting horsebox by a farm gateway.

Eventually we find the walled track that leads across green fields and flower-strewn banks to the ruins of Hatteringill. We're choosing a relatively easy route because Nicola's knee was dodgy on the steep descents from Ard Crags earlier in the summer, but after a month of physio-inspired exercises she's finding it no problem. "This is really nice, it's better than all those crags," she suggests, "it's much more like a walk in the country."

We head across the faint path, seeing a fine view of Lorton below and then Whiteside and accompanying fells across the valley.

"Dad, I think I like fellwalking again!" says a

revitalised Lola. "Why can't all the Lake District be like this?"

"Well, there are easy and difficult mountains. I'm glad you've got your mountain mojo back. It's only taken 11 years of therapy since Sharp Edge," I venture.

To our delight we see a shepherd's hut perched on a hill in the distance, looking very Hobbity. We stop for lunch by a gate and the first crisis of the day occurs — Nell has a blister. We thought they were the correct pair of boots from our collection, but it emerges they are an old pair of Lola's and are rubbing her heel raw. Luckily I have some blister plasters in my Gore-Tex pocket and administer first aid. Pasties and photo ops restore our spirits.

We walk on and find the ruins of Hatteringill, an old farmstead that must have been quite grand in its day. It's not as intact as in Wainwright's illustration; all is now a sad tumble of stone and lost lives. These farmers couldn't have had much of a social life — it's a long trek across the fell just to get down to the Wheatsheaf.

Someone has laid out a stone arrow on the grass, pointing the way along the path up by a fence. An ingenious and clever way of helping other walkers. It's a steep climb past the ruined wall, over a couple of stiles, and soon we are by the summit trig point. Lola has decided to walk barefoot like a natural hippy.

The first Wainwright of any holiday is always satisfying, though the flying ants have also got up here and are buzzing the trig point. Nicola waits with Vulcan by the fence and the rest of us tackle a series of up and down slopes to Low Fell. It's all grassy inclines and Lola continues to gambol barefoot. After half an hour of ups and downs we arrive at a summit with much better views — a classic glimpse of Crummock Water with mighty Mellbreak on one flank and Grasmoor on the other. I take a selfie of myself with the youngsters.

Then it's back up and down the dips to find Nicola, who has met several other Wainwright baggers during our hour away. We retrace out steps back to Low Lorton, feeling quite tired having walked 25,000 steps. Mercifully the Wheatsheaf is open, though they are short-staffed and not serving any more pub dinners. At least we get peanuts and crisps. We sit in the beer garden enjoying cold beer and large glasses of wine discussing the highlights of the day and the best Abba songs. Vulcan sits beneath the table exhausted by a walk that's more vigorous than his usual stroll down Stroud Green Road.

Our plan is to catch the last bus to Keswick on a Sunday at 18.44pm, which sounds risky. But standing on the patch of grass opposite the pub, we dutifully and hungrily wait for the bus while Nell and Lola explore the river. Then we have to shout at them to come back as the bus arrives a couple of minutes early.

"It's the last bus, you never know if it will come or not!" announces the chirpy driver. "Where can I take you?" We flash our return tickets and enjoy the ride back to Keswick. Here we divert to the chip shop, where we're joined by Lola's boyfriend Michael, who has just arrived from Edinburgh, via London. As we cross Fitz Park Nicola spots the BMX track for the local kids and insists on us running round its curves like a human bike, as you do.

It's been a great first day, bar Nell's blisters. Reading Wainwright's description of Fellbarrow you'd think it a bit nondescript, but all the party have enjoyed our outing.

Day two sees Nicola taking everyone but me paddleboarding from Derwent Water to Bassenthwaite, with the aid of local paddleboard guide John. Someone has to look after Vulcan, so today he's my walking companion. We're taking the X4 to the Castle Hotel and then making a bid to climb the set of brown contours on my OS map that is Binsey, an outlier at the very edge of the Northern fells.

The isolated side road to Binsey lodge isn't too busy, though when a white van does pass me it's doing 60mph. There are a few houses initially, then a set of barking Alsatians outside a barn full of logged wood. Side lanes lead to places with names like High Bewaldeth. The rounded form of Binsey starts to get closer. After a mile or so the charming Whitefield Cottage marks a sharp corner and after a short trek uphill I'm at the mock-Tudor Binsey Lodge, looking very similar to Wainwright's picture, except with added private property signs. Poignantly Wainwright writes that bus no 71 stops there — no chance of such a thing now.

Here's the path at last. Tying Vulcan's lead around the branch of a gorse tree, I stop for a pasty and some fruit. Vulcan is a good companion, and Wainwright would approve, as my canine pal is largely silent.

It's a fairly gentle but long path up to the summit. All is grass, gorse and heather until the stony top emerges. As Wainwright says, it's a summit deserving of a much higher fell. Much of it is an ancient tumulus (Wainwright playfully pictures himself as an ancient Briton alongside it), which non-archaeologists have fashioned into two rudimentary shelters. I sit inside one of them with Vulcan and tweet a photo of him. Like the Who, I can see for miles and miles. Flat land heading to the coast, the Coniston fells far away and great views of the back of Skiddaw. It's fun to trace out the route of last summer's Longlands to Great Cockup walk with Nicola and Nell.

Near the summit I find another dog walker with a collie. He's from Lancashire and has just walked the five fells of Longlands to Great Cockup and is now adding Binsey, though he's aided by having a car. This is his 93rd fell, and it's my 180th, not that Wainwright baggers spend all their days exchanging scores.

The road back to the Castle Hotel seems long and I've given up hope of catching the 3.12 bus, at least until I see it driving away as I arrive at the crossroads. Why do buses always do that? It's a two-hour wait for the next bus so I look for tea in the Castle Hotel, which is some kind of conference centre. Café and bar are closed but the receptionist is helpful. She says I can take a complimentary coffee from the urn for new arrivals and sit in reception in one of their comfy armchairs. It has a copy of the *i* newspaper and free wi-fi, while Vulcan enjoys lying down on the soft carpet and sleeping. People are helpful here.

When I do finally catch the bus there are two bus stops, one down the side road, one on the main road. I'm confused so flit awkwardly between them ready to dash across the road should the bus arrive at the other stop. You wait two hours for a bus and then two turn up. Bizarrely an unexpected 555 bus from Carlisle to Keswick arrives, closely followed by the X4 from Workington to Keswick. From their separate stops they move in convoy back to Keswick, picking up walkers with poles and backpacks on the way.

After a good sleep, a day off from the fells proves fun as Nicola and myself hire bikes and cycle down the re-opened Keswick to Threlkeld former railway line. Brundholme and White Moss bridges were swept away and Rawsome's bridge left at risk of collapse during Storm Desmond in 2015. Two hundred metres of the footpath was also destroyed. At a cost of several million pounds the footpath has now been re-opened, and the new bridges have a pleasing Victorian look to them.

Using the Keswick to Threlkeld path you realise just what a feat it was for those Victorian engineers to build so many bridges over the winding river and at times tunnel through solid rock. Ripping out this line was surely the most idiotic of all the train closures after Doctor Beeching's report. Tourism? That will never happen in the Lake District.

But at least it has become an invaluable footpath and cycleway, with an ice cream van happily situated by an old stone shelter. The walk ends with a short cycle path beside the A66 to Threlkeld, all in the shadow of Blencathra. We take the back roads and re-join the path via an unfeasibly steep lane, then cycle back through dappled cuttings and under the motorway flyover, finally reaching the old station.

"This reminds me of cycling in the Dordogne," says Nicola, which can't have been said of Keswick very often. Soon we're returning the bikes and joining Michael and Lola for a sneaky cocktail at the bar on Lake Road.

The Lake District is heating up. Extreme heat wasn't something I'd expected to be tackling on Rosthwaite Fell, but it's 26C in September. My cunning plan is to take the 8.30am bus to Stonethwaite and beat the worst of the heat. I follow a couple of blonde women in micro-shorts down the lane to Stonethwaite. They look like they could be on *Love Island* but are heading to the campsite beyond the village.

The campsite is active, full of campervans, tents and people in shades eating breakfast on fold-up tables. I find the path heading upwards by Little Stanger Gill. The day is already heating up, but with a peaked cap, lots of sun cream and a short-sleeved Mountain Ridge 'technical' t-shirt I feel prepared. It's a delightful climb by the ravine of the gill and the oak and silver birch trees keep it cool and shaded. Soon, the view back down Stonethwaite opens out behind me. The cleft becomes rockier. Passing dry stone walls built at impossible angles, I stop to take a picture of a mass of red berries on a group of rowan trees.

When the narrow path eventually joins the sky ahead I find an incredible enclosed valley. It's a natural amphitheatre, with Stanger Gill traversing sideways to its source beneath a set of craggy rock spurs. A thin path in the grass guides my way past several rounded tops and then veers left and up the back of Bessy Boot, aka Rosthwaite Fell.

Having not seen anyone all journey I discover two women on the summit, whom I shall call Thelma and Louise. "Can you hold this for us please?" says Thelma, handing me a sign reading "214". I've arrived at the exact moment they are completing their second round of 214 Wainwrights. We chat about bagging. They used to live in Chelmsford, Essex, but have now retired to live near Hallin Fell.

We find some things in common, and Louise knows my manor of Finsbury Park, having grown up nearby. They take a picture for me of my own bagging of Rosthwaite Fell as I lean on the triangular cairn. We discuss favourite fells and when I say I have yet to do Branstree, Selside, Tarn Crag and Grey Crag from Haweswater they advise me not to finish on those as they are quite boring. Perhaps the fells around Wasdale, Ennerdale or Eskdale might be better. What we all agree on is that Rosthwaite is a very underrated fell.

I walk down to the reedy shore of the evocatively-named Tarn at Leaves, a still body of water overlooked by the rugged stony outcrops of Glaramara. Walking back down the path above Comb Gill the sun starts to really kick in. I'm on my second bottle of water and intensely grateful when an isolated tree offers a moment's respite and some shade. Heatstroke must be a real danger for anyone setting out in the afternoon. Finally the path emerges at the main road between Seatoller and

Rosthwaite.

The obligatory bus rolls past just before I arrive at the bus stop. Phone messages are instructing me to meet Nicola and Nell at the Platty Plus paddleboarding centre opposite the Lodore Falls Hotel. After a wait in the cool stone of a bus shelter I arrive at the centre, take hold of Vulcan for them and enjoy a cold pint of Wainwright in the hotel, even if a sign does say it's for residents only. Sod that, I've walked a fell in Foreign Legion-type heat and I deserve a drink.

Back at the house that evening there's further drama with Lola. "Mum, mum, there's a tick stuck on me!" she cries. Indeed, nestling around her midriff is a brown grub. It must have been due to walking in a sports top up Fellbarrow and pretending to be her hero Taylor Swift singing *The Lakes*.

"I put two ticks on my Wainwright wall chart last night, perhaps one escaped," I suggest. Lola doesn't seem to appreciate my wit.

After much panic and talk of Lyme disease, we remove to the seat on the terrace and Nicola tugs at the gorging tick with a pair of tweezers. "It's alright, I've done this on Vulcan before," she says. But the bug comes away with its head still inside Lola. Google reveals this is the way to get infected. And maybe ticks lay eggs inside humans and they explode out of your stomach *Alien*-style.

Next day Lola visits the emergency clinic in Keswick and a nice nurse called Liz removes the offending bug's head, and reassures her that this is likely to be a sheep tick and it is deer tick that spread Lyme disease. Lola learns a lot about Liz, including the fact that she's worried about wearing her suede shoes at her friend's wedding the next day because rain is forecast. You don't get such friendliness in London's busy clinics.

Sir Ernest Shackleton had to survive on seal blubber, but we've had Nell's blisters and Lola's tick attack. Still, we've had good weather and it's all Michael's doing. He is clearly still some kind of rain god. He's now spent two week-long holidays in the Lakes without rain and is convinced you don't need a Gore-Tex in such a sunny place. If we take him every year Lakeland will never see precipitation again.

My final assault on a summit is an attempted climbing of Seathwaite Fell. Via Seathwaite Farm we walk on to Stockley Bridge. Nicola is worried by the lack of water in the wide stony course of Styhead Gill.

The immaculately made arches and walls by the bridge make a good spot to stop for a pasty. Nicola and Lola turn back after lunch but Nell, Vulcan and myself climb Styhead Pass to try and bag Seathwaite Fell, though cloud is drifting in and out of the higher peaks.

The views across to the vast scree banks on Base Brown are impressive as we trek up the steps of the fixed path. but as the pass weaves around Seathwaite Fell it's unclear where the path to the summit lies. There's what might be a faint track on the grass early on but we want the second easier route mentioned by Wainwright. And then the mist comes down. There is no sign of a clear path heading up to the fell and the pass itself is getting indistinct. Visibility is down to ten feet. "Wow, this is cool!" says Nell, who has never really been among the clouds before. I take a picture of her on a footbridge, shrouded in mist.

We take a little diversion up the side of Seathwaite Fell but it quickly gets boggy and Nell still has recovering blisters and is only wearing trainers, which won't keep out the water. I don't fancy getting up to the top and then becoming disorientated with no visibility. Best to save it for another day. We retrace our steps and are soon away from the wispy world of dragons in a foggy Middle Earth.

Just to prove the Lake District is full of surprises, on our final night we sit on the terrace and hear the sounds of Bad Manners wafting up from the park. Buster Bloodvessel and co are playing at the Keswick Mountain Festival. I never thought I'd be hearing *Lip Up Fatty* in the shadow of Skiddaw.

It's been another successful trip — a great cottage, a lot of paddleboarding for Nicola, my daughters entertained, the young people kept in beer, cocktails and pasties and four new fells completed.

13. UP HILL AND DOWN ESKDALE

Date: October 2021

Accommodation: Eskdale Youth Hostel.

Transport: Train from London Euston to Lancaster, train to Ravenglass, taxi to Eskdale.

Companions: Solo trip.

New Wainwrights bagged: 3 — Green Crag, Harter Fell, Hard Knott.

Total Wainwrights completed: 188

Total Wainwrights left: 26

There's been a landslide on the Ravenglass and Eskdale Railway, aka La'al Ratty. This is more like proper travel writing. George Monbiot wrote in his book *Poisoned Arrows* about being lost in the West Papua forest and surviving on rats and insects, then almost being stung to death by hornets and threatened by soldiers with Kalashnikovs. Maybe I can get that vibe in west Cumbria, dodging landslides and dealing with the lack of packed lunches at the youth hostel.

At least the Ravenglass light railway phoned me up to offer a refund. The landslide has occurred after heavy rain and will prove expensive for the whole region, putting the trains out of action for several weeks.

Travelling on the branch line from Lancaster to Ravenglass is a slow if scenic experience. After the rusting graveyard of Harry Potter-like ancient train carriages that is Carnforth station, the line curves around Morecambe Bay. It's all shining sands and marshy grass, reminding me of our walk across the bay with guide Cedric a few years earlier, following a trail of branch markers to dodge quicksand and wading through water with an emergency tractor at hand if needed.

The train stops at the faded grandeur of Grange-over-Sands the resort that was the base for my school's 1976 geography field trip —the first time I saw the visionary gleam of the Lake District as a 16-year-old.

On through small settlements with strange names like Cark-in-Cartmel. Past mudflats and watery sculptures amid coastal grass. Then the bigger town of Ulverston and Roose with its big estate of what look like Barratt Homes.

Past a derelict warehouse, a Union Jack and a lighthouse and into Barrow-in-Furness, full of cranes and red-bricked northern industrial homes. Then a swift change of train and my journey continues up the coast. The area feels increasingly remote, cut off from the rest of the country by mountains, with the train ambling slowly by the sea and most stops request only. It's a land of large river estuaries and ten-cottage villages. The outline of the mountains can be seen inland and as we approach Ravenglass station some outlying fells come right out to the coast.

My pre-booked taxi is at the station and the driver says it rained so hard last Saturday he thought it was going to be another Storm Desmond. He points out workmen in orange boiler suits working on the Ravenglass railway just outside Ravenglass. He reckons it'll be several weeks before the old mining railway is repaired, "which is a shame as it brings in money to the whole community."

In the northern lakes the taxi drivers often don't know much about the fells. But here my man is on his second round of the Wainwrights, while his wife is on her first. We discuss obscure fells. He says he doesn't know why people bother with Scafell Pike. As we drive down single lane roads past a couple of pubs he tells me of the direct route up Hard Knott from the Roman Fort via a wall and an array of directions which I can't really take in. As we drive past the Woolpack Inn and up the hostel drive he shows me the zig-zag peat road up to Green Crag. A good service for £20.

Eskdale YHA was purpose built in the 1930s and has to be one of Lakeland's best hostels, with its own stream and trees nestling beneath crags. After waiting a couple of hours for the five pm opening of reception — I get to read all the posters on Neolithic, Roman and Viking history in Eskdale — staffer Mick offers me a friendly guide to the hostel and a door code in the event of my going on a wild night out until the small hours. My room has a double-bed-sized bunk and a sink, which is a result in hostel terms. After unpacking it's down to reception for a pizza and pint of Cumberland ale.

The YHA still appears convinced that the only method of stopping Covid is sausage baps. I'm given the obligatory veggie sausage bap for breakfast, the same one you get at every other hostel, though it would be nice to have a little choice or even the offer of say an egg in a bap. The days of full English breakfasts seem a long while back.

I set off for Green Crag with a feeling of optimism. Past the Woolpack and over the road to Doctor Bridge, possibly named after an early appearance in Eskdale of

David Tennant. Then it's past Low Birker Farm and on to the old peat road. Half-way up I stop for a rest. "Are you shattered already?" asks a hearty Geordie with a shaved head and gaiters. "Just getting my walking head on," I mutter, letting him pace on way ahead.

Rather pleasingly, there's a roofless old peat hut on the peat road, discovered by this Pete. Today we need to save the peat up on the moors to help soak up carbon. But befitting his curmudgeonly image, Wainwright brings the nuclear power station into his guide, moaning that while we have newfangled atomic power, "peat is out of fashion. Alas!"

The top of Green Crag isn't what you can see from the road, the fell crosses a boggy expanse overlooked by Kepple Crag and Crook Crag. The bracken is russet brown as autumn sets in. Soon the path is skirting the remote Low Birker Tarn and I pass a lone walker in shorts and a green technical top heading back down to Eskdale: "It's not a bad day, the clouds are blowing through, at least we'll see something," he says.

Across the boggy brown marshland lies a striking Neolithic cairn, which was part of a Bronze Age hut circle and field system. It's a neat looking circle of stones, collapsed in the middle. What were those people from thousands of years ago doing up here? Did this area speak of the sublime to them too? Or were they just trying to keep warm? Was it a burial mound and marker of territory? Or just a place they lobbed stones when they cleared the fields for agriculture? There are many stone circles and field systems around Boot and clearly this was an important place in pre-history. They might even have had axe shops, which is more than the current Eskdale has.

The path takes me to a col between Crook Crag and Green Crag. There's a walker coming down. "These boots are not waterproof!" he complains, pointing at his lightweight footwear, "It's these wet rocks, I need some proper bog stompers."

Green Crag is a bee-hive shaped rocky lump, but a small detour to one side allows access to the excellent summit. There's plenty of water visible, Devoke Water to the west, Low Birker Tarn, and Blea Tarn and Burnmoor Tarn above Eskdale. The Scafells are standing in cloud. It's a fine top. You can see wide estuaries, the grey coast and matching grey cloud. I halt for a slightly stale bagel imported from Finsbury Park because the YHA has stopped doing packed lunches as a Covid precaution and the nearest shop is several miles away.

Across a marshy stretch of flat land lies the triangular top of Harter Fell. Descending between Crook Crag and Green Crag I head across what the YouTube videos say is a very boggy divide between the two Wainwrights. At first there's a faint path across a solid shoulder of fell. But then comes the flatter section and I have to head towards Hardknott Forest at the foot of Harter Fell.

It gets boggy quickly, though I've coped with Armboth Fell and Mungrisdale Common. Anything with heather growing on it is slightly more solid, while the light green patches are treacherous. Paths seem to go nowhere. Eventually I decide to leg it towards the forest, poking ahead with my walking poles to check the solidity of the surface. It all goes well until one step sees my right boot descend into the mire with a great slurp. Water surges into my boot and my pole descends ominously a pace ahead. Sod it. I reverse and try a different route over heather, moving quickly and thinking of *The Hound of the Baskervilles*, where huge bogs on Dartmoor swallow people.

Eventually I get across to the fence, scale the netting and find a path taking me to the start of Hardknott Forest.

I stop to take off my saturated boot and wring out my sock. At least there seems to be a path going up to Harter Fell by the neatly fenced forest. A couple descend from Harter Fell on their way to Green Crag and I warn them of the dangers of the bogs. The woman says it's 15 minutes to the top. "Only if you run!" says her partner.

Better get going. It's upwards with tired legs for the next 45 minutes. Soon the path moves into cloud. But I keep going and end up in a weird land of big rock turrets surrounded by white cloud. Finally I get to find the trig point and take a selfie. Visibility is nil but at least I've made it. Taking out my Wainwright book, he writes that this isn't even the true summit, it's the slab of sheer rock to my right. It looks unassailable even if Wainwright says there is a way up. Not being a pedant, the trig point will do me. Two Wainwrights in one day, not bad.

I'm back down at the forest at 4.30 where the path should, according to the map, take me back down to the Jubilee Bridge at the foot of Hard Knott pass. A stile indicates a path to the left, which is a short cut. It's a gamble in that should I go wrong darkness is rapidly approaching. It's a steep descent, but it works, after passing numerous tree plantations, the track descends through bracken to the River Esk and eventually passes Penny Hill Farm, where the footpath signs are confusingly listed in yards rather than miles.

After a pleasant amble along the sunken Penny Hill Lane I emerge at Doctor Bridge and miraculously arrive at the Woolpack Inn just before dusk. I treat myself to a pint of a citrus session beer by the Fyne brewery and a packet of cheese and onion crisps, before returning to the YHA's supper club meal of pasty and gravy in the cosy reception room warmed by a log burner. A productive day using the last of the October light before the clocks go back.

Another day soon begins with yet another sausage bap. Fill water, fold map in case, pick up sticks, pack lunch. My next objective is Hard Knott, via the Roman fort.

Travelling via Shanks' Pony I'm legging it up Hard Knott Pass, while being wary of passing cars in the narrow lane. It's clear the authorities have had problems with the increased number of visitors after lockdown. Every layby has signs instructing no overnight camping, saying that there are rangers on patrol. A big blue sign above a stone wall is headed "Respect", and adds, "take your litter home, no overnight camping, no BBQs or fires and remember there is limited parking." "Please do not block the gate," is on every field gate.

As the road starts to increase in gradient a sign warns, "Road suitable for cars and light vehicles only. Unsuitable for all vehicles in winter conditions." But it's not that bad by foot when you're used to climbing mountains and at least the surface is even. I step over the cattle grid, weave around the tarmac bends and then take the footpath on the left that goes up over a ridge to suddenly emerge at the exterior wall and west gate of Hardknott Roman Fort.

It's my ideal day, combining archaeology with a new fell. The walls are impressive, about the same height as the best bits of Hadrian's Wall, even if the top stones above the line of thin slates were re-installed by the Ministry of Works when Wainwright was writing his *Guide to the Southern Fells* in 1959.

Built in the second century AD during the reign of Hadrian, it has the typical oblong shape of a Roman fort, with four gates and the base of a square doorless tower at each corner (access would have been by the ramparts). Inside are the excavated lower walls of the granaries, headquarters and commanding officer's quarters.

A little way outside the walls are the remains of a sophisticated bath house, with hot and cold pools for the Romans to relax in. It looks a lot more spacious than the youth hostel's shower. Maybe the whole place was the Roman equivalent of a YHA, but with rather harsher punishments if you didn't finish your sausage bap.

The fort is in an immensely atmospheric position, overlooking a massive drop into the beautiful Eskdale valley and giving a commanding view down the pass to Ravenglass, where there was another Roman fort. It stood on the site of the old Roman road and would have controlled travel to Ambleside. Though perhaps the fort needed a little rebranding, as the original name of Mediobogdum isn't quite as catchy as Hardknott.

What must have the 500 men from the Cohort of Dalmations have felt while they were stationed here? When the winter mist came in were they scared of their hostile environment, or did they also feel a sense of awe. We'll never know, but walking across the grassy mounds of unexcavated structures you feel yourself transported back in time.

Returning to the road I weave my way around the hairpin bends. On some bends there are short stone walls designed as buffers to prevent motorists crashing down fearsome drops; you certainly wouldn't want to skid and end up in one of the ravines.

Soon I'm at the top of the pass where there's a layby for a few cars. From here I can see down into the Duddon valley and the rest of Wrynose pass snaking past Cold Pike and Pike O'Blisco. In the distance are the three distinctive bumps of Crinkle Crags. All my previous trips are starting to fit together.

A cairn marks the top of the pass and here is the path up to Hard Knott. The hard work has been done. It's an easy 500 feet of ascent up to the top — my sort of mountain. The path takes me to Border End. It's an exquisite spot, several small boggy tarns surrounded by a ridge, with a cairn marking the highest point and Harter Fell looming large above the pass.

From the far end there's a superb aerial view down to Hardknott Fort. The full outline of the fort is visible and you can see just what a commanding position it held, overlooking the corridor of green fields and woods that leads to the sea. The view down the Eskdale valley is spectacular too, brown and yellow vegetation merging with shattered rocks.

But it's here that I make my big mistake and assume that Border End is the true summit with its big cairn. When I post a picture of Border End on the *To Climb all 214 Wainwrights* Facebook group I'm corrected by many Wainwright baggers. The true summit is the slightly higher point to the east. Doh! I'm annoyed with Wainwright for not doing a proper map and only devoting one cursory page to the ascent of Hard Knott. But you set your own rules, it's going to be difficult to get to again and I'm claiming it, though I feel a little guilty.

The walk down the pass is a lot easier than going up. And after another amble round the Roman fort, where a sign forbids commercial photography and drone flying, it's back into the YHA for supper club. It's sausages and mash, after sausage in a bap for breakfast and a Greggs vegan sausage roll for lunch. Some are born to sausages some achieve sausages and some have sausages thrust upon them. Still, at least the YHA's Rachel admires my Tardis phone cover and the staff are always helpful, if a little sausage obsessed.

I'm joined by Francois, a talkative Belgian who doesn't do social distancing and is camping outside with his motor bike, plus Steve from Sheffield who discusses how the official rules of football were codified by

Sheffield FC, and describes Sheffield as the world's biggest village.

My final day is less fruitful. The terrace route from Wha House Farm up to Slight Side is a fine walk, with brilliant views over the wall to the Eskdale valley, but then it's a long boggy trudge over Quagrigg Moss. It's a wilderness of small streams and tussocky faded grass with not a single walker encountered anywhere.

Slight Side is covered in cloud and for once Wainwright's map doesn't appear to be that accurate. Occasionally the crags of Scafell loom out of the mist behind the rocky top of Slight Side. The faint path by the big boulder seems to take me up Horn Crag, which is steep and uninviting, and with the weather worsening, cloud dropping and daylight limited I decide to save it for a better day as I don't fancy getting lost on Quagrigg Moss. Slight Side is a big trek at 2499 feet, and might be a good fell to finish on. No walk is ever wasted, even if I've had to turn back today

Next morning a taxi takes me through Eskdale Green and back to Ravenglass station, where the light railway is still closed because of the landslide. It's been interesting coming at the mountains from the less populated side of Lakeland, though it must be difficult living here as the taxi driver says the nearest place to shop is Workington.

This time the train takes me north to Carlisle, past St Bees and the red cliffs that mark the start of Wainwright's Coast to Coast walk. All sorts of power generation is on display, from the square blocks of Sellafield to the wind farms out in the Atlantic and dotted along the coast. Despite hosting COP26, the government is also contemplating opening a coal mine here. On through Whitehaven, Maryport, Workington and eventually Carlisle, where after the seclusion of Eskdale I'm rather pleased to find Costa coffee and fresh food before catching the train to London.

Twenty six Wainwrights left to complete and probably no more climbing until next spring. But I'm getting there slowly and three of the more obscure southern fells have been added to my wallchart. It will take maybe three weeks to bag my remaining fells. Barring another pandemic, personal catastrophe or climate meltdown, next year should finally see the completion of my 214.

14. SETTING OUT MY BAKESTALL

Date: March 2022

Accommodation: Carlton Heights, Keswick.

Transport: Train from London Euston to Penrith, 508 bus Penrith to Keswick, taxi to Peter House Farm.

Companions: Nicola and Vulcan.

New Wainwrights bagged: 1 — Bakestall

Total Wainwrights completed: 189

Total Wainwrights left: 25

It's getting easier to understand how Alfred Wainwright must have felt walking the fells during the second world war. On February 24 Vladimir Putin's Russia invades Ukraine and suddenly there is war in Europe's back yard and the world seems to have turned into a history programme. Bombs are exploding on hospitals and theatres, port cities bombed to rubble. Ten million people have become refugees and Putin is making threats of a nuclear response if the western countries intervene. President Zelensky and the people of Ukraine are bravely refusing to surrender, Kiev is being shelled, the Russian tanks, manned by unwilling conscripts, aren't making the progress they expected and it looks like becoming a long war of attrition.

All this after two years of Covid and now the latest science indicating that the poles are melting at unprecedented rates due to global warming. It's easy to imagine how Wainwright might have found solace in the mountains as humanity seemed to be bent on self-destruction. We all need a break from doomscrolling.

We're travelling to Keswick for a mini-break before Nicola starts to run her paddleboarding course at Angel, Islington, for the rest of the summer. It's only giving us two days of walking but it's a chance to experience the Lakes in March again — the last time we did this lockdown started in 2020 and, envisaging roadblocks around London, Nicola made us rush back from Grasmere a day early.

It's a relief to wake up in our silent rented apartment with no Radio 4 *Today* programme bringing bad news. Peter House Farm is a good place to start our first day's walk, with the mountain weather information service promising a 90 per cent chance of cloud-free summits. We take a taxi from Keswick for £18, with a driver who recalls the floods and shows us where the River Greta would naturally flow without human-made detours.

"Let's take a selfie of the cow field," suggests Nicola as we pay the driver at Peter House Farm. Here is the very cowgate field where frisky bullocks terrified our daughter Nell as we attempted to leave Great Cockup and take the footpath to Bassenthwaite back in 2020.

The Cumbria Way path heading towards the Back o' Skiddaw is actually a rough road going to Skiddaw House, and very easy to follow. Vulcan the wonder dog sniffs the air and is alert to the long-distance views. There's something magical about this deserted place. As Wainwright points out, there are three isolated white farmhouses across the valley and that's it, no holiday homes or anything connected with tourism.

A mile or so along the road we find a parked van with a logo for a dry stone walling company on the side. A little further down the track we spot two men at work repairing a field wall down near the stream. It's odd, because we have been reading Wainwright, writing in 1961, saying, "sometimes a solitary farmworker can be seen tilling the few ploughed fields or repairing a wall." Very little has changed in 61 years.

We walk on past the evocatively-named Dead Crags, a dark chunk of rockface gouged out of the fell. The white ribbon of tumbling water that is Dash Falls comes into view. The path rises alongside Dash Beck and we sit for a snack break by a ghostly white tree, among heather and grass, overlooking the narrow rocky ravine containing the falls. The air feels remarkably fresh after London.

Just past the falls a track to the right heads up Birkett Edge to the summit of Bakestall, a good Wainwright to finally knock off. It's a steep climb by a wall and then a fence, very squelchy at first. After the initial pull I start to puff, feeling the effect of too many pints and packets of peanuts in London. The first walk of the year is always tough and my thighs burn for the 900-foot ascent. Nicola is handling it better, her core toughed by cycling, paddleboarding, exercise cushions, wobble cushions and a strange inability to relax on sofas.

The plod upwards seems to take an age and there's another mound ahead and then the top of Skiddaw. But eventually we reach the plateau above Dead Crags and a short walk takes us to the Bakestall summit cairn at 2189 feet. We find a rewarding view across to the Solway Firth and away to the hills of Galloway in Scotland.

As we stop for a photo another climber appears. Phil is doing the Birketts after his wife "passed on". He's done all 514 and is now on his second round. It gave him something to aim for, he tells us. Our new friend lives by the sea on the Solway Firth. “We get a lot of weather and there aren’t many facilities,” he says, “though the walking’s great.” He asks us where we’re going tomorrow and we mention Seathwaite Fell as a possibility, causing him to enthuse about the fact it used to be a vast volcano, before heading up towards Skiddaw.

As we descend back to the Cumbria Way, we see a white pick-up truck moving slowly along the road far below. “What if there’s a body in the boot?” asks Nicola. We shouldn’t have just binge-watched all six episodes of *The Tourist*. It’s really quite unlikely that a murderous Greek drug baron high on LSD has sent out a hit-man to find us here.

We stop for a pasty at the foot of Bakestall, which seems appropriate. The Cumbrian Way walkers in winter seem a determined and not very talkative bunch. One woman in gaiters steams past us without even stopping to admire Dash Falls.

As we carry on upwards I start to puff again. Nicola informs me that if I were one of her clients she would be worried and insists on carrying my backpack. Then some walkers emerge from the other direction.

“Give me my backpack back! I can’t be seen with a woman carrying two backpacks!” I exclaim.

“I love it when you’re sexist,” Nicola counters. Grabbing my backpack from her, I avoid embarrassment at the expense of perpetuating the patriarchy.

The path weaves around the bulk of Great Calva and soon we can see the square batch of trees that shield Skiddaw House from the Cumbrian winds. A quick read of my AW guide reveals a passage of peak Wainwright curmudgeonly prose, as he enthuses about the circular sheep folds: “In these decadent years of easy money and overmuch leisure, of easy consciences and slipshod work, it is refreshing to come across craftsmanship of the highest standard." And that was written in 1961. What would AW have later made of those layabout Beatles and Rolling Stones, let alone the permissive society?

We need to be back before darkness at six, but it's long been an ambition to walk this prominent green line on the OS map, a ten-mile trek from Peter House Farm to Keswick. We head over Dead Beck and see that white pick-up truck edging slowly down the track towards us. As it passes us we discover that it's actually driven by a female warden from the youth hostel at Skiddaw House and not Billy Nixon, the guy with the hat from *The Tourist*. We wonder if Amazon Prime would deliver out here. It's a big drive to get your groceries and you wouldn't want to get back to Skiddaw House only to remember you've forgotten a box of matches.

A short pull up the hill takes us to Skiddaw House, surrounded by trees with wind-battered tops. It's a good moment as I've only ever seen the place as a dot in the distance from the summit of Skiddaw. A sign tells us that it is re-opening as a hostel, despite reports it was up for sale. At 1550 foot above sea level it's the highest hostel in Britain. It was once a hunting lodge and shepherd's house, but as a hostel now boasts fleece lined walls, solar panel generated electricity, solar thermal hot water and a spring-fed water supply. Not to mention a piano and 22 beds in four rooms.

We walk on past some tumbled-down walls of old farm buildings and the winding path tacks across the edge of Lonscale Fell. Across the river valley are stone walls dividing even the boggiest bits of grass and then the upturned pudding of Mungrisdale Common. The walking is relatively flat if quite a long trudge. We stop to eat a buttered hot cross bun while sitting by Whit Beck.

Finally, in the lovely evening light, we make the car park on the lane from Ormathwaite, where Nicola discusses gaiters with a father and son. They say they are good for walking through long grass, but really you still need waterproof trousers as well, and they are not a lot of use for the sheep-cropped grass and clear paths we've been walking on.

From the road we descend past Latrigg and through Birkett Wood. I'm getting a bit of a second wind but Nicola is starting to feel her legs hurt as the path descends steeply. She's been saying that the Lakes are bereft of wildlife, beyond sheep and some chaffinches. She might have a point, though it's the sheep farming that has given Lakeland its distinctive fields and stone walls, as well as denuding the hills. So I tell Nicola that this is where a saw a red squirrel five years ago, as we head through trees towards the flyover over the A66. She suggests stopping to look, though obviously we won't see another squirrel.

"Look there's one up there!" Blimey. Miraculously, a red squirrel appears in the branches above us. We watch it gracefully leap from one tree across our path and on to another set of branches on a different tree.

"It's lovely. I never thought I'd see one ever," she says in a kind of reverie.

"I thought I'd lay that on for you, as you said you'd always wanted to see a red squirrel," I bluff.

On a path packed with Skiddaw walkers and next to a roaring motorway it seems amazing to have been plunged back into the world of Beatrix Potter and Squirrel Nutkin.

As we walk up Brundholme Road there's a woman in her garden holding a dog on a lead, which is barking at a wild Peter Rabbit sitting on the lawn, minus his waistcoat. "He hates those rabbits, he's been barking at them for two years!" the dog's owner says cheerfully.

We stagger into Keswick and back into our apartment to eat Indian food from Booths. The flat has underfloor heating, which feels luxurious, and fine views of the fells from every window. Then it's on to the Alhambra cinema where Nicola has booked tickets to see the documentary *River*. Before it starts we learn of the efforts to restore the fine old building as we buy drinks from David at the bar, meet a Yorkshire couple now retired to Portinscale and talk to an elderly lady who has tales of being born in the second world war, Calder cabbages and St Martin's Art College, all while annotating a novel by Richard Madeley.

On the second and final day of our mini-break it is solid rain, making us soon give up any idea of further summit-bagging. So we buy coffee and sit under the canopy outside the Yew Tree Farm Café at Rosthwaite, looking at the steam come off our cups and the rain drift over Castle Crag and the grassy fields.

A low-level walk in the rain by the murmuring River Derwent is delightful. And we finally get to find Millican Dalton's Cave, a long-standing ambition. Born in 1867 Millican grew up in London and worked as an insurance clerk. But in a strikingly modern tale, he downshifted to live in his Lakeland cave for fifty years — albeit retreating to a hut in the winter. He was a self-styled 'professor of adventure', offering rafting and climbing tours plus doing outrageous things like encouraging women to walk and climb up rock faces. These days he'd be offering paddleboarding and wild swimming and probably be derided by the *Daily Telegraph* for being woke.

A couple on the path hear us discuss the whereabouts of Millican's cave and helpfully tell us that it's not the first cave you find on the path to the left, you keep going up. In fact it's the third cave. We edge up over low branches and across moss, bracken and quarry spoil.

Dalton's cave is an old slate quarry with a low entrance, but inside it's wide enough to feel sheltered. At one side is a raised area known as the attic, leading to another smaller entrance. Millican's graffiti can still be seen etched into the rock, reading "Don't waste words (sic), jump to conclusions", though another version is that it was written by a Scottish friend of Millican's, after a heated debate.

The floor is a jumble of rocks and doesn't look too comfortable, though presumably Dalton fashioned some kind of bed. We walk around shining my torch, amid the sound of drips and the clatter of loose rocks.

In the middle of the lower cave there's a stone fire pit built by recent visitors. Someone has left a dusty sleeping mat on the floor among the stones. The cave has running water, some of it from the walls. We are tempted to make an offer, I suggest on Facebook, though John Manning the editor of *Lakeland Walker* says he's not commissioning from any second homers.

From Dalton's cave we head on through the trees by the river to Grange and then over a series of duckboards at the head of Derwent Water, stopping to look at frogspawn among the reeds before reaching the Lodore Falls Hotel and taking the bus back to Keswick.

It's been a short stay, truncated by my need to get back to see West Ham play Seville (and win!) in the Europa League and Nicola's season as a paddleboard teacher is about to start. Perhaps she is the Millican Dalton of north London.

The first Wainwright of the season has been scaled and tingling thighs persuaded to venture forth once more. Next time it's going to be Cockermouth where I'm making plans for my pal Nigel to join me with a car. Twenty five Wainwrights left to go — global conflict permitting, could 2022 be the year when I finally complete the Wainwrights?

15 GET YOUR KICKS ON THE A66

Date: May 2022

Accommodation: 2 Bridge Street, Cockermouth.

Transport: Nigel's Honda.

Companion: Nigel.

New Wainwrights bagged: 8 — Grike, Crag Fell, Lank Rigg, Selside Pike, Branstree, Burnbank Fell, Blake Fell, Gavel.

Total Wainwrights completed: 197

Total Wainwrights left: 17

For once I have wheels in the Lake District. Nigel, my fellow West Ham season-ticket holder, is keen to help me bag some of the more obscure Wainwrights and has offered to be my chauffeur. We're driving up from London for four days in Cockermouth. A letter recently emerged in which Wainwright admitted that he had used taxis and the odd lift while walking the Western Fells, so I'm hopefully allowed a little leeway in not doing absolutely everything by bus.

Nigel walked a lot of Lakeland fells with his dad when

he was younger, as well as the Coast to Coast footpath. While in his twenties he and his mate once walked both Blencathra and Skiddaw in one day, some 12,000 feet of ascent and descent. I'm not sure we'll quite manage that now we no longer have the impetuosity of youth. Luckily Nigel's not been to the Lakes since 2006, so he might now be as slow as me.

Our wives probably think we are going to be discussing emotions during our period of male bonding. Or we could try the news. Partygate is rumbling on as Boris Johnson proves the only way isn't ethics, the Ukraine war is continuing at huge human cost in the Donbas and there's a cost of living crisis as fuel prices soar. But we take the better option of compiling lists, as Nigel talks me through his top 30 guitar solos. Ritchie Blackmore's work on *Highway Star* from Deep Purple's live album *Made In Japan* gets his vote as number one. Listing my top ten Lakeland mountains proves more problematic, as I end up with about fifty on my short-list.

As we drive down the M1 we listen to West Ham winning 4-0 at Norwich — which means that whenever West Ham play away again we have to be driving to Cockermouth as it's clearly a lucky omen.

We arrive in Cockermouth at seven and unpack at our cottage in Bridge Street, right next to the River Derwent. It would have been inundated during the great floods of 2009. A marker on Main Street shows the flood level up to the top of the doors at the Black Bull pub.

The next morning our bagging adventures begin. It's a rare luxury to have a motor. The bus to Ennerdale Bridge goes once a week — not one you'd want to miss. Nigel's Honda glides off the roundabout by the Travelodge and down the A5086, before we take a back road to Ennerdale Bridge. Here is the sleepy village which Nicola and myself stayed on the Coast to Coast walk back in 1997 and we can see the back of the Fox and Hounds pub. Driving through the hamlet we take the evocatively-named Cold Fell Lane up Scarny Brow and stop at the car park just before Kinniside stone circle. Having a car has gained us a bit of height, though as Nigel doesn't believe in sat nav I've had to work hard with my OS Map to find the start of the walk.

The Kinniside stone circle was actually rebuilt a hundred years ago, the original stones having apparently been re-purposed for farm buildings. The stones were meant to match the old holes, but no-one can be sure they are the correct ones. Still, it's a good approximation of what it might have looked like in antiquity. Though some sources maintain the whole thing is a fake.

We delve into the car boot for our footwear, walking poles and backpacks and then we're off, trying to beat the forecast rain in the afternoon. A man in a dog grooming van has parked ahead of us and is off up the fells. We find the track and head through a forest of conifers and then on to bare fell. It's a simple walk through a stile and then over open grass to the top of Grike. First Wainwright of the day achieved after an hour's walk. The summit has a triangular cairn and a stone wind shelter. The view to the coast is excellent; we're able to make out wind turbines in the ocean and the Isle of Man on the horizon. We can't see Ennerdale Water, which lies down in the valley, but the Loweswater fells make a fine backdrop to our north.

A clear path heads on to Crag Fell, with the unusual navigation aid of a radio mast in the depression between the two fells. It was the sort of thing Wainwright would have hated, though in his guidebook it is marked but escapes without a curmudgeonly comment. It's over a stile and then a bit of a trudge upwards to another flat grassy dome.

The summit of Crag Fell has a cairn and a great view

down to the leaden surface of Ennerdale Water far below. We can see the forest plantations on the north shore through which belted Galloway cattle now roam — better than sheep for biodiversity apparently — and the grey mass of screes on the flank of Great Borne.

Everybody walks differently, and I notice that Nigel, in control of the Wainwright book while I have the map, likes to look at Wainwright's view diagrams and pick out the panorama of fell silhouettes in the distance. He's excited to spot Pillar, which he once walked to from Black Sail youth hostel. We can also make out Great Gable and the Scafells. The effort of identifying every top through the mist must have been massive for AW.

After taking a selfie of two men in West Ham hats, the bulk of Lank Rigg is our next objective. We find a path heading down across a mass of clear-felled branches, trunks and detritus, and the large wall that takes walkers on to Caw Fell is clearly visible. That's going to be a bit much for our first day and Nigel's first Lakeland hike since 2006, so we follow the wall and then take a short-cut across a boggy valley towards the ridge of Whoap. Perhaps this name is onomatopoeic. When failing to watch my feet crossing the moss and finding a right boot full of cold bog water I do indeed exclaim, "Whoap!"

Whoap is a Birkett fell topped by a solitary white stone amid a sea of grass. That is one of the 541 peaks described in Bill Birkett's 1994 book, beloved of those Lakeland anoraks who have moved beyond Wainwright. From the top of Whoap a col can be seen stretching to Lank Rigg.

Lank Rigg is certainly big. Wainwright says that it is ten miles to walk round its base and that should you die here it's unlikely your body will be found as meeting another human is "outside the realms of possibility." And you feel AW rather enjoyed that sense of isolation for there is something enticing about the seemingly dreary Lank Rigg. It's isolated from the rest of the Lake District, an outlier by the sea, but full of ancient history, a bit like AW himself.

The summit is marked by a trig point, and nearby is a small shallow tarn. The principle view is a magnificent circular sweep of coast; a mix of fields, wind turbines and the chimneys of Sellafield, the Isle of Man and Scotland.

Not far from the summit is a huge mound of loose stones, which is an ancient tumulus. The fell has many more ancient monuments on its seaward side at Tongue How and Latterbarrow, a series of cairns, field systems, hut circles and settlements — or as the OS map plainly puts it, a "pile of stones". Probably dating to Bronze Age or Neolithic times, when there would have been more trees around, these settlements indicate it was once an important area. Perhaps one of those liminal regions marking the border between sea, flat land and massive mountains. Or maybe it was simply a community of ancient Wainwright fans.

We head back on a path down Whoap Beck, which opens out into an excellent view down the Calder valley. We walk through a small herd of cows, but still no humans anywhere. After a long walk and some map indecision about where the ford is, we head over some boulder-strewn brown water, round Blakeley Fell and eventually on to the lonely Cold Fell Road.

Once we're in the car heavy rain starts. Perfect timing and a tribute to the weather app Nigel has found. We stop for a pot of tea at Ennerdale in the Fox and Hounds, where the landlady is joshing with a group of *Last of the Summer Wine*-style Coast to Coast walkers at the bar.

Back in Cockermouth we enjoy a pub dinner at the Bitter End, which brews its own beer and has a whole side of veggie/vegan food on the menu. We have found an Islington-style pub in Cockermouth, though should anyone want to order a meal after 7.30pm in Cumbria you'll struggle.

Meanwhile news reaches us on the BBC that American ultrarunner and superman John Kelly has just run all 214 fells in five days, 12 hours and 14 minutes, with barely one or two hours' sleep per night. It might take me a little longer. "But I bet he doesn't know as much about West Ham as us," says Nigel, reassuringly.

We then discuss Russ Moorhouse, who has recently spent a year camping on every Wainwright fell, including through several winter storms. Rather than do a ridge walk, Russ would draw a name from a hat each morning and camp wherever luck took him.

Our next excursion is to Haweswater for an attempt to scale Selside Pike and Branstree. Nigel drives to Penrith down the A66 and then on the long and winding back road to Bampton, where we stop at the village shop for coffee. Three elderly ladies are enjoying a natter and locals pop in and out with hearty banter. Baristas haven't quite made it to Bampton as our coffee is improbably frothy, though the chocolate homemade cookies are very good.

"Hiya Neil, how are you? We'll see you at the meeting." A middle-aged man saunters in and out. Nigel looks almost as excited as when he ticked off his 92nd and final league ground to become a bona fide groundhopper.

"That's Neil out of *Seven Up*!"

"The TV series?"

"Yes, he was the one who slept rough in the Highlands, became a vicar and is now a Lib Dem councillor."

"I vaguely remember it."

"He was the most interesting. He had mental health problems and dropped out of Oxford, I must ring Carolyn and tell her, we're big fans!"

Little did we expect to be meeting reality TV stars in Bampton. Nigel and his wife Carolyn have seen all the series of *Seven Up*. Though perhaps there is something in the Lakeland air. Looking for the loo I spot a guest room called Uncle Monty's. It seems we have gone on holiday by mistake. I ask the man behind the counter if *Withnail and I* was filmed here and he says it was indeed part filmed in this very village, the red phone box we have driven past was where Withnail phoned his agent. While the scenes at Uncle Monty's house were filmed at Sleddale Hall, just across the other side of the range by Haweswater.

Slightly delirious with excess TV information, we drive on past the local pub that is sadly threatened with closure, past the dam and on the well-made road that weaves along the shoreline of Haweswater reservoir. The forced immersion of Mardale village is a sad story, but it's still an attractive body of water, even if Wainwright hated its abrupt white shorelines.

We drive past the Haweswater Hotel where Nicola and myself last stayed in 1998 shortly before the birth of our first child. The car park is now full of top-of-the-range cars. It's a peaceful spot, with the ridge of High Street on the far bank and sad dry stone walls leading down into the depths instead of the old fields. We find a parking spot in a layby by the old Corpse Road. The wooded island of Wood Howe would once have been joined to the land, but now makes a good backdrop for a waterside snap.

The Corpse Road was where the villagers of Mardale took their dead over the fells for burial at the consecrated church at Shap, until 1736 when they got their own church. We set off up the steep path on a blustery afternoon. A few hundred feet up we stop by the two ruined stone buildings at High Loup and Low Loup, which are mentioned in the book *Wild Fell* by the RSPB site manager for Haweswater, Lee Schofield. The book's been doing well and is in the window of the New Bookshop in Cockermouth. It's a passionate work all about trying to increase the numbers of flowers and birds in the area.

Schofield argues that the number of sheep doubled after the second world war and with intensive farming concentrating on maximising food production biodiversity suffered and rare flowers only flourished in out-of-the-way gullies. His solution is fewer sheep, mixed and less-intensive farming, restoring river meanders and a change of emphasis in government subsidies towards rewilding. All of which has proved controversial with some local farmers.

A door lintel is still present in the ruin, and it's perhaps most likely that the buildings were peat huts or maybe summer accommodation for shepherds. They seem too close to the old village to have been used as a resting point for the corpse carriers. The ruins offer a fine view over the reservoir and also a very impressive set of waterfalls just off the path. This is Rowantreethwaite Beck gorge, an area of rare plants that Schofield enthuses about in *Wild Fell.*

The corpse road eventually levels out on to the plateau of coarse grass and moss that is Mardale Common. From the top of the range the view opens out eastwards, with the outline of the Pennines prominent. The rarely visited valley of Swindale lies far below, vivid green with a winding beck, and beyond that the town of Shap and the M6, marking the end of the Lake District.

On the top the wind is approaching 40 mph and it's getting pretty gusty. We see another human, a fit northerner moving past us quickly with a cursory greeting.

We press on up Selside End and emerge at the stone shelter that appears to be a re-designated ancient cairn. A straight wire fence stretches across the ridge, keeping sheep out of unwanted areas. We hunker down in the shelter away from the wind as I enjoy a cheese and onion pasty. Braving the wind a short walk away from the shelter reveals views of the tarns Small Water and Blea Water beneath High Street.

Following the fence line we move into the splendidly-named Captain Whelter Bog. Who was Captain Whelter, and did he come to a soggy end up here? This area has some spectacular nomenclature, including Willy Winder Hill, Geordie Greathead Crag and the Tolkien-esque Hobgrumble Gill.

Gore-Tex hoods flap in the wind as we trudge on up to Artle Crag, which is marked by two tall circular cairns, works of some craftsmanship. One of the objects of interest is the stone survey post left by the water engineers when they made the dam. Suddenly a group of 20 or so students emerge silhouetted against the horizon making their way towards the survey post and on to Howe.

The summit of Branstree is at the angle where a well-made stone wall joins the wire fence. There's not much here except grass and some patches of water and it's difficult to stand in the wind for our selfie.

Second Wainwright bagged, we head down by the fence towards Gatescarth Pass. The wind drops in the pass as we clamber over several waterlogged patches by Gatescarth Beck. It's a wide path, the sun comes out and the crags of Harter Fell to our left are sheer and imposing, much more the rocky scenery that Wainwright favoured. Though even Branstree gets to offer a few scree slopes on this face. We meet a pair of probable Shoreditch refugees with a print-out looking for the path up to Branstree. We direct them to the fence, though afterwards Nigel points out that the woman's boots were suede and looked ill-equipped to deal with bogs. Let's hope they don't follow us and demand to know why we didn't warn then about Captain Whelter's Bog. We carry on. The sun illuminates patches of fell across the reservoir and Haweswater looks lovely in the distance.

Emerging at the Mardale Head car park there's a sign from the United Water Utilities telling the story of the villages Mardale Green and Measand that were sunk beneath the water in 1929. Today it supplies a quarter of the north-west's drinking water. During times of drought the dry stone walls and fields of Chapel Bridge can still re-emerge, though the buildings, including the Dun Bull Hotel and the church, were all demolished.

"The good news is that because it has been protected by water extraction many of Haweswater's historic and archaeological features are unspoilt and exceptionally well-preserved," reads the board. "At United Utilities we respect Haweswater's great heritage and are trying to enhance it for future generations." Though on balance I'd say the heritage might have been better preserved if the old state-controlled water company hadn't flooded the villages. It's hard to forgive the industry for denying us a pint in the Dun Bull.

We walk up the road, not passed by a single car, looking at the walls and former fields heading into the depths and a series of "no swimming" signs. Soon we're in the car again and motoring past pubs that are all closed on a Tuesday night, presumably as a hangover from Covid.

Aware of the pubs' tendency to stop serving food early we stop at the Horse and Farrier at Threlkeld on the way back. They only have seats outside and we spend an hour beneath a gazebo, turning on an outdoor heater as the night starts to chill. After an hour the staff catch up with their orders and eventually our burger and lasagne arrives. The Sharp Edge beer is good though and it's a satisfying day all round. Haweswater is practically impossible to get to by public transport so it's again been massively useful to have Nigel's wheels at my disposal. I've also enjoyed his company and now I'm down to just 20 Wainwright fells left.

Our final day's walking begins with a trip to the Kirkstile Inn at Loweswater for a morning coffee. We sit under the low beams taking in the smell of woodsmoke from the open fire. While we drink our coffees the bar staff tell us that Loweswater Gold used to be brewed here but has now been outsourced, though the pub still has a very creditable range of real ales. We discuss famous Cumbrians after I mention that the Wainwright biographer Hunter Davies lives in Loweswater. Nigel says that Melvyn Bragg comes from Aspatria and so does the newsreader Anna Ford. Not that we like lists.

We drive back to the other end of the lake and set off for Burnbank Fell from the car park at Waterend. Only Nigel's had a disaster and forgotten his walking socks. Left with only thin day socks he opts to use his West Ham hat as a makeshift sock for his right foot. Sir Edmund Hilary and all the other great explorers would be proud of such ingenuity.

We walk through tree-lined fields and a couple of farms to reach the brow of the fell. It's a relatively easy walk upwards and we stop for lunch at the cairn overlooking Loweswater for lunch. Even though it's not the summit, Wainwright says it's the best spot for views, with Low Fell and Fellbarrow prominent and the grey mass of Grasmoor across the Buttermere valley.

Discussing Mark Noble's forthcoming retirement at West Ham we end up trying to list the Premier League's longest-serving one-club players and after a quick Google Nigel discovers that Everton's Seamus Coleman and Burnley's Jack Cork are the next longest-serving players after Nobes. We then take a picture by the cairn.

"Are you going to include me then lads?" asks the cockney voice of a man who has appeared from nowhere. He's wearing a luminous blue tracksuit top and gaiters, and has a yellow scarf tied over his bald head. It looks like the sort of thing Greta Garbo would wear. He's a talkative type, and lives in Norfolk, though he has a caravan in south Lakeland that he rents from a farmer. We ask if he's bagging Wainwrights and he tells us his story.

"I had a hip operation and I was so grateful to walk again that I decided to do all the 214 fells. I've just been back to do Burnbank Fell and Blake Fell, I was knackered last time. That book by Graham Uney says do all five Loweswater fells in one day, which is impossible. I'm never using him again. I prefer the one by Karen and Dan Parker with the foreword by Steve Burkinshaw. How many have you got left to do?"

"Nineteen," I say, assuming we get to the top of Burnbank. "And hopefully 17 by the end of the day."

"I've still got 86 left. What do you plan to finish on?"

"Difficult to know as I've not done it logically. Maybe Slight Side. I've done Great End already."

"My favourite fell is Dodd, the views of Bassenthwaite are fantastic."

Our new friend bids us farewell and sets off to return to his caravan.

"You got respect for that, when you said you only had 19 left," muses Nigel. I feel rather pleased. "I wonder why he opted for Dodd as his favourite rather than one of the classics? Maybe it's a good conversation opener."

The summit of Burnbank Fell is a rusting straining

post next to a small cairn. It's another grass dome but provides a striking circular panorama of the coast. The walk to Blake Fell is a straightforward down and up stroll by the fence. You feel in the middle of everything here and can see Crummock Water, Buttermere and Ennerdale Water. The inland view stretches across all the northern mountains to Skiddaw and a piece of Blencathra. We enter the low stone shelter where a family assure us that Gavel Fell is directly along the fence line.

It's an easy walk across grass to the cairn at Gavel Fell, from where we can see the beached whale outlines of Hen Comb and the mighty Mellbreak, set among the soggy moss, which I recall from my previous wet trip up the Floutern Pass. Looking back at Blake Fell there's a rockier side of it we can now see. Our third fell of the day and now there are just 17 Wainwrights left to complete.

After a little map pondering we opt to head down by the fence and towards the path that runs alongside Whiteoak beck. The track back to Maggie's Bridge is idyllic in the sun, looking up at the flank of Hen Comb and down at the winding beck and its stony flood plain. On past the ravaged front of Carling Knott and a heart-shaped tarn. Then we are among fields, walls and oaks with sheep grazing in the sunshine.

After going through High Nook Farm we take a left and walk alongside the gently lolling water of Loweswater. We're now in the lower part of Holme Wood strolling among grand old trees, bluebells and holly.

"Maybe Hunter Davies, Anna Ford and Melvyn Bragg are all sharing a few pints in the Kirkstile Inn," I suggest to Nigel.

"That would be unlikely as Anna lives in west London, though Hunter and Melvyn might be there," suggests Nigel.

Sadly they are not at the bar when we arrive, though I do enjoy a pint of Loweswater Gold in the beer garden while driver Nigel has a pint of Coke. And what a great view of the seemingly impregnable face of Mellbreak.

We return to Cockermouth to further experience the rather puritanical attitude to late-ish eating. "We can do dinner if you get here in five minutes," says the barmaid at the Bush Inn when we phone. It's only 7.25pm. We make it just in time for fish and chips. Perhaps it's Brexit that has caused so many pub staff shortages. Is there a chef in Cumbria who works after 8pm?

We're sad to leave the cottage in Bridge Street the next day. As we walk along Main Street and on to the bridge over the two rivers a lady rushes out of the deli. "Can you undo this?" she asks us, handing over a large jar of gherkins. Despite our fell-walking triumphs we can't, though we suggest running it under hot water and that works. We end up buying some strong local cheese and learn that the shop lady is from Maryport. "We have a promenade and a lovely pier, you must visit next time you're here," she says in the Geordie-like accent of northern Cumbria. Her son's living in Port Isaac, Cornwall, where they film *Doc Martin*. People are certainly friendly in these parts.

Driving back to London Nigel takes the scenic route, cutting down to Ullswater through Dockray (this is James Rebanks country) and then along the Kirkstone Pass and eventually the M6. At the services we sit drinking Costa coffee looking at the traffic roar by. "It's not Loweswater is it?" says Nigel wistfully. It takes forever to get back to London compared to the train as we encounter jams around spaghetti junction, but eventually I'm dropped off at Arnos Grove tube.

With a car we've explored three of the more inaccessible by public transport regions in Ennerdale,

Loweswater and Haweswater. It's been good of Nigel to act as my chauffeur and I sense that his Wainwright wall chart might soon be in further action. For me it's seventeen fells left — and as long as the Ukraine conflict doesn't go nuclear I might just get to my 214.

16. OVER LAND AND SEATALLAN

Date: July 2022

Accommodation: Forest How Guest House, Eskdale.

Transport: Dave's Ford S-Max. Train London to York, train Windermere to London.

Companion: David.

New Wainwrights bagged: 5 — Middle Fell, Seatallan, Buckbarrow, Caw Fell, Haycock.

Old Wainwrights Bagged: 1 — Hard Knott.

Total Wainwrights completed: 202

Total Wainwrights left: 12

The subsidence men have moved in and our house is full of builders and plaster dust. For years our London gaff has been a literal crack den, necessitating years of monitoring for ground movement. Now, having agreed we have subsidence, the insurers have put most of our stuff in storage while the builders work around us. Only in an epic blunder, my Osprey backpack, containing waterproofs, torch, compass, whistle, map case and survival bag, has been taken away by over-zealous storage men. Shackleton must have felt like this when he saw the *Endurance* trapped in ice like a nut in a chocolate bar. Will I be one of those idiots derided by Mountain Rescue for not having the proper gear as I'm carried off the fells? Still, I've found an old Gore-Tex coat, which isn't completely waterproof, but is better than nothing, even if it does smell of wet dog.

The builders need supervising and a constant supply of parking vouchers, but Nicola has agreed to look after them on Monday. So I'm taking a long weekend with my second cousin Dave, who lives in York. Dave now works for the local council running their parks, but in a previous job has worked in an outward-bound centre near Ullswater. He's done things like ski mountaineering across bits of Canada, walk to the foot of Mont Blanc and is an experienced rock climber and caver. Dave recently walked the length of the Roman High Street from Staveley to Penrith, while training to climb Mont Blanc. He has a 65-year old friend who does Iron Man contests. I've explained that I'm a plodder and not an iron man — in fact more of a jelly belly man — and he's agreed to walk at my sedate 62-year-old Londoner's pace.

It's been an eventful week. Boris has finally resigned as PM (except he's clinging on as a caretaker) after being economic with the truth about lots of things, including parties, sorry "work events", at Number Ten. A Tory leadership race is now under way. Nicola is off for the day doing a paddleboarding qualification in Norfolk, our kitchen wall has been stripped to lathe and crumbling plaster, and I'm now on the Friday night train to York.

Dave picks me up at the station and after an overnight stay and couple of beers at his house we leave at 9pm the next morning and are soon driving through the Dales in his Ford S-Max, feeling a little like James Herriot and

Tristan Farnham. The road hugs the Settle-Carlisle railway line and we can see the flat peak of Ingleborough in the distance. Dave spots a kite and then a buzzard. He explains that with rock climbing he's probably been up quite a lot of Wainwrights over the years, but couldn't now remember which of the routes actually ended up on the summits. A bit like my lost Wainwrights at Lancaster University hiking club, when I never took a note of where we were climbing. Dave's bought a Wainwright wallchart though and I think he might be getting the bug.

After a couple of hours we are in the Lakes (or the "Lakes peninsula" as it's now marketed on the road signs), driving round the southern fells towards Wasdale. Sat nav takes us up over Birker Fell on a rattling, bendy road across moorland. The more rugged mountains of Eskdale can be seen in the distance, but this is a lonely traverse across an open fell that feels more like Yorkshire. "I'm always surprised that in Britain you can live so far from other people," says Dave. We drive past a rocky river valley and then along the narrow lanes of Eskdale, before eventually coming alongside the fabulous screes on the far shore of Wastwater.

The shore is packed with cars and daytrippers, the result of a heatwave hitting Britain. Children play in the shallows and it brings back memories of my own children hopping on and off a tiny island on the lake. "Children don't need much, do they?" remarks Dave, watching kids happily frolic in the clear water.

Greenhead is a little farm on the road to Gosforth. We park up and eat our sandwiches, smear on sun block and put on peaked hats. The grey crags of Buckbarrow are immediately impressive rising 1000 feet from the farmland. It's 1.30pm but we should still have time to walk the circular route of Middle Fell, Seatallan and Buckbarrow.

We head past Greendale Gill and then turn right up a grassy path. The gradient soon gets steep and Dave is down to his vest, while his shorts seem more suitable for the climb than my long Craghoppers. The 30-year-old Karrimor backpack I've borrowed from him is heavy compared to modern packs, but feels sturdy, if not indestructible. "They made them to last back then," he says. "It doesn't have any side pockets either. I always say if it doesn't fit inside your pack, don't take it."

Soon we have a brilliant view of Wast Water and its famous screes, shimmering in a purple heat haze, every ridge and undulation clear with great big fans of grey stone at the bottom of each chute. We pass foxgloves, bracken and small yellow flowers in the grass, which Dave identifies as tormentil.

"I'd say you're close to the top but I'd be lying!" quips a man on the way down as we trudge upwards. Over a few false summits we eventually reach the top. Middle Fell has a rather dull name and surely deserves something a bit more lyrical. I've never seen the Scafells from this angle before, and they look spectacular, two great grey lumps with Mickledore seemingly a huge bite-sized gap in the rock between them. I take some pictures by the triangular cairn. The views of Wast Water, Yewbarrow and Great Gable all make this a great vantage point.

We chat to a young couple in North Face t-shirts doing the same horseshoe walk. Dave is rather bemused that they don't have any gear with them, just water, and are on their 14th Wainwright. Such is the optimism of youth, though thanks to my storage faux pas, I'm also without my survival bag, waterproof trousers, compass, whistle and torch for the first time in living memory.

We head down north from the rocky outcrops of Middle Tarn and into the boggy area towards Seatallan.

Here lies Greendale Tarn, a remote body of water that few people ever get to sit beside. From here the path goes 750 feet straight up the side of Seatallan. At this point I discover that Dave really is a bit of a mountain goat as he shoots up it ahead of me. The gradient is fierce, my ligaments stretch painfully and every twenty paces I need a rest, though this does give me a chance to admire the deserted valley containing Nether Beck. Then more earthy steps up towards the clear blue sky. "That was hard work," says Dave as we meet up on the top, "you just have to look at your feet and keep going" — though he might just be being tactful saying that.

Seatallan's summit contains a huge mound of stones; a tumulus now re-purposed as a rock shelter, which seems rather disrespectful to whoever was buried there. There's also a trig point and views across to the isolated Caw Fell and Haycock and out to the coast across flat fields with Sellafield and the Isle of Man prominent.

It's a flat stony area with what Wainwright considers to be the best profile of the Scafells in the entire district. There's a slight breeze, which is cold enough to ensure I put on a light fleece despite it being 24C at sea level. It's six o'clock and Dave starts to worry that we might miss our check-in at the guest house and 7.45pm booking for a meal at the Bower House Inn. He wonders if we should miss out Buckbarrow and I look a little horrified, if not homicidal. I suggest we keep going as it's downhill from here. We've come too far to miss a third Wainwright bagging.

We make good time walking downwards along Nether Wasdale Common, the boggy ridge of Seatallan, and admiring another perfect isolated valley where the River Bleng flows far below. It's easy walking and soon we are at the turning point of Cat Bields, then the best rounded cairn of the day at Glade How, followed by the cairn marking the summit of Buckbarrow. We're almost blasé now about the views of the Wasdale screes.

Dave then puts on the after-burners as we head down a steep rocky path to the road as I trail behind with my poles. Everything hurts as we clamber down the rocky trail. Eventually we arrive back at the road and it's a ten-minute walk back to the car. We're checking in at the guest house by 7.10pm. Forest How is down a small lane and over two hump-backed bridges, but feels like an enclave of tranquillity at the foot of Muncaster Fell. We meet our host Corinne, fill in our breakfast forms and after changing shirts (for the benefit of all in the pub) drive back to the Bower House where we've booked dinner. There's a marquee outside and the sound of Toploader's *Dancing in the Moonlight* being played at full volume at a rowdy wedding disco. It's not as quiet in Eskdale as you'd think.

We sit down for our pub dinners and pints as the paddleboarding group on the next table discuss how they hate Spurs, which is understandable. We then have another pint of Bluebird in the bar. "I've got a friend who once said, "serious walking is a conversation killer'," remarks Dave, as we slump in silence at the table shattered by the Greendale Round.

Back at the B & B I take a welcome hot bath and wash away the grime of a sweaty day. Dave says he could hear several signs, moans and groans coming from our en-suite bathroom. He takes a shower and we crash out on our twin beds in a deep sleep.

Enjoying a fine full breakfast with the sun streaming into the breakfast room the following morning, we meet a Dutch couple who saw a badger in the grounds last night. We drive off, feeling slightly stiff, to tackle the inaccessible Ennerdale fells of Caw Fell and Haycock. After going out towards the coast we then come inland to find sat nav taking us up a steep hill and then the lonely Cold Fell Road, which I recognise from my previous trip to Grike, Crag Fell and Lank Rigg.

The car park is a mile or so outside Ennerdale Bridge, and this walk would be a couple of miles longer if you were using foot power and staying in one of the pubs in Ennerdale. Even with a car it's an extra three miles down the lake and three miles back to add on to the arduous climb up to the ridge. These are probably two of the most isolated Wainwrights and if you get in trouble you're a long way from help. As AW warns, there's only one farm in the whole of his map of the Caw Fell and Haycock area.

It's another searing day as we set off along the southern shore of Ennerdale, wearing shorts and shades. On the far shore Great Borne, Starling Dodd and the High Stile Range are looking magnificent above the green forest plantations. Dave stops to admire the crags of Bowness Knott across the water and wonder if climbers have listed routes up it. The trees provide some shade and it's mainly flat, though the section upwards round Anglers' Crag stretches my tired calves again. We walk past a solitary woman reading a book by the pebbly shore and then get on to the important business of naming Lakeland mountains that share their name with footballers.

"There's Alan Dodd of Stoke," begins Dave.

"And Geoff Pike of West Ham," I add.

"Plus Norman Whiteside…"

"How about Robert Green Gable?"

"And Robinson of course."

"Or Joe Hart Crag…"

"Brian Clough Head…"

This could go on a long time, but it passes the time during a pleasant and mainly shaded stroll along the lake.

Soon after the lake ends we enter a forested area, cross a footbridge and start to scramble up the brow of Tongue End. The trees end at a stile and it's up through heather and grass, flanked by Deep Gill on one side and Silvercove Beck on the other. Dave races ahead again but waits further up and I find him admiring a tiny bird the size of a finger, a meadow pipit. Later he spots an orchid among the coarse grass.

At least there's a slight breeze the higher we go, though the sun is still intense. In a series of stages we make our way to the ridge where a sturdy stone wall divides the two valleys. Its double thickness indicates a real statement wall. It was built to mark the boundary of the Muncaster Estate — Muncaster Castle is open to visitors near Ravenglasss — and the wall is remarkably intact apart from one section that has suffered some collapses.

Close to the wall is the small summit cairn of Caw Fell. Although Wainwright dismisses the top as uninteresting, it's full of superb views. Caw blimey. A peek over the wall reveals yesterday's mountains of Seatallan and Middle Fell and there's another great angle for the Scafells. To the north we can see over to the High Stile Range and Whiteside and to the west the sea glistens in the distance.

We walk down the ridge back to the col and then up towards the rockier peak of Haycock, all the time following the ever-present wall and weaving around Little Gowder Crag. The top of Haycock is full of shattered rock and at 2618 feet is the highest fell of our trip. Over a stile in the wall lies a rough shelter and a spectacular view of Ennerdale Water and the vast Cumbrian coast. The wall marches on through a depression to Steeple and Pillar beyond, while there's a fine view of the high-level, seldom-visited Scoat Tarn, described by Wainwright as "the grandest of the Western tarns". All around are some of Lakeland's most iconic peaks.

Haycock is a challenge to any Wainwright bagger but we have made it. After a celebratory Tunnock's Caramel Wafer and glug of water we take a new route back to Ennerdale Water. At the depression between Haycock and Scoat the OS map shows a thick green path going down over Tewit How. But paths are often not as clear as they seem on the map. The ground is moist and pleasantly springy, but the track takes some following. Looking back we see the twin peaks of Scoat and Haycock and the spectacular rock amphitheatre of Great Cove.

After losing the path in heather we find it again and begin a steep descent by a wire fence through trees. It's a path that needs fixing, full of displaced rocks and awkward drops. But eventually we return to welcome flat ground and turn to head back around Ennerdale Water. "It's the concentration that's tiring," says Dave as I arrive with sweat dripping down my face. By this stage I've drunk both my big bottle and small bottle of water and feeling dehydrated top up my supply from a fast-running stream by the lake, hoping it's not full of anything deadly.

The only sounds are the baas of sheep and the gentle wind. The water looks glorious with the evening sun on it as we pass geese on the shore, head up the climb over Anglers Crag and then pass a group of paddleboarders at the lake's end. After removing boots and sweaty socks we drive to the Fox and Horses to re-hydrate and possibly eat. "Sorry, you've missed your food by 45 minutes!" says the barman, who clearly hasn't just been up two massive fells like us. It's 8.30pm and surely someone in Lakeland could make a killing by offering meals for late and hungry exhausted walkers arriving after 8pm. But the Citra IPA is refreshing and we make do with two packets of crisps.

We drive on to the Bower House Inn for another drink plus peanuts and decide we aren't bothered with food having had a big breakfast and a packed lunch. We've had no dinner, but rather like the Sex Pistols we don't care and we're each £15 better off. The day has lasted 12 hours, if you include pub and driving time, and we've covered 37,000 paces, a definite Lakeland adventure.

The following day we enjoy a good breakfast enlivened by the appearance of a red squirrel at the French windows. Local naturalist Peter Trimming comes to stay and has written a book, *Belinda: the Forest How Squirrel*, reveals landlady Corinne's daughter Kate, showing us a copy. As we pay the bill we learn from Kate that they moved into this old farmhouse a year ago from Dartmoor, and despite fears they'd be regarded as incomers, everyone in Eskdale has been tremendously welcoming.

I'm not up to a big walk and am catching the train later, but Dave offers to help with some unfinished business. As we're driving up Wrynose Pass we can stop and make the short 550-foot climb to Hard Knott. I confess to Dave that last autumn I climbed up to Hard Knott and, possibly exhausted after walking from the youth hostel up the pass, bagged Border End, which isn't the true summit of Hard Knott, even if it does have a great vista of the Roman fort below.

"No one would know except me, but it would play on my mind if I don't complete the true summit," I tell him.

"The one true summit, it sounds like a religion," chuckles Dave.

"Oh it is for Wainwright baggers. Forgive me AW for I have sinned… We already have the holy texts and holy artefacts such as a pipe and cap."

It's a much easier walk from a car than my last yomp to the top by foot from the YHA down at Eskdale. Dave spots one of Britain's only two carnivorous plants on the way up, a butterwort. We cross over the plateau and round a couple of knolls to the one true summit. Redemption! Time for a loiter.

The profile of Slight Side and Scafell is particularly striking across the Eskdale valley and Dave suddenly recognises a rockface he has climbed many years ago. A short walk from the summit we even get to glimpse the elusive Eskdale needle, a pillar of rock in the mould of the Napes Needle on Great Gable. We stroll to Border End where I show Dave the Roman fort far below. Then it's back down, past a man with a dog listening to the Rolling Stones on his phone, and into the car for the scenic drive to Ambleside. We stop for a farewell pint in the Golden Rule, listening to American tourists talking about Beatrix Potter. Dave is pleased to have visited fells he would never have thought of before. We finish our pints in the sun before Dave drives home and I loiter in town then catch the train from Windermere to London.

It's a long journey home as the heat has affected the railways. My train to Euston is cancelled at Preston, then I have to take a train to Crewe and wait for a train to Euston that is delayed by an hour because of points failure. I arrive home two hours late at 1.30am but it's a small gripe to end a very productive trip. And there's been no need for my missing waterproofs.

Five more out of the way names on the map have been completed, plus one conscience-tugger, and I ceremonially fill them in on my wallchart the following morning. Twelve peaks left now and the finish is on the horizon. Two or three more trips should do it.

17. I'M MISTER SLIGHT SIDE

Date: August-September 2022

Accommodation: Eskdale YHA

Transport: Train from London Euston to Ravenglass, Ravenglass and Eskdale Railway to Dalegarth. Taxi from Eskdale to Ravenglass for return journey.

Companions: Solo trip.

New Wainwrights bagged: 1 — Slight Side

Total Wainwrights completed: 203

Total Wainwrights left: 11

If Alfred Wainwright had used Avanti West Coast trains then he might have become even more curmudgeonly. I've booked three nights at Eskdale Youth Hostel, though trying to get a train ticket there is proving problematic. Avanti West Coast has scrapped its old timetable and a search of Train Line, National Rail Enquiries and the Avanti website reveals that tickets to Ravenglass via Lancaster have not been released. In desperation I put out a request for advice on the Facebook group *To Climb The 214 Wainwright Fells*. As usual there's lots of helpful advice and a number of stories of double-booked seats and delays.

And I'm travelling on a bank holiday Sunday. What could possibly go wrong? Will I make the Ravenglass railway connection? I don't blame the railway staff; in Britain we have a culture of huge bonuses for the bosses and big dividends for the shareholders of private companies while there's supposedly nothing left for the workers, the staff who got us through the pandemic. And no railway should rely on its workers routinely working overtime to function. But it still feels a little like I'm Sir Ranulph Fiennes, who probably crossed the Antarctica continent with less difficulty than I'm encountering reaching Ravenglass.

There's also the problem of lunch. Emails to the youth hostel reveal that they are still not providing packed lunches and the nearest shop is several miles away, so I will have to bring my own supplies. This is an odd policy, as it seems to assume that everyone travels in by car and can stock up on provisions at the nearest town.

It's been an eventful summer, which we've spent covered in plaster dust and welcoming builders every morning at eight am and scrabbling for parking vouchers, as the subsidence work continues on our Victorian house. Externally we've had a heatwave with a hosepipe ban, and two days of 40C temperatures in London with wildfires burning down houses in Essex. This was followed by floods and in rather an apt metaphor for the country, the water companies have been in trouble for dumping sewage into our rivers and sea. Energy prices are set to massively increase due to Russia cutting gas supplies in retaliation for western sanctions and some energy companies profiteering. The Tory leadership contest between Rishi Sunak and Liz Truss is seemingly lasting forever and inflation is soaring. So more than ever an escape to the Lakes offers respite from the weight of the world.

My Wainwright bagging has been very unsystematic, an ad hoc journey over 40 years. This trip will hopefully tick off Slight Side, the one remaining fell left in the hard-to-reach Wasdale region. After that I can concentrate on the more accessible fells around Keswick, plus the Nab at Glenridding and Grey Crag and Tarn Crag down the lengthy valley of Longsleddale.

Four days before my journey the tickets are finally released and I manage to buy some direct from the Avanti West Coast website. My Sunday trip goes surprisingly well. Avanti West Coast has done such a good job deterring passengers that the train from Euston is only half-full. Admittedly there's a twenty-minute delay at Lancaster as the Carlisle via Barrow train waits for staff to arrive. But the train wends pleasantly around the sands and estuaries of the Cumbrian coast and soon I'm at Ravenglass

Despite the delay I'm still at Ravenglass in time to make the last train to Dalegarth on the Ravenglass and Eskdale Railway at 3.50pm, and buy a packet of Piper's crisps for the journey. A reproduction 1930s poster at the station announces: "Visit the HIGHEST mountain, the DEEPEST lake and almost the SMALLEST Church in England — BY THE SMALLEST RAILWAY IN THE WORLD." This is marketing speak not quite telling the truth, as Wastwater, St Olaf's Church and Scafell Pike are a few miles from the railway, though it is a very pleasant ride from the coast into the heart of the fells.

Luckily I have a tiny open carriage to myself, so it can safely accommodate both my suitcase and backpack. With a whistle the train sets off for Hogwarts. It trundles past a river and sheep, through silver birches and bracken and on past Muncaster Fell. Irton Road reminds me of my recent trip with Dave to Eskdale as we gently move on via Beckfoot to the terminus of Dalegarth. Excited families get out to wait for the return train while I enjoy a cup of tea at the café and note that it provides sandwiches in what is otherwise a takeaway desert.

From Dalegarth I wheel my suitcase a mile along the small road to Eskdale YHA. After my recent forays into motor travel it feels good to be arriving somewhere difficult entirely by public transport. After checking in to my room (a solo dorm with a double bed) it's time for pasta and a beer in the dining room and an early night.

In the morning my assault on Slight Side begins with putting some slices of Emmental cheese into the bagels I've brought up and adding some nuts, dried mango pieces, a Tunnock's Caramel Wafer and a banana I've nicked from the hostel breakfast. That's my packed lunch sorted.

It's technical top-only weather as I set out from the YHA, smeared in sun cream and wearing a peaked cap. As I start to ascend the path opposite Wha' House Farm a woman shouts up, "Excuse me, is that your van?" I tell her the camper van in the lay-by isn't mine. She then knocks on the window, waking the couple sleeping inside. I'm not sure if she's a park warden, but she deals with the couple tactfully, directing them to official campsites after telling them overnight camping is prohibited.

Soon I'm at the three drystone wall sheep folds and then follow the wall out on the terrace route, overlooking the enticing bends of the river in the Eskdale valley and the serrated crags of Hard Knott. A couple come past and when I mention Slight Side the woman asks if I'm going to view the plane wrecks. I say the only plane wreck I know is on Great Carrs. "Oh there are about 500 of them. I know it's morbid but I've ordered a book on them from

Amazon," she tells me. They tell me they are about to complete their 214 by climbing Slight Side and Scafell today, so I wish them luck and good wreck spotting. A little Googling that evening reveals that she's right, two airmen died on the fell in 1941, when after flying through cloud they crashed into the rocky flank of Slight Side, killing both Polish pilots, Zygmund Hohne and Stanislaw Karubin. Bits of rusting wreckage are still to be found among the scree.

The rocks here are old, cracked and tumbled, as if shattered by some mighty cosmic force, with a lonely hawthorn tree emerging from the top of the crags. Soon I'm pacing upwards through bracken and boulders and crossing the marshy hinterland around Cowcove Beck as Slight Side comes into view. It looks like a big hunk of a mountain in its own right from here, not just a spur of Scafell. It's 2499 feet tall, which as Wainwright points out, is a rather pedantic height, surely a more romantic surveyor might have made it 2500 feet?

There's a ridge to my left and the silhouette of a couple of walkers suggests that's the route up. Last year I was defeated by cloud, Wainwright's rather vague instructions, taking the wrong path and impending nightfall. This time it's sunny and I've watched quite a few YouTube videos to check the route. Walking along the valley to a large landmark boulder, I go left following small cairns to the ridge and a path up the flank through heavy scree.

It gets steep very quickly and I'm slowly puffing my way upwards as I'm passed by Rachel from the YHA. She and her husband Mick have worked there for 18 years she tells me, and she walks whenever she has a day off. I can tell that by the speed she takes off ahead of me up the scree. Slowly the path makes progress even if I do have to rest on my poles every 20 paces. Eventually it rounds a series of rocky outcrops and reaches the summit. It's one of the best tops in Lakeland, steel-coloured smooth rock tapering to a couple of pointed summits. It's not clear which is highest, but after scrambling up one mound I find a thirty-something couple, the man in shorts and the woman in bush hat, both checking their watches. They have some kind of smart watch that measures height and tell me that the top to our east is slightly higher.

The summit is an exhilarating place. The north side tapers steeply up to Scafell, but the rest of it feels like you are on top of a mighty peak, with big drops and vast views over to Burnmoor Tarn and then across Eskdale and out to the sea. I'm reluctant to leave the few square feet of rock on the summit, but deciding that Scafell is a climb too far, I head back down the steep scree path. As I reach the level ground I'm passed by Rachel from the YHA, who says that it was amusing to see only a few people on Scafell but crowds of bank holiday visitors on top of Scafell Pike. She then heads off at pace to descend via Eel Tarn. I try to take the same ridge route, but at a junction mistakenly take a lower path and end up walking down the way I came up, though it's still worthwhile for the view of huge chunks of rock gouged out of the cliffs beneath Hardknott Fort.

Back at the YHA it's time for a can of Neck Oil as Mick tells me that the rocks of the summit have a lovely sparkle in the sunlight. The staff here are certainly interesting. I also enjoy a chat with Kirsten, a Spurs fan who as well being a former footballer for Fulham, works at the Antarctica research station in the winter, as you do. Mind you, Antarctica probably has more shops than Eskdale and they might even provide a packed lunch.

Slight Side was my last Wainwright left in the area, so the following day sees the luxury of a lower-level walk. I take the Corpse Road from Boot up to Burnmoor Tarn.

It's a pleasant low gradient walk past bracken and yellow flowering gorse, accompanied by the sound of gushing water. Cumbria seems to have more corpse roads than you could shake a dead body at. This Corpse Road was once used by the inhabitants of Wasdale to take their dead up to the church in Eskdale.

Burnmoor Tarn is looking majestic, sitting beneath a blue sky with woolly clouds. The tarn lies between Scafell and Ilgill Head and has a riveting view down to the Wasdale fells. A bonus is that it has what looks like a grey-rendered council house parked alongside it. Burnmoor Lodge was formerly used for fishing and is now run by the Burnmoor Lodge Club as a base for walking and climbing. It has drystone walls around it and sits in a sheltered enclave accompanied by an outhouse and several struggling trees. The few windows tell of the harsh winter conditions, but it looks a cosy place to spend a night on the fells should you be a member.

From Burnmoor Tarn I walk back over the fell towards Boot and stop at the Neolithic bonanza of stone circles and cairns. The rounded burial cairns have lost their tops but are still big enough to get inside and near-perfectly preserved. Big things were happening here. I find an astonishing network of five stone circles some of them with cairns inside. It seems to have been an important ceremonial site, a place to remember the ancestors perhaps. Looking at one upright stone in a circle that seems to align with a cleft in the side of Whin Rigg I wonder if there was a fertility theme too. It's a fascinating spot.

The path down to Boot has ruined peat huts, one with a smelly dead sheep in it, and a derelict station house at what would have been the terminus of the old mine railway. Walking past the Boot Inn — the local of former Southend pub rocker Mickey Jupp, the man who composed Dr Feelgood's hit *Down at the Doctors,* according to a recent *Guardian* piece — I opt for the other Boot pub, the Brook House Inn, where an outside table is a splendid place to drink a fine pint of He's Not the Messiah pale ale.

It's been a swift visit to tick off Slight Side, and the next day I'm off in a taxi at 8.30am to catch the train from Ravenglass. The Wainwright-bagging driver tells me of some of the challenges his firm has faced over the years, from Chernobyl fallout to foot and mouth disease and Covid. Then it's a trouble-free journey back to London apart from the obligatory double reservation booking with Avanti, but at least there are plenty of spare seats. Bagging Slight Side feels like positive progress and means resources can now be directed away from this difficult-to-reach but enticing region. Eleven Wainwrights left now and a family holiday in Keswick coming up.

18. THE CARROCK AND STICK APPROACH

Date: September 2022

Accommodation: Wainwright House in Keswick.

Transport: Train to Penrith, Hannah's van, 78 bus, taxi to Longsleddale, lift with Emily and Johnny from York.

Companions: Nicola, Lola, Michael, Hannah and Vulcan.

New Wainwrights bagged: 8 — Carrock Fell, High Pike, Great Calva, Knott, Whiteside, Seathwaite Fell, Grey Crag, Tarn Crag.

Old Wainwrights bagged: 2 — Hopegill Head, Grisedale Pike.

Total Wainwrights completed: 211

Total Wainwrights left: 3

The Queen is dead. It's pretty obvious what has happened in the afternoon as the newsreaders on the BBC don black ties and announce that the Queen in "unwell". The news comes through at 6.30pm as I'm standing outside West Ham's London Stadium awaiting the Europa Conference game against FCSB. The game goes ahead and there's a minute's silence at the start plus a spontaneous chorus of *God Save the Queen.* At half-time a picture of the Queen handing Bobby Moore the World Cup trophy goes up on the big screens before West Ham win 3-1.

The next morning Nicola, myself and Vulcan the dog head off on a train to Penrith ready for our week's holiday in Keswick. The newspapers and TV are full of saturation coverage of the Queen's life and death. There's a portrait of her up where the ads normally go at Euston. I can't agree with the principle of an unelected monarchy, though if you are to have a royal head of state then the Queen made a pretty good job of it. She's been there all our lives; a couple of days later when the man selling tickets for the Derwent Water ferry tells us that he's going down to London for the Queen's funeral it's clear she brought a lot of pleasure to many people.

Outside Penrith station we meet daughter Lola and boyfriend Michael, down from their gaff in Edinburgh. Michael has again brought the gift of good weather; he's starting his third holiday in the Lake District without seeing a drop of precipitation. Lola is a little miffed that Vulcan makes more fuss of me returning from the booking office than her after a gap of two months. We're only missing younger daughter Nell, who is away for the summer working at Camp America in Pennsylvania.

We take the bus to Keswick and find the aptly-named Wainwright house, which has three good bedrooms and fine views of Latrigg. Our friend Hannah from Wales, who is more used to the hills of Powys, completes our party. She's arrived in a big black van and is offering to take me to some of the more obscure northern fells. Communal spaghetti is cooked and everyone is happy to be here.

We wake up to lots of royal mourning on breakfast

TV, accompanied by Hannah's bread and excellent home-made marmalade. She's also arrived with a box of vegetables. After breakfast and a trip to the Cornish Pasty shop for lunchtime provisions, Hannah drives us along the A66 towards the poetically-named Apron of Stones. We turn left through Mungrisdale with its pub, village hall and church, on through Mosedale and then pull up on a grassy verge.

As the name implies the ground around Apron of Stones is littered with deposited boulders that may or may not have fallen from a giant's apron. Carrock Fell looks steep and imposing in front of us but thanks to my YouTube video watching — Hannah thinks this a very bizarre idea preferring spontaneity — I suggest the best plan is to head up the path towards the tree on the brow.

Carrock Fell is Wainwright's favourite northern fell after Blencathra and Skiddaw. For the geology student it has gabbro volcanic rock, not usually found in the lakes, and several other ore deposits used for tungsten. A number of disused mines lie around its flanks.

It's a steep climb through bracken. Hannah is clearly a quick walker and carries a wooden stick with a natural fork at the top, a rural riposte to those of us with metal poles. Michael and Lola tackle it with the alacrity of twenty somethings while I follow behind Nicola, who is holding Vulcan. Sweat is running down my brow, but we're soon up.

Once we are on the less-steep section we start to see the billowing chutes of paragliders flying over us like something from the film *Flash Gordon*. Their riders are leaping from the side of the fell and enjoying sweeping views across the network of flat fields towards Penrith and the Pennines.

We carry on upwards on a clear path heading towards the cloud-covered top. We reach the Iron Age fort, which is now a massive ring of collapsed stones. It would once have been three to four metres tall. It is oval in shape and has two gateways. The ring of fallen stones is now several metres wide, but in one spot the foundations of the laid stones can still be seen. It must have once been a massive structure. Was it defensive or ceremonial or just Iron Age bling? Did the Romans destroy it? It's hard to find much information, but it's certainly in a superb defensive position. In the cloud it's not hard to imagine an Iron Age person, or Robin from *Ghosts*, stepping out of the mist.

In the middle of the fort is a shelter, which Wainwright thinks has been fashioned from a tumulus. The five of us huddle inside it to eat our pasties. The walls are higher and better made than the average shelter. If it is the burial place of some Iron Age chieftain, hopefully they won't mind sharing a lunch break with us. We move on to take photos at the well-made circular cairn on the summit. Charles Dickens and Wilkie Collins once walked up here on a Cumbrian tour so we're in good company.

Clag is now all around us and the next problem is how to get to High Pike. We ask a couple of sturdy looking chaps arriving at the top. "It's that way but it's very boggy and lots of different paths. Have you got a compass?" asks the one with the beard. Oh no. I have to confess that mine is still in storage with the subsidence people, feeling that I have become one of those compass-shunning dolts who trouble the mountain rescue service. "You could try downloading one," suggests the beardy man.

Michael obliges, managing to get a data signal and download one on the OS Locate app. "Just keep going west and you should be ok." This prompts a quick chorus of *Go West* by the Pet Shop Boys. We head downwards into the mist but there is a path of sorts across the boggy mulch. Michael checks we're still going west and eventually we hit a wide track and a thrilling view emerges again, of the valley stretching down to the road and a short climb up to High Pike. As we climb towards High Pike we hear engines as a couple of scrambling bikes emerge on the Cumbria Way. AW would probably think that the world was going to hell in a scrambling bike.

On top is something every summit should have, a slate bench, with a poignant dedication to the memory of 16-year-old Mick Lewis, "who loved these fells" and died on May 8 1944. He'd surely be happy that his seat gives solace to so many weary legs.

There's also a large mound of stones fashioned into a crude shelter (maybe another tumulus?) and a neatly-fashioned OS trig point. We're right on the edge of the northern fells here, and can see across the Solway Firth to Scotland.

We discuss routes down with a retired husband and wife who have arrived by the seat. They moved up here 18 years ago and have children in Walthamstow and Hackney and the dad gets quite nostalgic as he reminisces about London house prices. "I was renting in Kensington for £3 a week when I was young, we never thought of buying. Worth a fortune now."

But property prices and Hannah wait for no man and we drop down to the old miner's track that runs beside Carrock Beck. You can still see some mounds of spoil but the old mining buildings have been demolished and the shafts landscaped, which is a shame as it's part of the area's industrial heritage and Carrock Fell was once a much busier place than it is now.

It's a peaceful walk back to the road and we get a fine view of Carrock Fell, now out of the cloud. Anyone attacking the fort from this side would have had a near impossible task. Nicola suggests a competition to photo the hang gliders jumping off the fell and we all take shots of the flying humans. The competition is judged later by Nell, who is in America, but available on WhatsApp.

We cross a ford and on the way to the van meet Julie and Ben, cyclists from Dorset, who are carrying their border terrier Gilbert in a basket on the saddle rack. They fashioned the makeshift dogmobile from a basket and some wire mesh for gardens. Gilbert and Vulcan sniff each other, and as is often the case in the Lakes, we learn quite a lot in a few minutes. Their last dog, another border terrier called Wilf, had two cruciate ligament operations and died six months ago. They still miss him. Vulcan thankfully, is still walking well despite his 13 years and some wobbly teeth.

We say our goodbyes and drive past vans loading up paragliders, motor cyclists and a farmer on a quad bike. I request a refreshment stop at the Mill Inn at Mungrisdale.

This is where Lola came for her A level Geography field trip and visited the village hall to do a survey of the local facilities for teenagers. As a Londoner she was quite appalled by the lack of entertainment. “Lola, there’s a woman putting up a sign in the noticeboard,” says Nicola. Lola goes across the river bridge to look and returns with her findings. “It was a tribute to the Queen from the Parish council,” reveals Lola, who had been hoping for some exciting local events like a secret Taylor Swift gig. “See, we told you there was stuff going on,” we laugh.

We head back to the cottage in Keswick and cook dinner, feeling tired and contented. We award the Lake District Cup (a triangular wedge of wood adapted by Nicola into a holiday trophy) to Hannah for outstanding driving services. She admits that the Lake District is indeed beautiful and almost as good as her native Wales.

Hannah doesn’t quite understand my obsession, but is

keen to help. Before everyone goes paddle boarding the next day, she drives me to Peter House Farm, saving me a £30 taxi fare. My goal is to bag Great Calva and Knott, the last two Northern Fells left on my wallchart. Having walked this section of the Cumbria Way with Nicola in March, there are no navigation problems. It's up past Dash Falls and soon I can see the bulk of Great Calva to my left and the trees around Skiddaw House in the distance.

Wainwright claims there's a path to Great Calva just past Dead Beck — whoever named the features round here seems to have been a bit of a gloomy Goth as I've already walked past Dead Crags. The path is indistinct at first but a little investigation soon reveals a path cutting through the peat and heather. It's so eroded that it's easy to follow and it's always satisfying to walk up a mountain that tapers to a clearly-defined summit. Soon I'm up at the top, taking a selfie by the cairn, which is topped off by a several rusting fence posts. Surprisingly there's a view to the Helvellyn range and Thirlmere through the valley between Blencathra and Lonscale Fell.

From Great Calva my next target is Knott. This involves descending to a very boggy area towards Little Calva; still a man who has been on Mungrisdale Common and Armboth Fell can cope with bog standard squelching and slurping. I'm passed by a puffing man, the first person I've seen all day. "It's not quite as boggy as Wainwright says," I remark cheerfully.

"Aye, I'm working on my fitness, I've got a Cumbria Way party below but I thought I'd come up to Little Calva. I haven't been in the fells for four months!" he answers in a Geordie accent. I wonder what he's like when he's fully fit as he pounds onwards.

I can see Knott looking quite a distance away across a col. How to get to the col is unclear as the path meanders across the bog but after cutting across to the wire fence I find a stile and slight track through the tufty grass.

After reaching the col, it's a straightforward climb of 400 feet up short grass to the flat summit of Knott. There's a real feeling of isolation here, round the back o' Skiddaw, with its green shapely fells and the ghosts of ancient forests. I'm passed by a woman in shorts, but eventually make it to the top after some puffing. It's a flat area with a small pile of stones — Wainwright suggested you could play a cricket match on it. Still, four peaks bagged this trip and just seven left now.

The rain starts at the summit and I have to put on my old Gore-Tex, which still smells of wet dog. I walk down to the col with the patter of raindrops on my hood, regretting that my waterproof trousers are still in storage.

Put off by the bogginess around Great Calva I abandon my plan to retrace my steps and decide to take a short cut at the col heading down by Burn Tod into a fabulous ravine. Several spurs of rock covered in delicate green moss make it a corridor of delight as I descend by Hause Gill, stopping to look at discarded mine spoil and white lumps of quartz.

There's a message on my phone saying the others have booked dinner for six pm at the Sun Inn in Bassenthwaite, which I'm not going to make at this rate. Once the path reaches the valley it diverges confusingly and taking the upper section finds me wandering lost across the flank of Great Cockup in the drizzle. But spotting a wall from above I drop down to a seemingly never-ending farm track. Eventually it reaches the road. I head past Horsemoor Hills farm and at Cassbeck Bridge spot a side-road going to Bassenthwaite.

It's now six, I've done 26,000 paces and I'm exhausted. I don't want to put too many demands on Hannah, but with my battery low I try a text to Nicola, reading: "Now 5 minutes from Peter House Farm Shall I walk to Sun Inn? Sign says one and a half miles to Bassenthwaite." Luckily Hannah understands the emotional subtext of my message and realises that I am desperate to be picked up.

Fine minutes later Hannah's black van is meeting me on the road and I slump in her front seat muttering thanks. Inside the pub Nicola, Lola and Michael have ordered dinner and my vegetable lasagne has arrived at that very moment. They send me to the bar to get a welcome drink. Only there's a man at the bar that is ordering a list of drinks slightly longer than the average Charles Dickens novel. Beer, wine, liqueur, coffee, Tia Maria, he's ordering every drink known to humanity.

"Sorry, I hope you're not desperate for a drink!" he comments.

"I've just walked 13 miles, I'm trying to do all the Wainwrights and I could murder a pint!" I explain.

To my astonishment he takes a look at my muddy wet trousers, smelly old second-choice Gore-Tex, dishevelled hair and face covered in sweat and rain, and buys me a pint of Bassenthwaite Beauty. Now that's a result. I retreat to eat my lasagne as a happy man. Two days walking and I've cracked the difficult northern fells of Carrock Fell, High Pike, Great Calva and Knott, all ending with a free pint.

After a rest day and a cruise around Derwent Water with Nicola it's time to return to the purity of Wainwright-style bus routes as Hannah and her van have gone back to Wales. The 77 burns a fair amount of rubber getting round Catbells and up Honister Pass. After a mass exodus of pensioners at Buttermere, it's just myself and one woman walker getting off at Lanthwaite Green Farm. She tells me it's good to see someone else looking at a paper map, and her son who is in the military is always saying that she's the last person to still use maps. We have a little chat and then I let her walk ahead.

The climb up to Whiteside is exhilarating. Initially it's a steep slog up to the spur of Whin Ben but then it turns into a gentle amble across heather and then another steep pull up to the top. From Whin Ben there are dramatic views into the stark ravine of Gasgale Gill, a magnificent v-shaped cleft in the fells, with a tiny stream far below next to a winding grey path that takes the walker to Coledale Hause.

The summit of Whiteside is reached quickly and it's another Wainwright completed. The views back to Crummock Water and out to the coast are inspiring, as is the pasty consumed by the small cairn. As Wainwright mentioned, even the Fellbarrow range looks insignificant from up here.

The ridge walk back to Braithwaite is superb. First it's a stroll along the grassy ridge, looking down the arêtes of Gasgale Crags to the tiny gill far below, before arriving at the triangular summit of Hopegill Head. From Hopegill Head a giant bite seems to have been taken out of the mountain, in the form of the 500-foot slate cliffs of Hobcarton Crag. It's exhilarating looking over the edge of the forbidding drop, cast in deep afternoon shadow, and seeing the green Hobcarton valley far below.

On the steep descent I slump down by the path to eat an apple, one leg tucked under me. "I thought the bottom of your leg was some kind of a yoga cushion!" says a posh gent who creeps up behind me. At least I can still impress someone with my flexibility.

Soon Derwent Water comes into view and the mining valley of Greendale. It's upwards past a tumbled down wall to the summit of Grisedale Pike, at 2593 feet the highest point of the walk. It's a long descent down a stony path, but the white houses of Braithwaite and

Keswick look inviting in the distance beneath a clear blue sky. After a breathless descent I even make the 6.10pm bus back to Keswick. It feels a real achievement to have come from Buttermere to Braithwaite via the tops.

Our final family day out is a climb to Seathwaite Fell with Nicola, Lola and Michael. Off the bus at Seatoller then down the lane to Seathwaite Farm. One excellent addition to the path is the Seathwaite Snack Shack, a small shed selling chocolates, cakes and cans in aid of Borrowdale Primary School. We place our money in the honesty tin and take four packets of kettle crisps.

Soon we're along the path to Stockley Bridge and then heading past the rocky downfall of Base Brown and up to Sty Head Pass. A very faint path heads up by a small stream towards Seathwaite Fell. Last time I was here with Nell the mist came down, but today it's clear and although steep, Lola and Michael find their scrambling legs and are soon heading up towards the rocky top.

The green forests and fields of Borrowdale are resplendent in the distance and we can now see Derwent Water, nestling beneath Skiddaw. The summit is an enticing place, a series of knolls and patches of water. Five fells left to complete now. We are joined by a party from Cambridge asking if they can get down the way we came up. It's steep but they can, I tell them. We follow the path they arrived on, take in the second summit and scramble down a steep slope towards Sty Head Tarn. The rocky dome of Great Gable looms magnificently over the scene as we head back down the path to Seathwaite.

We make it back to the Glaramara Hotel for a drink before the bus comes. Nicola starts chatting with Graham and Miles, an Aussie father and son who are doing the Coast to Coast walk. Graham has worked in Essex. We explain who Wainwright is and show them my guidebook, before discussing the Australian election and climate change. Graham changed his vote to the Labor Party because of environmental concerns and the fires and floods in Australia. They're also football fans and planning on taking in a Brentford game. A woman at the other table tells us that she's walked eight tops to get here. Nicola wonders why everyone we meet has walked further than us, though I explain that it's quality not quantity that matters. She almost believes me.

Our week in the cottage comes to and end and we see Lola and Michael off on their way to Edinburgh. But Nicola, Vulcan and myself are now moving on to the Travelodge at Kendal for two nights. It's down by the river and takes some finding, but Kendal is a likeable place with its shopping yards and riverfront. We walk up to the ruined castle in the evening light, which is a peaceful spot, well-used by the locals. I've not been in Kendal since my geography field trip in 1976 and it is all a pleasant surprise.

My final mission is an attempt to get down Longsleddale and bag Grey Crag and Tarn Crag, two of the most inaccessible Wainwrights. Taxi driver Roger says he wishes he was coming with me. He's originally from Morecambe but has lived in Kendal 20-odd years and has been up Longsleddale to walk the Kentmere round. Not all his friends are so keen: "I said to my mate let's do something exciting like the Coast to Coast and I never heard from him again!"

A good five miles out of Kendal we turn down the long winding lane that takes us five miles along the valley of Longsleddale. It's a glimpse of a place that can't have changed in centuries, isolated farms, dry stone walls, green fields, small woods and an air of timelessness.

"That phone box is the only place in the whole valley where you can get a signal," says Roger. "I had to pick up a soaking couple from there, we get a lot of calls and it's a couple of miles from Sadgill so it's quite a trek. Make sure you book a taxi from the summit as you won't be able to do it at the bottom unless you're very lucky."

We arrive at Sadgill, which has a charming bridge, a bench, a farmhouse, black bags of silage in a field, a row of houses and several walkers' cars parked by the start of the Garburn Pass. After paying my £29 fare it's off through a gate and across a permissive path (my late mum was always worried I was on this, ever since the Rolling Stones were pictured weeing outside a garage in the 1960s) up the side of Grey Crag.

The path skirts the crag of Grey Howe and has excellent views back down the valley. It soon flattens out into a trudge across grass, and a turn right to the small top of Grey Crag. Wainwright is right when he says that this moorland doesn't feel quite like Lakeland, but the bonus is superlative views across to the Pennines and down to the Howgill Fells.

Getting to Tarn Crag involves crossing a boggy area. but this is achieved with only minor slurping and soon I'm heading upwards to something that looks like an obelisk from *2001*. It's actually a tower of stone and concrete, a survey post left by the Manchester Corporation when they built Haweswater Reservoir and the Longsleddale aqueduct in the 1920s. When Wainwright was writing in 1956 it still had a wooden platform around it, that's now gone leaving what looks a little like the base of a stone Dalek surveying the fell. Nearby is a small cairn signifying the summit and here I run into Bob and Jane from Bournemouth, who unsurprisingly are also Wainwright baggers. They have two fells left and plan to finish, like a lot of people, on Great End — and then their grandson wants to do them all again with them.

From Tarn Crag I phone the taxi company only to be

told unhelpfully that they can't order a cab two hours in advance. I'm going to have to try to get a signal down below. But I'm feeling high as I weave down the old track that heads towards a disused quarry on the Garburn Pass. These are two fells I would not have got anywhere near but for my Wainwright quest.

Tarn Crag and Grey Crag feel flat and featureless on top, but from the Pass there's a fine view of their best side, a set of precipitous fragmented crags and a jumble of loose rock. The odd brave tree has stuck its roots into the crevices of this wall of rock, safe from gnawing sheep.

The path to Sadgill is long and stony, but I'm down by 4.30pm. Only there really is no phone signal and I'm stuck. I consider the alternatives; walking up the side of Grey Crag to try to get a signal, possibly walking across the path to Kentmere and then four miles to Staveley; or walking down the road a couple of miles to the phone box. I sit on the wooden bench feeling deflated. But then I spot a young couple getting into their car. "Can you get a phone signal at all, I'm trying to get a taxi back to Kendal?" I ask, while trying my best to look old and feeble and all of my 63 years.

They can't get a signal either, but Emily starts to look sorry for me. "Are we going that way Johnny?" It turns out they are going to go by Kendal on the way back to York and they very kindly offer me a lift.

Emily is doing a PhD in environmental studies at York University and Johnny is also an academic there. They started to drive to the Lakes during lockdown and have been coming ever since.

I tell them about the Facebook group for Wainwright baggers and my own links with York University, my daughter having just finished her degree there and my wife having studied politics at York back in the 1980s.

What nice people. They turn down my offer of petrol money and drop me by the river in Kendal. That night I post a thank you on the Facebook group and admire the camaraderie of fellwalkers. Emily and Johnny have also saved me £29 in a taxi fare and prevented a bit of extra carbon gong into the atmosphere.

Meeting Nicola and Vulcan, who have been exploring the yards of Kendal, we head to a craft beer bar and then have soup, bread and beer in the Ring 'O Bells. "Nicola, I guess we'll always have Kendal," I mumble like an Essex version of Humphrey Bogart. I'm feeling elated at having got down Longsleddale without having to own a car. It's been a really productive nine days.

Back in London I dutifully add the fells climbed to my rather battered Wainwright wallchart, which is not on my wall, but folded on my desk. There's recently been some dispute about the best method of recording summits on the Facebook group *To Climb the 214 Wainwright Fells*. Some users make their own Excel spreadsheets, others recommend apps like British Hills, WalkLakes, Harold Street, AmintLakes, All Trails, Strava, Climbed-IT, Summit Bag, Hill Lists and Hill Bagging.

But who needs tech? There is something much more satisfying about pen on paper, putting in a tick and writing the month and year of ascent. My wallchart is starting to crack along the folds and some judicious use of Sellotape will soon be necessary. But it is more of a friend than an app will ever be. If Mr Wainwright compiled his guides by hand then that's good enough for me. And now there are just three empty spaces to complete.

19 GREAT BORNE AGAIN

Date: November 2022

Accommodation: Keswick Youth Hostel

Transport: Train London Euston to Penrith, X5 bus to Keswick, 77 bus to Buttermere, taxi Buttermere to Keswick.

Companions: Solo trip.

New Wainwrights bagged: 1 — Great Borne.

Old Wainwrights bagged: 2 — Red Pike, Starling Dodd.

Total Wainwrights completed: 212

Total Wainwrights left: 2

I'm sitting in the darkness on a clump of heather by the wettest footpath in England wondering if I have become benighted. It's five pm and the cold is setting in. Is it time to get out my survival bag and spend a very cold night by Crummock Water? Will my body be found years later and like George Mallory they'll look for my phone camera to search for evidence that I really did reach the summit? Is this where Wainwright bagging has got me? Caught out in search of that elusive number 212.

There's a stream in spate and a beautiful full Moon. I think of my family and vow to keep going. But most of all I think of my Wainwright wallchart. Nothing is going to stop me putting a tick next to sodden Great Borne...

October ends not with a bang but much whimpering. Finally Covid has got me. My Australian-based sister Pam is taking a cruise from Barcelona back to Perth, strangely preferring this route to a trip around Derwent Water. We haven't met for three years so it's a good opportunity for my younger sister Kaz and myself to go to Barcelona to meet her for a couple of days. But somewhere amid the Eurostar train to Paris and a seven-hour train journey to Barcelona, or on the wide streets of cafes and parks, or perhaps while touring the Sagrada Familia or staying in hotels, I pick up the virus.

It manifests itself a couple of days after my return and results in five days in bed feeling like I've completed the Bob Graham Round while carrying all of Wainwright's coffee table books. I have nine days of testing positive. Nicola does a fine job giving me toast, soup and fruit in the spare room, even if I do feel like Gregor in Kafka's *Metamorphosis*. But the couple of days we spent together after my return mean that I have also inadvertently infected her; she goes down with it a week after me. So with our combined illnesses, three weeks is lost, a period when I had been planning another trip to the Lakes to complete my 214 fells — though thankfully neither of us is seriously ill or affected with long Covid.

By early November it seems there is a conspiracy against long-distance Wainwright bagging. The rail unions have, quite justifiably when you look at the inflation rate and their wages and working conditions, called a series of strikes on Saturday November 5, Monday November 7 and Wednesday November 9, plus there's a tube strike on Thursday November 10. To compound these logistical problems the Lakes summer bus timetable ends on November 6th and that's my last chance of getting the Honister Rambler to Buttermere. Oh, and the clocks have gone forward at the end of October, meaning it now gets dark at five instead of six pm. It would be no surprise to see my Aviva West Coast train hit by stray meteorites as well.

The news headlines only add to the end of days feeling. A suspension bridge collapse in India has killed at least 141 people, there's been a massive Halloween crush in South Korea killing at least 156 people, Russia's President Putin is cruelly bombing Ukraine's energy infrastructure and a UN Report is warning of imminent catastrophe unless the world takes action to just stop oil. Liz Truss has lasted all of 49 days as Prime Minister while crashing the economy. It seems we've had more PMs than Wainwright fells. On top of all that Matt Hancock is going to be appearing on *I'm a Celebrity... Get Me Out Of Here!*

When my train gets into Penrith the 5.20pm X5 bus to Keswick simply doesn't turn up. So it's a long wait with a group of frustrated passengers in a rain-spattered bus shelter for the 6.20pm bus to arrive. It's odd to be travelling to Keswick in the dark. The bus windows are misted up, all we can see are white lines, glimpses of road signs, kerbs and grass illuminated in the headlights. The Lakes in winter becomes a scarier place of elemental nature and black night sky.

Finally checking in at Keswick YHA I use my phone to log on to the Mountain Weather Information Service. The forecast for the next day is terrible. The chance of cloud free summits is 30 per cent going down to nil. While the wind speed is going to be between 40 and 70 mph. It warns that on the mountain tops, "mobility will become tortuous". The MWIS forecast isn't usually so descriptive and the word "tortuous" is giving me a clear steer. This has to be one of the gloomiest ever MWIS forecasts. I head out to the Keswickian chip shop, which is already full of leaves on the floor. "I'm growing trees!" says the man behind the counter to his colleague as he sweeps up the leaves that have blown in.

It's a good decision not to walk. Broom Fell will have to wait. At first the weather looks ok but by noon there are white horses on Derwent Water as the storm moves in. Catbells is shrouded in misty rain and the storm moves up through the jaws of Borrowdale and Castle Crag disappears. The trees quiver and rain cascades down as the mountains are enveloped by mist. Main Street is shining black in the downpour as people scurry past with umbrellas. There's pooling water by the museum where I've stopped for a coffee. The only option is to retreat to the YHA and put my soaked Gore-Tex in the drying room, From my room on the top floor I can hear the hypnotic gushing of the River Greta as the water level rises, but thankfully stays below the decking outside the café/bar. The floods of recent years have left me a little nervous.

The next day's forecast is better with lower winds and only isolated showers. It's an early start to catch the 8.30am 77 Honister Rambler bus to Buttermere. Packed in summer, today the bus only has a few passengers. We judder up the Honister Pass and then down again. Buttermere is full of autumnal beauty when I disembark, butterscotch-coloured leaves on the trees by the lake and a white torrent gushing down the cleft of Sour Milk Ghyll.

After grappling with the public toilet, which takes 50p off my debit card but doesn't let me in, it's off on the path to Red Pike. Yesterday's storm has gone, leaving a lot of surface water and a chill in the air. The sky is a mix of grey clouds and the odd shaft of blue.

My plan is to climb the well-made path to Red Pike and then cut across to Starling Dodd and finally reach my target of Great Borne. People with cars do it from Ennerdale but the only way to get to it via bus is from Buttermere. From my previous walk to Startling Dodd I know that the alternative path up via Scales Force is a difficult slog, so hope this route up to Red Pike might be a bit easier.

Soon I'm climbing up the steps through Burtness Wood, then cutting across the fell towards Sour Milk Gill. Enticing views appear of Buttermere and the patchwork fields between the two lakes, which are the bright green of a goalkeeper's jersey. Thankfully my lungs seem to be coping after my recent bout of Covid.

Eventually I reach the brown water of Bleaberry Tarn, scattered stones nestling just beneath its flat surface. It's a great spot with a classic hanging valley overlooking the tarn and a clear path heading diagonally up the flank of Red Pike. The track really does become red thanks to the syenite igneous rocks. The last section is unmade and over loose rocks, heading up towards the pyramidal summit. It's hard work and by the time I reach the summit it's been a three-hour trek — I've never been a fast walker and at 63 uphill is becoming more of a struggle, while Covid might have affected my stamina. It's going to be a race to get up the next two tops before darkness falls and the last bus goes.

Red Pike is a fine summit, with views across the whole of the Buttermere valley towards the grey screes of Grasmoor. On the other side is the deep drop to the Ennerdale valley. By the shelter I find a walker and his nephew who say they had to come up a different route from Ennerdale because of the swollen rivers.

Descending from Red Pike I take the path across the grassy col to Starling Dodd. The route is now familiar from my walk in 2019 and in an hour or so I'm up on Starling Dodd with its small cairn crowned by rusting metal fence posts. Great Borne still looks like a fair walk across the depression but it's two o'clock and I'm determined not to be thwarted scaling it a second time having been defeated by cloud and rain three years ago.

It's one and a quarter miles and 650 feet of ascent along a sometimes boggy grass path that eventually follows a fence. It seems to veer away from the summit but then turns upwards. The summit of Great Borne appears, a great heap of stones, resembling a giant tumulus.

One final push and I'm on top of the rock-strewn plateau. Strangely enough there's a dog sitting on top of the neat trig point, being photographed. Her owner is Bob from Carlisle, while the dog is being snapped by Bob's son Matt. Molly the Jack Russell is 13, he says, the same age as our border terrier Vulcan. "They were born for it," he says when we compare the mountain exploits of our elderly dogs. Matt takes a picture of me by the trig point and we fall into a discussion. When I say that I live near Arsenal but support West Ham we get into a discussion about football. Bob reminisces about watching Carlisle when they briefly topped the old First Division and I mention that I saw that side play at West Ham in the 1970s, reeling off the names of Bill Green (who went on to play for the Hammers) and Ray Train. You have some unlikely discussions on the fells and talking about the merits of Bill Green is one of them.

Bob and Matt head back down to Ennerdale. Great Borne has an otherworldly feel, with lots of scattered rocks, a small shelter and views back down the invariably boggy Floutern Pass to Crummock Water. It would be nice to explore its edges but it's three o'clock and time to get down quickly, with darkness arriving by five. My plan now is to return to Starling Dodd then head down the path that follows Scale Beck to Crummock Water. I've walked this route before, so hope that even in semi-darkness that familiarity will help.

My legs are tired walking the mile back to Stybarrow Dodd and there's no time to dawdle. A drizzle is now falling and my waterproof trousers are needed. It's going to be a struggle to get down in time so I take a short cut across the bouncy and sometimes boggy heather, eventually hitting the path from Red Pike down to Scale Force. It's full of loose eroded red rocks, but eventually starts to run parallel to Scale Beck.

From four pm the light starts to fade. It's an up and down path and I have to be careful not to slip over the drops by the beck. I put on my distance glasses to try and counter the twilight but they keep misting up. Every step requires concentration. As the path descends the river valley my feet suddenly give way. I stick out a walking pole and land on my backside while also receiving a few grazes to my knuckle.

The path is longer than I'd remembered. Was I foolish to attempt to bag that missing Wainwright at the risk of safety? It's a relief to see the trees above Scale Force finally appear though the rocks are slippy and I take a couple more tumbles before reaching Scale Force at 4.30pm. The wooden foot bridge is a welcome sign of civilisation though it's now almost dark. But I can see Crummock Water in the distance so should now be safe.

The problem is that yesterday's storms have left the path even more saturated that normal. I sit down for a second and get my torch out. To my relief the Maglite's batteries are fresh and the light good, though trying to see where the path goes is difficult in the dark. I stumble down what seems like a boulder-strewn stream but is in fact the path. The sky is now an ominous black.

It should be easy to get to the lake but suddenly I'm stuck. The beck is in spate after all the rain and I seem to be wedged into a triangular piece of land between two roaring cataracts. As my sense of panic increases I sit on a piece of heather and look at my map by torchlight. Think clearly; you have a survival bag and a phone and you are off the high-level fells. Though it would be embarrassing to be one of those duffers who has to call out Mountain Rescue through getting their timings all wrong. The path should go down to the lake so let's take another look. To my relief a footbridge appears in the beam of my torch, straddling the roaring beck.

The path is several inches deep with water, but edging on by torchlight I reach another footbridge and a right turn towards Buttermere. Only the path doesn't follow the shore of the lake but meanders confusingly. Sometimes it's not clear at all where the path goes and I have to use all my fell-walking experience to detect signs of worn grass in the torchlight. It's getting cold too.

But a full Moon is now shining on the pools of water that cover the path. It's eerily beautiful though the rest of the sky is darker than a Nick Cave album. The distant lights of Buttermere shine like something from a sci-fi film. As long as I keep parallel to the lake I should be ok, but progress is slow and I might not make the last bus at 6.20pm. But really I'll just be glad to reach habitation and somewhere with light. Thankfully my batteries hold out and eventually, after edging through endless floods, I reach the bridge of land between the two lakes. To my immense relief I find the straight path at Scale Bridge that heads to the village of Buttermere, the yellow footpath arrow on the gate gleaming in my flash-light like an old friend. I've done it.

I stagger past the Buttermere Court Hotel and on to the bus stop only to discover that the last bus went ten minutes earlier. I'm going to have to stay the night in one of the two pubs, if a room is available, or maybe kip in the public loo or the church, but at least I'm safe and there's electric light. Farm tractors are still working by their headlights. I enter the bar of the Bridge Hotel and sit down, exhausted after navigating in the blackness. If my torch had given out I'd have been in trouble. But here it's warm and smells of food and beer.

It's waitress service only, but my glasses keep steaming up, so I have to get the waitress to read out the beers to me, and opt for a pint of Blonde. I take off my wet waterproof trousers and sup the very welcome ale. How to get to Keswick? I try to look like an old man and explain my predicament to an Aussie lady who seems to be in charge, and she's very helpful.

"Ah, you'll need to ring Iain for a taxi. They don't always come out to us but it depends if he's busy or not." My phone battery has now died and she phones Iain from reception. He's not busy and can be there in half an hour. I can finish my pint in comfort.

The taxi is a welcome sight at the pub entrance. Iain is based in Penrith but works from Keswick. "I don't normally go over Newlands Hause if it's less than 5C," he says, "but I thought I'd take a chance even though it's just hit 4C." I'm thankful he did. Iain is a friendly driver and tells me about the time he skidded on ice into a ditch on Newlands Hause. He had to wait to be rescued for four hours and everyone at the Bridge Hotel was very helpful — the manager even offered to lend him his car to drive back to Keswick.

"Did you enjoy your pint? It's amazing how you always want a cold pint, you'd think they would have invented something hot for walkers by now," he says.

Iain runs the taxi firm from Penrith with his dad and his conversation covers the farmer who got in trouble for burning all the detritus the illicit lockdown campers left, the big roadworks on the A66 and the new Premier Inn at Keswick. When he drops me off by the steps to Keswick YHA it seems a very good use of £29 to be back in my room removing my walking gear and not sleeping on a boggy path by Crummock Water. I've even got back in time to have a lasagne and beer in the YHA restaurant.

The next morning is spent checking out and resting before catching the train to London. My body aches after the stress of yesterday but a particularly obstinate Wainwright outlier has been scaled. The train journey home confirms that nothing now runs to plan in Britain. It takes six hours instead of three, after a fatality at Wigan, then getting stuck behind a broken down freight train at Warrington and having to divert to London via Manchester.

I do get to learn a lot about the people on the table ahead of me who bond during the long day's journey into night; 27-year-old Keeley from Wigan who works for Virgin and is on her way to a party in Islington to meet her long-distance boyfriend; Alice a geography student from Lancaster University; a Welshman in the music industry; and a 64-year-old Scottish photographer going to buy a car in south London and then drive it back across the border to beat tomorrow's strike. Only now the Twitter rumour is that tomorrow's strike is off. Everyone remains remarkably stoic in our battle to reach Euston. And at least I might get a refund as the train arrives three hours late.

It's perhaps fitting that my epic walk up Great Borne is bookended by difficulties. It's an awkward fell to get up and one I'm really pleased to have finally completed. It has come at a price though, My left hand starts to go septic and Nicola painstakingly uses a needle to remove some 14 tiny gorse thorns from my palm— the legacy of slipping over in the dark on my way down to Crummock Water. Sir Ranulph Fiennes lost his fingers to frostbite after a failed expedition to the North Pole in 2000 — cutting off his mummified fingers himself at his home, as you do. Dr Beck Weathers lost one hand, his fingers and his nose (thankfully now reconstructed) to frostbite in the disastrous 1996 expedition to climb Everest detailed in John Krakauer's book *Into Thin Air*. And now I have my thorn wounds, a tragic legacy of serious Wainwright bagging in terrible conditions, but soon sterilised with Savlon and not as yet requiring any amputations.

Two more fells to go, though the long nights and my unsettling nocturnal experience by Crummock Water mean my next foray will now be in the spring when the days are longer. As Bruce Springsteen might observe, there's darkness on the edge of tarn in the Lakes, and it gets a bit scary. But somehow Great Borne has been scaled at last. The end is almost in sight.

20. NABBING THE WAINWRIGHTS

Date: March 2023

Accommodation: Old Water View, Patterdale.

Transport: Train London St Pancras to Penrith, 508 bus to Patterdale.

Companion: Nicola.

New Wainwrights bagged: 1 — The Nab.

Old Wainwrights bagged: 1 — Rest Dodd.

Total Wainwrights completed: 213

Total Wainwrights left: 1

I'm taking Nicola on a romantic mini-break romping through bogs, if all the descriptions of The Nab are accurate. The fact the Nab is part of a "deer forest" makes it a difficult fell to visit. Martindale and The Nab is home to the oldest pure-bred red deer herd in England and is a UNESCO World Heritage Site. As it's a red deer conservation area the owners, the Dalemain estate, try to ensure the deer are not disturbed. Wainwright trespassed to get up it from Martindale in 1956 and warned that even his route from Rest Dodd was technically illicit.

Things are a bit more relaxed regarding access now, but when I phone the Dalemain estate office they politely say that they prefer walkers to take the longer Rest Dodd route rather than go up the nose of The Nab from Dale Head, though in bad weather it's permitted to come straight down that way. My plan is to first complete the Nab and then finish my 214 on Broom Fell in April, when we have a cottage booked in Keswick.

It's been a four-month wait from completing Great Borne to making an attempt on The Nab. We're visiting in mid-March which is a bit of a risk, as the clocks haven't gone forward yet, but at least the days are now longer and spring is partially here.

After a surprisingly efficient Aviva West Coast train journey to Penrith and a bus ride to Patterdale — which is only £2 as a temporary incentive across England to use public transport — we arrive at the Old Water View guest house. It's an old slate building in an excellent location, set on a bend above Goldrill Beck, with gardens and benches sloping down to the water. Shelves of home-made marmalade line the reception area.

"Wainwright used to stay here, look we've got his signature from the guest book," says co-owner Dave, who has run the B&B with his wife Andrea for six years, pointing out a set of framed Wainwright memorabilia on the wall. "Of course it would have been known as Ullswater View then."

And there on the wall is that distinctive script, reading, "A Wainwright, 19 Castle Grove, Kendal." He stayed here in 1929 and also for four days with his cousin Eric in 1945. It's possible he could have used the hotel as a base for researching some of his *Eastern Fells* guidebook.

"Wainwright might have slept in this very room," I tell

Nicola, as we admire the view through the window of the meandering Goldrill Beck with its arched stone bridge and in the distance the beige flanks of Sheffield Pike and Glenridding Dodd.

The White Lion pub is closed due to staff and managerial difficulties, which is a shame as it has so many memories and is ideally positioned for the Coast-to-Coast walk. But luckily Old Water View has a cosy bar with a log burner, even if it doesn't do evening meals. In the evenings Dave and Andrea go to their cottage in the grounds, leaving us to write on an honesty sheet what we've drunk and eaten.

After a drink of Old Faithful beer and white wine plus some crisps we head to nearby Patterdale Youth Hostel for dinner. The staff are very friendly at the hostel where it's their first food night of the season. Over lasagne and curry we chat to a young staff member who has worked at Buttermere and Wasdale YHAs and is halfway through the Wainwrights. It turns out that during the post-covid sausage in a bap period at Buttermere he was the person who responded to Nicola's controversial request for tomatoes in a bap instead.

Next morning, after a fine breakfast and much sampling of Old Water View marmalades, we set out in search of The Nab. Cloud hangs over Place Fell as we step outside. The Mountain Weather Information Service forecast says there will be rain and only a 30 per cent chance of cloud free summits, but we opt to give The Nab a go anyway. Soon we are trudging up the familiar diagonal path to Boredale Hause, though I can't resist a sit-down on the Victorian iron bench near the start. Two walkers trot past us holding their phones, saying they are "doing the loop".

Nicola has been reading *The Nutmeg's Curse, Parables for a Planet in Crisis*, by Amitav Ghosh, and it's made her go a bit mystical. "Remember we have to ask the mountain spirits for permission to be here," she says.

"But I've already asked the Dalemain estate for permission to go up the front end of the Nab, and they said no. Do we have to ask the wood sprites as well? Or can we just make do with the spirit of Mr Wainwright?"

"Larks!" declares Nicola.

"Yes, what larks!" I reply, thinking of Joe Gargery in *Great Expectations*.

"No, listen to the larks! I didn't think they'd be here so early. It's so lovely and quiet, just the birdsong." Indeed, the songs of the larks are better than anything on Twitter and with the Kirkstone Pass being closed for roadworks there's no traffic noise apart from the odd tractor or highways dumper truck.

Soon we're at Boredale Hause and looking at the ruins of the "Chapel in the Hause" as it's named on the OS map. Once the chapel served the opposite valleys of Patterdale and Boredale, necessitating a 30-minute walk for worshippers to get to the windy plateau. Today the chapel walls are just a few stones high and the interior is full of grass.

We head upwards to move past the stumpy twin summits of Angle Tarn Pikes and enjoy the view of the tapered end of Hartsop Dodd, while also looking down into the Kirkstone Pass and seeing the recent work done to add some more natural meanders to the previously straightened Goldrill Beck. This work has been done by the Environment Agency and other partners in order to boost wildlife and reduce the flow in periods of flood.

Angle Tarn is one of my favourite Lakeland tarns. It's high up yet feels enclosed, surrounded by fells and crags. It has two islands, one with a few windswept trees, a peninsula and scattered rocks half-submerged in its silvery shallows.

We sit by the tarn and Nicola gets out her Thermos flask. Normally I don't carry flasks because of the extra weight, but Nicola was insistent she needed tea and it's very pleasant and English to be enjoying a cuppa on the grass by this gentle sheet of water.

We chat to a couple walking past. They are also going up to Rest Dodd and The Nab, and have 20 Wainwrights left to complete their set. He is 70 and she is 69 today. They get free travel on the buses and we end up discussing senior railcards and the temporary £2 bus fares in Cumbria.

After finishing our tea we set off on the relatively level path to Satura Crag. The bed of clouds above us has turned from dishwater grey to brooding black and as the rain starts we put on waterproof trousers to add to our Gore-Tex coats. We head through the gateless posts by the dry stone wall and are passed by two men jogging along in shorts and cagoules. "We're mapping out the route to Shap. We'll be running in the dark in the race!" answers a not-very breathless man when Nicola asks him where they are going. It's preparation for a fell-running race on Saturday, not that we'll be joining them as walking seems arduous enough after four months away from the fells.

We can see the great bulk of Grey Crag towering over Hayeswater and the path heading down and then up to High Street. The higher fells have small patches of snow on their sides. Soon we depart from the Coast to Coast path for a lesser path etched into the flank of Great Dodd. We climb upwards towards the dry stone wall that divides Great Dodd from The Nab.

There is an option to head straight on to The Nab, but encouragingly Nicola decides that she can't miss Rest Dodd. At this rate she might soon be getting a

Wainwright wallchart. We head up the grassy slope towards the rounded top of Rest Dodd and flop down by the small pile of stones. The wind rustles my Gore-Tex and all we can see is the rounded top shrouded in clag. Nicola takes a celebratory photo of me at the summit cairn holding my snack of choice, a Tunnock's Caramel Wafer.

The drizzle has faded and cloud now moves in and out of the peaks. As the clouds blow on we see that the patches of snow on the High Street range are a brilliant white. Suddenly the sun sneaks through the cloudbase and a rainbow appears above the Rampsgill valley, an unexpectedly vivid glimpse of orange, yellow and purple against the brown and grey fells. This seems like a good sign.

From Rest Dodd we can see the head of The Nab rising above a depression full of black lines, which are the infamous peat hags. We're joined by a man carrying a large backpack who has just trudged up the steep path from the Nab. We ask him how boggy it is.

"You'll do it, but there's a couple of gruffs," he says.

"What are gruffs?" asks Nicola, wondering why a Gruffalo might be here.

"Oh, it's a Peak District word. You'd call them peat hags."

Our new friend is looking for somewhere to camp around the Knott, which is brave in windy and wet March, and walks on having defeated the gruffs. We take the steep path down towards The Nab. Thanks to some physio work Nicola's knees are much less troublesome. As she forges ahead I slip and take a painful tumble on to my elbow, but luckily she doesn't see.

We reach the wall, still mainly intact and staggeringly well-built considering it's across a wasteland, and find a path through a gap. As we reach the dip between Rest

Dodd and The Nab the ground becomes squelchy. Soon we are at the hags, dark brown overhangs of mulchy peat above four-foot drops into watery mud. It looks like something from the Somme.

We edge round the first hag but this makes it difficult to get back to what passes for a path. For the next one we decide to follow the boot prints and go straight through. Taking soundings with our poles, we hop across the mud where it looks least likely to submerge us.

"It's not as deep as it looks!" says a relieved Nicola. Soon she is running across the myriad channels, and then jumping them as if she's on a horse. "This is fun, it's like jumping fences!"

"Look out for the gruffs!" I shout, pleased with our word of the day.

"Don't worry, I can handle gruffs!"

We see the 70 and 69-year old couple we met earlier edging round the hags having made it up The Nab. We keep to the more direct route and with the aid of good boots get through the assault course of peat and start to head upwards on a sodden path. The Nab has been strangely enjoyable. The peat hags might be the worst in the district, but the sense of adventure getting across them makes it feel like a real achievement.

The broad expanse of boggy fell narrows to form a proper mountain summit. As Wainwright says, viewed from Martindale, it looks like a "lofty wedge" rather than a boggy morass. It's still surrounded by mist and looks like the sort of dramatic spot where in *Doctor Who* a Time Lord might regenerate

Eventually we reach the small summit cairn, made with a few stones, and overlooking the few farms and woods of Martindale far below.

"How do you feel having bagged your penultimate Wainwright?" asks Nicola.

"Brilliant if tired. It's been quite a trek. And I'm aware we've got to get back across the peat hags to the wall and it's a long way to get back before dark. But bloody hell, we made it. Never thought we'd do it when I saw the clouds this morning. And now the sun's come out."

Though actually it's hard for this Wainwright bagger to feel too much beyond exhaustion. It's mainly relief at having finally made it up a stubborn fell to crack, but later will come a moment of quiet reflection when I'm safely home. I first saw the outline of the Nab when Nicola and myself went wrong in a hailstorm amid 50mph winds on the Coast to Coast path back in 1997. It's taken a few failed attempts and 26 years to finally reach its boggy top. Contours on a map now have a memory attached. And I'm proud to be so close to reaching the 214, even if it's taken 40-odd years of long-distance fellwalking.

The Nab's rounded top is tussocky grass, yellow and brown in this early spring. But to the west we can see down into Bannerdale valley where the deer live, a peaceful place without what Mr Wainwright would term "habitations". The summit is flanked by Beda Fell and Wether Hill across the two valleys. The Nab really does feel a long way from anywhere. No wonder it's taken so long to get here.

It gets dark soon after six so we set off on our return leg. Buoyed by six weeks of Pilates Nicola enjoys the trek down to the peat hags, holding her running sticks out and shouting "Wheeee! This is fun!" in the fashion of our kids when they were seven. She urges me to join her in running, but I can't raise more than a trudge. Well she is four and a half years younger than me and doesn't train on peanuts and beer.

Then it's over the peat hags again. This time I nearly suffer a waterlogged boot, but manage to vault out of the mire by scrambling up the edge on my knees. It's quite easy to get trapped in the depressions. We pass an ascending group of walkers with their dog who say they have come up from Hartsop. Soon we're at the wall and following a parallel path up the lower slopes of Rest Dodd.

"Look I can see deer!" exclaims Nicola. "Down there in the valley. There are two groups of them." We can indeed see the deer in the distance, dotted across the lower slopes. We count 28 of them. They must be able to smell us but don't seem too worried by silly baggers. We get my survival bag out and sit on the waterlogged grass for a few minutes, feeling lucky to have seen the elusive creatures. We're pleased to have kept well away from them by avoiding the direct route up the front of the Nab. It's hard to tell if there's an old stag who resembles Alfred Wainwright.

We follow the dry stone wall relentlessly upwards. At the crest of the wall we veer off on the rough path that takes us back to Satura Crag. Then it's along by Angle Tarn again, the stones in the water gleaming in unexpected sunlight and then a steady walk down to Patterdale. Old Water View is pleasingly close to the path and we stagger into our bedroom for a cup of tea and a shower. We've covered 11 miles and 28,000 paces, while Nicola's Strava suggests we have hit a not-that-fast 1.8 km an hour. Then it's off to the youth hostel for another dinner of vegetable lasagne before collapsing into bed with tired limbs and a sense of achievement.

Having allowed two days in Patterdale in case of bad weather we have the luxury of a Sunday of low level walking, which is just as well as the first walk of the year always results in aches and strains. After a hearty breakfast we walk into Glenridding to look at the shops and then take the footpath from Patterdale to Hartsop. It's a beautiful path, dotted with cottages and following Greensill Beck. We admire the massive trunk of a mighty oak set next to a holly bush, and then a bank of wild daffodils.

Sitting by a moss-covered oak, we stop for a picnic and a cup of hot tea on a slope overlooking the beck. Looking at a set of huge trees, they remind Nicola of those she used to climb in the grounds of her posh school. It's clearly been a popular picnic spot for years. An old tree trunk, long since felled, has hundreds of lucky coins embedded in it.

We chat to a lady from Cambridge who visits the Patterdale estate every six months to volunteer, clearing rhododendrons and doing other work. "I drive up every March and September and always get excited when I see the first signs for Cumbria. It sets me up for the year," she tells us, before recommending we visit the Wool Farm Shop on the path.

We walk on to Hartsop, stopping to admire a set of three waterfalls tumbling down Angletarn Beck. They're not particularly famous but are just as good as any of Lakeland's more celebrated falls. Then, near the farm with luxury glamping, we look at the restored meanders in Goldrill Beck from close up.

Turning round we head back along the path to Patterdale, stopping at the Wool Farm Shop. Nicola thinks it's called Wool Farm, though it might just be a farm shop that sells wool. We meet Mary inside who shows us pictures of the goats, now sold, used to produce mohair, plus more pictures of sheep. We end up buying two pairs of the special socks and a greeting card with a picture of her favourite sheep Blossom.

Sunday is rounded off by being greeted like old friends in the youth hostel, as we hungrily consume our third dinner of the holiday. The next morning we head off on the bus laden with goodies from Old Water View, including two jars of their own marmalade and a Coast to Coast mug.

The Nab has seemed like an insurmountable obstacle for much of the winter. But now it's been successfully scaled, the peaty gulches traversed and the bogs stomped. One more Wainwright to go.

21. BROOM WITH A VIEW

Date: April 2023

Accommodation: Primrose Cottage, Keswick.

Transport: Train to Penrith, X5 bus to Keswick and Powter How.

Companions: Nicola, Nell, Vulcan.

New Wainwrights bagged: 1 — Broom Fell.

Old Wainwrights bagged: 2 — Barf, Lord's Seat.

Total Wainwrights completed: 214

Total Wainwrights left: 0

Is this where I make a clean sweep of the Wainwrights on Broom Fell? Nicola, Nell and myself have booked an Easter week in Keswick, hoping for enough clear days to complete my 214. The bank holiday track works don't make it easy. Our trip from London takes slightly less time than a manned flight to Mars. From St Pancras International we have to take a train to Bedford. From Bedford we queue in the spring sunshine for a juddering rail replacement bus service to Milton Keynes. And then from Milton Keynes it's another train to Penrith, followed by the X5 bus. Six hours later we're in Keswick.

Primrose Cottage is in a new part of town for us, just off the Penrith Road. Landlord Steve is a Carlisle fan and very talkative. He's originally from Hull, his late wife was a teacher here and his son is a railway enthusiast who has filled the house with old railway posters and made raised flowerbeds from railway sleepers. The house belonged to Steve's mother-in-law. It was built in 1805 and still has many of its old fixtures and fittings such as built-in wooden cupboards. We like the place and enjoy visiting the Spar at the nearby garage. It's also fun looking at Calvert's Bridge where Wordsworth once walked to see Coleridge at Greta Hall. We explore the disused railway footpath and enjoy a pint in the Twa Dogs Inn while admiring their stuffed "Cumbrian bogart", a half fox and half badger creation set in a glass case by the entrance. It's said to roam the slopes Skiddaw, mainly on April 1st.

The weather forecast is relatively good for our first full day so on Easter Sunday, after hastily packing sandwiches, we take the X5 bus to the site of the former Swan Hotel at Powter Howe on the edge of Thornthwaite. On a cloudy but dry day, the rounded hulk of Barf looms above us. We can see the Bishop of Barf, a pinnacle of rock that's painted white, a local landmark, visible from the main road. Tradition claims that in 1783 the Bishop of Derry, while staying at the Swan Hotel, drunkenly wagered that he could ride his pony up to the top of this steep fell, but came to grief where the rock stands, the fall killing both the Bishop and horse. Ever since the rock was repainted by staff at the Swan Hotel, which is now holiday flats. The story, which may not be true, claims that the bishop and his horse are buried under a lower white-painted rock, the Clerk.

We know the wooded footpath from our previous trip up to Barf and Lord's Seat, but climbing up the side of Beckstones Gill we receive a shock. What was previously a claustrophobic and steep scramble over tree roots amid dark and dense woodland has now become apocalyptic. A massive square of pine forest has been clear felled. The mountain is now open to the sky, with a carpet of dead branches and trunks left to prevent land slippage. Nicola picks up some small twigs to whittle later, having arrived in Keswick armed with a whittling knife.

A sign from Forestry England thanks us for our patience while tree-felling operations took place and hopes that we enjoy the "more open views" now the path is open again. It says that over the next couple of years the slope below the forest road will be replanted with native trees while the area above the forest road will be a mix of, "conifers and some broadleaves to ensure the forest continues to contribute to the demand for timber into the future." The break from the old monoculture is welcome.

Nell starts to feel her asthma as we head upwards, but a burst of her reliever helps. Vulcan is doing well climbing, even if his back legs are stiffer now he's pushing 14-years-old. It's a steep slog with one bit of scrambling up wet rock, but soon we're at the forest road and heading over the gill and up a heathery dome to the top of Barf. Here it's short grass with the odd rock peeking through. The last time we ascended was on a misty day, but now we have a great vista of Bassenthwaite Lake and Skiddaw, rising up in three stages from the lakeside. Barf is a smallish fell with a big view. We can see across the Solway Firth to Scotland too.

The section between Barf and Lord's Seat is all

Hobbity hills and undulations, with the odd stray conifer growing among the heather away from the regimented plantations. It doesn't feel like a mountaintop at all. We pass some people working off their Easter eggs and a couple who don't know where they are but are following the person in front. The path is clear up to Lord's Seat. Soon we're on top sitting by some exposed rock and the remains of a metal fence post.

Am I really going to finish? There's a clear path to the next top but I start to panic, wondering if that really is Broom Fell. I check the map, which indicates you turn north from Lord's Seat and so this has to be it. Perhaps I just don't want it to end. Maybe like in *Thelma and Louise* we've come too far to turn back and we'll just keep on walking right into Wythop Moss.

It's an easy stroll across the grass. There's a stile over a wire fence and a splendid rounded cairn comes into view. Nicola videos my big moment. "So this is Pete's final Wainwright. It's Broom Fell and it's that bit of wall there. He's going over the stile athletically and he's going to do a little victory salute. Look how tall it is. Hooray! Clatter clatter goes his stick. Quickly, out with the sign. Yes!"

I touch the huge summit cairn with my walking pole. The cairn is much more spectacular than I had imagined, being some seven-feet tall. I had expected a few stones on some tufts of grass. So it really is a fine top to end on. As Wainwright writes, a mysterious and now collapsed dry stone wall goes right up to the summit, before abruptly ending. Strangely this wall is fencing in nothing. Some of the tumbled stones have been put to good use for building the summit cairn and also a curved semi-circular shelter with a stone seat.

Nicola has painted a "214" sign, which I remove from my backpack and hold up while standing next to the cairn. I beam for Nicola and Nell's photos. I've done it at last. Two hundred and fourteen fells. An objective in life has been reached and my not so aimless wanderings have ended. Can you hear me Mr Wainwright? I gave your fells one hell of a walking.

"We should get a picture of the whole team," I suggest.

Nicola accosts a family who are arriving at the stile. "Do you mind taking a picture of us? Pete's just completed his 214 Wainwrights."

"Wow you've done all 214!" says the man, taking a picture on Nicola's phone of myself, Nicola, Nell and Vulcan.

"It's taken 40 years though," I say self-deprecatingly, but enjoying the praise. It's not such a bad fell to end on at all. We sit in the shelter and enjoy sandwiches and Tunnock's Caramel Wafers. Ling Fell and Sale Fell are in the distance, right at the edge of the Lake District and beyond them the sea.

We are going back on the same route to catch the X5 bus. "You look so happy!" says Nicola as we walk back up to Lord's Seat. Looking at the photos I seem to look younger. Maybe the fells allow a *Doctor Who*-style regeneration.

It's a triumphant procession back to Lord's Seat. Vulcan is tired and so we slump down for a rest. Then it's down the heathery slopes and folds and up to Barf for another look at the metallic water of Bassenthwaite. As Nicola and Nell descend on the still-yellow grass there's a lovely view across the gill to the wooded slopes and winding logging road.

Four-year old George and his mum pass us on the way up to bag Barf and we offer words of encouragement to a new generation of summit baggers. Vulcan perks up when he sees sheep on the downward trail. We descend on the steep path we came up on and end up outside the Swan apartments slumped on my survival bag, with an hour's wait for the bus. Nell can't believe we can chill for 55 minutes without social media, but we encourage her to read our book club book Philip K Dick's *Do Androids Dream of Electric Sheep*, which Nicola is carrying in her backpack, and time soon passes. It's blissful to lie down and rest tired limbs and listen to the birdsong while feeling a glow of post-Wainwright satisfaction.

Soon we're back in Keswick and Nell and myself stake out the Wainwright pub while Nicola takes Vulcan back to the cottage for his dinner. When she returns we finally bag a table. I order a celebratory falafel burger and chips with onion rings and an aptly-named pint of Theakston's Summit Pale Ale. The walls are covered in Wainwright memorabilia. The pub is full of walkers and there's a TV screen playing videos of people skiing from White Side and Raise in winter. It feels like an apt place to mark my finish.

The next step is to post my triumph on the *To Climb The 214 Wainwright Fells* Facebook group, pointing out that it's taken 40 years and promising to run my next round in five and a half days, possibly. I'm overwhelmed by the number of likes, 232 and counting. Most people say things like "Congratulations. Welcome to the club." And it does feel like I've joined a club of like-minded souls.

Kerry Sheridan comments: "Slow and steady wins the race! And it's not about how long it takes but that you enjoy the adventure as you go! Well done." Stephen Vardy says: "Congratulations. I've been at it for over 50 years. Only four to go, so this might be the year for me to join the club." Kate Leahy writes: "Well done it doesn't matter how long it takes it is all about enjoying the experience." Richard Ratcliffe comments: "Well done, completing at a steady pace all the way from London must feel very satisfying," while Nita Wiltshire says, "Ah many congratulations. I still have a few to do. Isn't it a marvellous experience? I love the fells."

The next day Nicola and Nell go paddleboarding at Portinscale while Vulcan and myself walk by Derwent Water and reflect on fulfilled ambition. Then there's Twitter and Instagram to be informed. Though it doesn't go unnoticed on my West Ham WhatsApp group that at the same time as I was completing my 214 fells a group of people high (in every sense) on magic mushrooms had to be helped off the fells by the Keswick Mountain Rescue team. Drugs in the Lake District? It makes you wonder what Mr Wainwright really had in his pipe. I have to explain to my friends that it wasn't me and my support team over-celebrating. With admirable tact the rescue team report comments in deadpan fashion: "The casualties were walked down and given advice by the team medic regarding the timing of their onward travel."

It's lucky we walked on the first day. A walk along the disused railway track to Threlkeld for afternoon tea goes well, but as Nell's university friend Aaron the Spurs fan joins us in the evening, the rain starts. It's big Lake District rain, soaking through waterproofs and saturating the soul. We awake to hail outside and snow on top of Skiddaw and Causey Pike. So it's a low-level trek through mossy temperate rainforest by the River Derwent from Rosthwaite to Grange, sheltering in Millican Dalton's cave. Then an expedition to the Keswick Museum and on to the Lingholm Estate at Portinscale. On our final day we take Aaron for a walk up to Latrigg, his first Wainwright, in fine weather. I wonder if this might be the first Wainwright on my second round of 214. But by the afternoon we're sheltering in a Main Street cafe drinking bubble tea under a canopy as giant hailstones pound the town for an hour, followed by a massive downpour.

Meanwhile a lot of people are asking on social media what I'll do next. Actually I'm rather looking forward to climbing any Lake District mountain I like rather than trying to scale unknown fells. There are plenty of peaks I can hardly remember from 20 or 30 years ago and plenty of new routes to explore. The Scottish Munros might be too big and distant, ditto the Alps, but there are still the Lakeland circular walks to try again, maybe the Birketts, and there's a book by Wainwright on the Outlying Fells in Bookends bookshop that looks rather interesting.

There's a lot to say for knowing an area intimately. It's been a big adventure that has taken me to unexpected places. Without Wainwright bagging you wouldn't have found me stuck in Longsleddale minus a phone signal and begging a lift. Or running across the liminal bogs of Armboth Fell, squelching over Mungrisdale Common and dodging frisky bullocks near Great Cockup. Or indeed sitting amid an iron age fort on Carrock Fell; heading up the Corpse Road to Selside Pike; gazing at a Roman fort from near the top of Hard Knott; strolling down Ing Lane to Troutbeck Tongue on a glorious summer day; meeting the man who loved Dodd most of all on Burnbank Fell; and desperately trying to get off Great Borne by torchlight. I never thought I'd be leaping across huge peat hags on The Nab and certainly not walking for 20 miles from Grey Crag to Glenridding, only to miss out on a pub dinner.

It's been emotional, but with the help of the man who loved the Lakes I've got there. Now it's time to place the final tick on my wallchart. Thank you Mr Wainwright for giving me summit for the weekend.

22. LAKE DISTRICT LISTS

TEN EXAMPLES OF WAINWRIGHT HAVING A LAUGH

In *The Far Eastern Fells*, when writing about ascending The Nab through the protected deer forest, AW reveals that although he trespassed he might not have been detected due to his due to marked resemblance to "an old stag."

In his *Pennine Way Companion* Wainwright has much fun with the name Shitlington, describing, it as sounding "a trifle earthy" and suggesting it might be better to revert to the former name of Shotlyngton Hall.

In his entry for the summit of Binsey in *The Northern Fells* AW draws a picture of himself on the summit describing it as a prehistoric tumulus accompanied by an "ancient Briton."

In his *Pennine Way Companion* Wainwright writes that on Cam Fell a freezing east wind, "so shrivelled some of the body organs necessary for a full and enjoyable life" that he feared they might be perished forever.

In the TV version of *Wainwright's Coast to Coast Walk* AW and Eric Robson look at the visitors book in the White Hart in Danby Wiske and finds a comment from two Coast to Coast walkers earlier that morning reading,

"Wainwright should come here now!" AW writes his own entry reading simply: "He did!"

What did Wainwright get up to in Dufton? AW warns in his *Pennine Way Companion* that accommodation in Dufton is scarce and that, "Wise virgins book their beds in advance."

In *The Western Fells* Wainwright's Yewbarrow section contains a picture of himself and a talking sheep, with the sheep wondering if Wainwright is wearing a cap because he must be going bald.

His entry for Coniston in *The Southern Fells* has a cartoon of tourists on the summit looking for Blackpool Tower, boy scouts and a solitary fellwalker who is, looking north to the hills.

In the *North Western Fells* AW has a warning about the dangers of outdoor ablutions. He writes that "a certain function" is unwise on the Knott Rigg ridge as the silhouettes of walkers are in full view from both valleys.

In *The Western Fells* his ascent of Kirk Fell by the steep but direct route from Wasdale has AW describing losing his braces' and features a picture of a tired walker with his head between his legs looking backwards at a superb upside-down view of Wasdale Head.

TEN TIMES WAINWRIGHT REVEALS HIMSELF TO BE RATHER CURMUDGEONLY

When AW was on Radio 4's *Desert Island Discs* presenter Sue Lawley enquired about his first wife. She was answered with a terse, "I don't know how she stuck it for 30 years. Right, what's your next question?"

Mungrisdale Common merits much grumpiness. In *The Northern Fells* AW likened it to an upturned pudding that could not be photographed well and went on to write there was is point in drawing diagrams that will never be used.

In the *Western Fells* Hen Comb gets the withering comment that it was pleasant enough, "for anyone who doesn't want to get excited."

In *Wainwright: The Biography* Hunter Davies reveals that AW wrote a letter to his publisher Michael Joseph declaring that the designer Susan, "wants her bottom smacking" for suggesting cutting some passages and photos from AW's first coffee table books.

In his *Pennine Way Companion* AW remarks that a series of farmhouses have character, "which is more than can be said for the rubbish being built today."

Wainwright was clearly having a bad day on Branstree while trekking up from Longsleddale, remarking that, "By any standards and by any route, the climbing of this flank is completely uninteresting."

The ridge route from Armboth Fell to High Tove receives the bleak summary of "dreariness and desolation" in *The*

Central Fells.

AW had a miserable first marriage and at times it shows. His Great Gable entry in *The Western Fells*, contains the aside, "nagging wives should be left to paddle their feet in Styhead Tarn."

His notes at the end of *A Coast to Coast Walk* contain a rant against bad walkers who ignore the country code and a diatribe against those who can't read maps and the "complete nogs" who have never seen a map.

Wainwright's notes on Blencathra contain a long rant against road widening, complaining that Lakeland is being opened up to those who ate aliens in a place of natural beauty. He concludes: "We should be putting up barriers to keep them out, not facilitating their entry."

TEN VERY LITERALLY-NAMED FELLS

The Lake District is full of poetically-names fells such as Blencathra, Helvellyn, Lord's Seat and Glaramara. And also some much more prosaic monikers...

COLD PIKE
Cold Pike overlooks Wrynose Pass and is a mini-version of the much more imaginatively-named Crinkle Crags. Anyone who has ever visited the Lake District will know that any of the 214 Wainwright fells might justifiably be described as cold. The committee of Cumbrian farmers that perhaps named Cold Fell certainly didn't waste any time on undue flights of description. "Aye, it's a bit parky up there. Right, Cold Pike it is then."

HIGH CRAG
The Lake District is an area of mountains, and mountains are by any definition high. High doesn't really tell us much. But High Crag does dominate Buttermere and is indeed high. Many fells are higher than their lower neighbours. But couldn't someone have come up with something a little more original?

LOW FELL
Mountains can be high or low, and many mountains are lower than others. But as with High fells, Low isn't a great name. Low Fell is a lovely fell overlooking Crummock Water, while Low Pike is a small fell on the Fairfield Horseshoe, next to the equally blandly-named High Pike.

GREY CRAG
There's a Gray Crag near Hartsop and a Grey Crag in

Longsleddale. Most rocks in the Lake District are pretty grey, and most mountains have a grey aspect to their crags. Was this really the best name they could come up with?

WETHER HILL

The Lake District has weather, as anyone who has been caught in a downpour or freezing mist can testify. But Wether Hill doesn't really tell us much and could be the name of any fell in Cumbria as they all get weather.

DODD

A Dodd is a Lakeland word for a rounded hill, usually a subsidiary of another mountain. Around Helvellyn we have Stybarrow Dodd, Watson's Dodd and the more prosaic Great Dodd. But at Skiddaw we find a fell top simply named Dodd. Did no-one have time to give it a better name? Huge Dodd, Massive Dodd, Round Dodd, Diddy Dodd, Inominate Dodd, Boring Dodd, In Dodd We Trust? Any name would be better than just Dodd.

MIDDLE FELL

Someone around Wastwater could surely have come up with a superior name to Middle Fell. Yes it is a fell, and it is between Buckbarrow and Yewbarrow. But surely all those lonely shepherds and early Viking fellrunners could have thought of something a bit better?

CRAG FELL

Most mountains in the Lake District have crags in a few places. Crag Fell is part of the Lank Rigg group overlooking Ennerdale Water and is, erm, rather craggy.

HIGH RAISE

High Raise is part of the High Street group of fells, and is quite high and has a little raise to get to the top. Inspired naming.

GREEN CRAG

Green Crag is in Eskdale and like a lot of fells is covered in grass and quite green, as well as having a crag.

TOP TEN BOGGY WALKS

ARMBOTH FELL
The boggiest of them all. Best completed at a bouncing trot as you leap from soggy moss to mossy bog. The summit is one of the few rather unimpressive rocks that litter this watery summit.

MUNGRISDALE COMMON
Wainwright's "upturned pudding" is a wet wet wet trek from whatever angle you tackle it. It's hard to tell which is the highest point, but a few apologetic stones form a tiny cairn that is always surrounded by water.

REST DODD TO THE NAB
Descending from Rest Dodd the path crosses a series of peat hags, some of which come up to your waist. Even the deer tend to give this bit of bog a miss.

HIGH TOVE TO ULLSCARF
A remarkably saturated walk from just below High Tove on the flank of Armboth Fell towards the isolated, rather striking Blea Tarn. Once you ascend by the fence to Ullscarf things improve with dreary but solid flat ground.

GREEN CRAG TO HARTER FELL
Another proper bog stomper. Descending from Green Crag you cross a wet and pathless heathery wilderness and eventually reach the bottom of Harter Fell, often with a saturated boot.

BUTTERMERE TO SCALE FORCE
In wet conditions this pleasant lakeside path becomes a veritable river. Many a day-tripper has been caught out by

the unexpected stream at their feet.

GREAT CALVA TO KNOTT

It's a very wet walk from Great Calva along a teetering fence and then down to the col and up to Knott. As Wainwright writes, if your boots let in water you'll soon know.

CRUMMOCK WATER TO FLOUTERN TARN

From Crummock Water the path that goes across the marshes of Mosedale is a spongy morass. Even the tottering fence posts seem about to give up. Better to stick to the foot of Gale Fell for drier ground.

CARROCK FELL TO HIGH PIKE

The route from Carrock Fell to High Tarn crosses featureless marshes. The Iron Age inhabitants of the fort on Carrock Fell would have seen this as an extra form of defence.

GREY CRAG TO TARN CRAG

An area of liminal marsh at Greycrag Tarn (which isn't really a tarn) divides Grey Crag from Tarn Crag. The survey post on top of Tarn Crag, put up by the builders of the Haweswater Reservoir, is invariably surrounded by pools of water.

TEN UNDERRATED FELLS

GREAT END

Usually ignored in favour of Scafell Pike, Great End is an enticing rocky plateau with striking views down its five gullies and of the tarns on the corridor route. It's very peaceful compared to its more popular neighbour, an awesome slab of rock that dominates the view as you ascend from Borrowdale.

CASTLE CRAG

It might be the smallest Wainwright but Castle Crag has a secluded wooded top, a war memorial, upturned slates and a hermit's cave in the form of adventurer Millican Dalton's old home. Plus you are in the heart of Borrowdale, surrounded by larger imposing giants in your own castle.

SLIGHT SIDE

Slight Side looks like a proper mountain rather than a subsidiary of Scafell when approached from Eskdale. It is "the neatest and best" of the Scafell group's many tops according to Wainwright. An excellent rocky summit with inspiring views out to the coast.

ROSTHWAITE FELL

A lovely walk up from Stonethwaite through a wooded ravine, following Stanger Gill to its source beneath a set of craggy rock spurs. Then come several rounded tops and the ascent of Bessy Boot. Going down via the poetically-named Tarn at Leaves is another delight.

MIDDLE FELL

Not the most inventive of names, and Middle Fell is often

ignored by visitors to Wasdale. But it has views of the Scafells from a unique angle, two great grey lumps with a huge bite-sized gap in the rock between them. Great views of Wastwater and its screes, Yewbarrow and Great Gable.

LOUGHRIGG FELL

Small and easily accessible from Ambleside, the terrace has fine views of Rydal Water and a mining cavern. On top it's a pleasing labyrinth of small hills and heather, a fine place to read a book or amble away an afternoon.

HARD KNOTT

It might be relatively easy to climb from Hardknott Pass, but this has twin tops and from Border End you can really see the outline of the Roman Fort far below. You can also view the Eskdale Needle from the main summit and enjoy the Scafells and Crinkle Crags.

CARROCK FELL

This is surprisingly steep and rocky for one of the Northern fells, flanked by scree slopes. The climb from Stone End Farm is exciting and on top are the ruins of a massive Iron Age fort and a tumulus. Was this an early community of Wainwright baggers?

ST SUNDAY CRAG

While most visitors to Patterdale head straight up to Helvellyn, St Sunday Crag offers an excellent view of Striding Edge from a different angle and a path on to Fairfield. It's a peaceful plateau away from the crowds with fine views down into Grisedale and Deepdale.

HOLME FELL

Small but has a fine double top with views of Coniston

and the Langdale Pikes, Can be combined with starting at Yew Tree Tarn and then descending to view a man-made attraction, the great gulch of Hodge Close. The former quarry is a massive hole in the ground full of green water, the Lake District's own Grand Canyon.

TOP TEN CIRCULAR WALKS

HELVELLYN VIA STRIDING EDGE
From Red Tarn, which is a delight in itself, it's a thrilling walk along Striding Edge up to the summit of Helvellyn, then back down Swirral Edge. End the day with a detour up Catstycam, a great mountain in its own right, before returning to Glenridding.

THE FAIRFIELD ROUND
A great way to knock off eight Wainwrights from Ambleside. Starts with a walk along the idyllic Sweden Bridge Lane before ascending Low Pike, High Pike, Dove Crag, Hart Crag, Fairfield, Great Rigg, Heron Pike and Nab Scar. Thrilling views of Brothers Water and Ullswater and St Sunday Crag and Helvellyn from Fairfield, plus a great descent into Rydal to meet the spirit of Mr Wordsworth.

THE HIGH STILE RANGE
Fantastic walk from Buttermere along the shore of the lake, then over High Crag, High Stile and Red Pike before descending to the lovely village of Buttermere through woods. Great views of Buttermere and Crummock Water and to the south the Ennerdale valley.

THE COLEDALE ROUND
Starting at Braithwaite this is an epic walk up Grisedale Pike with excellent views of the Coledale valley and Force Crag Mine. The route continues to Hopegill Head and a thrilling ridge walk along Eel Crag and down to Outerside and Barrow before ending up in Braithwaite for a well-deserved drink,

THE NEWLANDS HORSESHOE

This begins at the small but beautiful Newlands church. The route goes up Hindscarth to Dale Head for a superb view of the isolated Newlands valley, then back via High Spy, Maiden Moor and the distinctive ridge of Catbells above Derwent Water.

THE LANGDALE PIKES

Ascend via Stickle Ghyll to Stickle Tarn, going either round or, if daring, across the great rock mass of Pavey Ark, via Jack's Rake. Four Wainwrights can be completed, Pavey Ark, Harrison Stickle, Pike o' Stickle and Loft Crag, each offering a rocky turret and castle-eye view of Langdale below. Descend via Loft Crag and Mark Gate to the Old Dungeon Ghyll Hotel.

THE MOSEDALE HORSESHOE

Starts from the best pub ever, the Wasdale Head Inn. The route takes in Pillar, the high-rise altar of Steeple, Scoat Fell and Red Pike, before descending via the bumpy rock chute of Dore Head. Spectacular views into the unspoilt Mosedale Valley and across to Ennerdale.

HIGH STREET, HARTER FELL AND MARDALE ILL BELL

Starting from the far end of Haweswater this walk takes you up the Rigg to High Street, offering fine vistas of the excellent Blea Tarn. Then on to Mardale Ill Bell and Harter Fell, and down the Gatescarth Pass back to the starting point.

THE KENTMERE ROUND

The tiny hamlet of Kentmere, at the southern edge of Lakeland, offers a circuit of seven fells, Yoke, Ill Bell, Froswick, Thornthwaite Crag, Mardale Ill Bell, Kentmere

Pike and Shipman Knotts. Kentmere Reservoir lies far below while there are also fine vistas of the Troutbeck valley and Longsleddale.

THE CONISTON FELLS

The Coniston fells lend themselves to a first-rate circular walk, heading up Walna Scar to Dow Crag then on to Coniston Old Man, Brim Fell, Swirl How and Wetherlam, and descending into Coniston.

TEN TOP TARNS

INOMINATE TARN
The tarn where Alfred Wainwright's ashes are scattered, so be careful where you step. A lovely secluded rocky spot overlooking Buttermere and surrounded by Fleetwith Pike, Great Gable, High Stile and some of Lakeland's finest fells. You're in the centre of glorious Lakeland here.

STICKLE TARN
This was my first glimpse of a Lakeland tarn. Stickle Tarn is dramatically overlooked by the vast face of Pavey Ark and the Langdale Pikes. It's also very convenient for a quick climb from the Dungeon Ghyll Inn.

RED TARN
Superbly situated in its own rock amphitheatre with Striding Edge and Swirral Edge at its boundaries. Sit and watch Red Tarn's waters lapping at the imposing bulk of Helvellyn while ant-like figures crawl along Striding Edge. Always busy, but a haven away from the Helvellyn baggers.

BURNMOOR TARN
Unique in that it has a building by it, the Burnmoor Lodge. A fine stop-off point between Eskdale and Wasdale, it's in an epic pre-history landscape with several stone circles nearby above Boot. Overlooked by Ilgill Head and Scafell it has a stunning view down into Wasdale Head.

BOWSCALE TARN
The Victorians loved it so much that they built a road to it

to accommodate tourists riding on ponies. Great views of Carrock Fell and surrounded by imposing cliffs. It is said to contain two immortal fish, which can't be bad.

ANGLE TARN (Patterdale)
Some beautiful islands adorn the tarn. It's not far from Patterdale and is a peaceful spot with views of Angle Tarn Pikes. A fine spot for lunch on the Coast to Coast walk or for wild-camping. The nearby twin peaks of Angle Tarn Pikes are an easy climb.

ANGLE TARN (Bowfell)
Dark and mysterious, with the craggy flank of Bowfell leading down to it. Angle Tarn feels wild and remote despite being close to a well-used route, with the Bowfell links, a striking rock formation above it.

SCOAT TARN
Wainwright described this as the grandest of the high-level western tarns and worth a day's walk on its own. It's a shy tarn that can only be seen from a few places, but it's thrilling to get a glimpse of the oval tarn as you ascend Haycock or Scoat Fell.

BLEABERRY TARN
An excellent stopping point on the route from Buttermere up to Red Pike. Bleaberry Tarn is notable for the superb hanging valley above it, a feature which will please all A level Geography students The red rocks on the ridge to Red Pike also give it a pleasing USP.

BLEA TARN (Langdale)
Beloved of holiday snaps and *Countryfile* features, the tarn is crowned by fantastic views of the Langdale Pikes, a rugged silhouette that will always raise the spirits.

There's also a wood alongside and wildflowers in summer. The tarn is now a Site of Special Scientific Interest, as the sediment in it hasn't been disturbed since the Ice Age. Pollen analysis has revealed evidence of forest clearances from 3000-2000 BC.

TEN FINE WALKERS' PUBS IN THE LAKE DISTRICT

THE WASDALE HEAD INN
Possibly the best pub in the world, set in the isolated heart of some epic routes at the end of Wasdale. Beer brewed on the premises, a lovely old wood-panelled bar for hotel guests, hearty food in the walkers' bar, a great packhorse bridge near the garden and brilliant views of Kirk Fell, Great Gable and the Mosedale valley. Lots of climbing history too as British mountaineering started there.

THE KIRKSTILE INN
The smell of woodsmoke from a real fire and pints of Loweswater Gold beer brewed locally. This 16th Century pub has a great beer garden overlooking a stream. It sits underneath a classic view of Mellbreak looking rather like the Matterhorn.

THE OLD DUNGEON GHYLL HOTEL
An excellent pub at the end of the *Postman Pat*-style road to Langdale. The Walkers Bar is a converted barn and this former farmhouse is a great place to stop for a pint after a trip up the Langdale Pikes, Crinkle Crags or Bowfell. A more exclusive bar for guests at the hotel too. Middle Bridge nearby was used for the final scene of *Brief Encounter*.

THE KIRKSTONE INN
After a walk from Ambleside and then up The Struggle the Kirkstone Inn is a welcome sight at the top of the Kirkstone Pass. It's one of Britain's highest pubs. A cosy beamed enclave is inside and it's a fine place to visit after

climbing Red Screes or Caudale Moor.

THE WHITE LION

The triangular shape of the White Lion is a welcome sight after descending from Angle Tarn Pikes to Patterdale or seeking refreshment while on the Coast to Coast path. Its rooms offer a superb view of Place Fell. Cosy interior and chips with gravy. What more could you want? Wainwright sold his first books in the now closed Post Office opposite.

THE BRIDGE HOTEL

Sat in the heart of Buttermere, the Bridge Hotel is a fine old pub with beams, beer, food and a garden with mountain views. It's dog friendly and overlooks a river. Well worth a trip over the Honister Pass to visit. Plus they are helpful if you've missed the last bus to Keswick.

THE WAINWRIGHT

Hard to argue with a pub called the Wainwright. It has a splendid selection of ales and craft beers, plus excellent falafel burgers with onion rings. Can get crowded, but is the best pub in Keswick and excellent for a pint after climbing Skiddaw.

THE SUN

The Sun in Bassenthwaite is a lovely old pub dating back to the 16th century and has a distinctive drawing of the Sun on its exterior. The ideal place to refresh with a pint of Bassenthwaite Beauty after walking some of the more obscure Northern fells.

THE TRAVELLERS REST

Nothing better than finding a pub as you descend into Glenridding from Striding Edge. This old miners' haunt is atmospheric and cosy inside and has good food for the mountain famished

BROOK HOUSE INN

One of two pubs in Boot — the other is the Boot Inn — Brook House has a great selection of craft beers. Sit outside at the front to watch the cars head up Hardknott Pass and enjoy a great view towards Green Crag.

ALSO BY PETE MAY

What Are Words Worth?

Man About Tarn

Goodbye to Boleyn

Whovian Dad

The Joy of Essex

World Cup Expert: Teams

World Cup Expert: Players

Flying So High: West Ham's Cup Finals

There's A Hippo In My Cistern

Hammers In the Heart

Ageing Body, Confused Mind

Football and its Followers

Rent Boy

West Ham: Irons in the Soul

Sunday Muddy Sunday

The Lad Done Bad (with Denis Campbell and Andrew Shields)

Printed in Great Britain
by Amazon

31245107R00150